Talking to My Selves

Learning to Love
the Voices in Your Head

by

DEBBIE UNTERMAN

To Raka,
Here's to you
finding all your Selves!
Have Fun! All the best,
Debbie Unterman
P.S. FREEDOM!

with a foreword by
David Quigley
Creator of Alchemical Hypnotherapy

What people are saying about
Talking to My Selves:
Learning to Love the Voices in Your Head

This is the first easy-to-read book I have found that I could give my clients to explain inner dialogue therapies. It is fun, thoroughly entertaining, and immensely insightful. Debbie Unterman gives readers a real glimpse into the inner workings of their heart, mind and spirit.

—*Tricia McCannon, Internationally acclaimed Therapist,*
Teacher and Author, **Dialogues with the Angels**

Unterman's work is a tour de force in transformation. She provides thoughtful and logical insight into persistent behaviors that limit us—and offers a powerful and easy method that permanently transforms those limiting behaviors into the experiences we dream of.

—*Jeanette Angela Gyles, Attorney and Author,*
The Foreign Student Survival Guide

Talking to My Selves is a book that finally gives people permission to accept themselves as they are: a roadmap for the pilgrim on a sacred journey. It not only allows us to see why we think or behave in certain ways, but goes further to help us consciously choose to make changes—literally, to transform. At a time when the energy of our Universe is shifting, this book provides an invaluable tool to its readers.

—*Jacqueline Robinson, Freelance Writer*

Talking to My Selves gives you more than an understanding—the information provides the answers to help you become and achieve more.

—*Dr. Michael J. Duckett, Speaker, Social Scientist,*
Author, **The Mental Codes**

Theater of the mind—it's all right here! This book is a simple and engaging explanation of the human psyche and how to work with it to create health, happiness and the abundant life. Its wonderful blend of magic, myth and psycho-spirituality are inspirational for the layperson and professional alike. Three cheers for *Talking to My Selves!*

—*Judy Winters, M.A. Psychology, and student of the shamanic art of play*

Talking to My Selves is a fabulous book! The writing is exquisite. This material is perfect for school systems, college psychology departments and drama classes as a primer on human behavior. What an inspiring project.

—*John Trevett, LMT, Licensed Massage Therapist*

Wow, I'm so glad to see that somebody has finally put information into a book that I can give my clients to help them identify their many selves. I have never read anything else that puts it as precisely as Debbie has. Some of the characters in it, such as The Queen and Ms. Perfect, were all too familiar to me, but as Debbie encourages in the book—just embrace and love them all!

—*Rev. Candace Zellner, Spiritual Counselor*

What a breath of fresh air! I recommend *Talking to My Selves* to my clients all the time. The chapters on Co-dependency alone are worth the cost of the book.

—*Bill Dare, CHT, Alchemical Hypnotherapist*

A must-read for parents or anyone dealing with children.

—*Phyllis McNeal, National Parenting Consultant*

Debbie Unterman has done an incredible job of taking complex material about the workings of the psyche and making it approachable. The book is so easy to read and so full of insight. There are layers of complexity that affect me deeper each time I read her words. In fact I had an epiphany thanks to what I just read. I believe this book is a great gift to the world, and so is Debbie.

—*Janee Barrett, Architect, Artist, trauma survivor*

I love this book! What a valuable reference tool full of excellent examples and appropriate humor. Thank you for all your work pulling together this incredible book on Sub-personality theory.

—*Lindsay Morgan, B.S. Nursing, CHT*

Talking to My Selves is definitely a page-turner. I found it informative, eye-opening and straight forward. I learned from reading it that I have been a "Rescuer" all my life and realize that now it's time to rescue myself and begin mothering me. Thanks to the exercises at the end of each chapter, I've already begun charting a path to a healthier life.

—*K. Jeffries, Retired Office Administrator*

The mark of greatness
is being true to
one's own
seed and
nature.

—Romany Gypsy saying

*This book is lovingly dedicated
to the memory of my mother,*

Eileen Unterman

CONTENTS

ILLUSTRATIONS

ACKNOWLEDGMENTS

I would like to thank all of my friends and family who read the manuscript for this book as I was writing it and took the time to give me their feedback about grammatical errors, typos, and philosophical disagreements. I know that the finished product has been improved because of them. There are some friends whose help was so invaluable that I must single them out. Thank you to DeAnna Hohnhorst and Shari Aizenman for reading every chapter as I finished it, and "suffering over words" with me to make sure I always chose the right ones.

A special shout out to Nalini Persaud for her tenacity and vision in helping choose the best representatives and descriptions for each character in the tables at the back of the book. The brainstorming you did with me to flesh out every archetype was invaluable.

To my editor, Ann Kempner Fisher, thank you for being my proverbial safety net, allowing me to write my heart out with the faith that you would be there to catch any mistakes and not let me fall.

Much gratitude and love to my father, Lewis Unterman, for allowing me to speak about our relationship so openly within these pages, and for supporting me in my eternal quest for emotional health through honest self-examination. His support has been unwavering as he pored through each chapter, with corrections and praise, acting as editor and advocate, championing me on to the finish line, while cheering for me all the way. If anything, this book has actually brought us closer together.

To David Quigley, I must thank you first of all for creating the Alchemical Hypnotherapy process, to which I owe my life as I know it. In rising to the top ranks of the Institute as an Alchemy Trainer, I've always known that Spirit placed me in the first class you taught twenty-five years ago because I was meant to be a vital cog in spreading the message of this gift to the world. The notes on the book I received from you stretched me to dig into areas no one else could have taken me. Our disagreements over content sometimes got animated, as they often do between peers, but through the fires of our heated discussions, the steel was tempered and the concepts were sharpened to perfection.

Thanks go out to any clients and peers who let me tell their stories, albeit anonymously, except for the one or two who told me to use their real names. I would also like to go on record as stating that although I may have changed some personal details about clients' lives to protect their identities, the examples used in the book are all based on actual sessions I have done.

To my mother, who this book is dedicated to, I want to say to your Spirit how sorry I am that you were never able to face the demons of your childhood. Your brilliant mind was, unfortunately, slowly and painfully extinguished by Alzheimer's disease in 2001 when you were only seventy-two. My personal belief is that had you been able to deal with your childhood abuse, it could have helped prevent the deterioration of your consciousness. Perhaps one day more research will be done to see if a link exists between emotional complexes and degenerative diseases of the brain. But I know you spent your whole life trying, in your own way, to protect me from the emotional pain you suffered.

And finally, I must acknowledge the part that every session I received over this last quarter century has had in transforming my psyche. Without being able to mention every Alchemist who guided me, many thanks go out to Krista Dauphin, Bill Stampler, Susan Stowe, John Trevett, Kari Dianich, Arjuna da Silva, Susan Marriott, Erin O'Malley, Heidi Wolf, Carl Miller and Richard Beyer.

A special note of thanks to Dianne Magnatta who came to me in my dream on that fateful night in 1983 to announce that she had made an investment for me and I was rich, and then went on to gift me with my first session. Who knows where I would be now without her?

FOREWORD

According to the Upanishads, "To know oneself is to know God." And it is certainly in following this path of self-exploration that each one of us comes to a deeper understanding and peace within our own beings. Over the past three decades, it has been my pleasure to be at the heart of a profound revolution of self-healing. Illuminated within the pages of this book are the tools that that have changed the lives of thousands worldwide. *Talking to My Selves: Learning to Love the Voices in Your Head,* takes us on a journey of self-discovery into the exciting world of Alchemical Hypnotherapy which has been transforming hypnosis therapy for the last twenty-five years.

Debbie Unterman, one of the world's foremost Alchemical Therapists and Trainers, was a seminal member of the first graduating class of our Institute in the early 1980's. Even then, I could tell by her brilliance and enthusiasm that Debbie was destined to be a mover and a shaker in this emerging new field. Since then I have witnessed her blossom into one of the top experts in this discipline. Her twin specialties of working with childhood abuse and trauma, as well as her work with Sub-personalities, which I call "Conference Room Therapy," have contributed a great deal to the advancement of this cutting edge technology.

As you doubtlessly will find in the pages of this book, her insights, sense of humor, and stories of profound healing will be an inspiration to each one of you on your journey. Because it is much more than merely a therapeutic textbook that you now hold in your hands; these pages outline a journey of self-discovery that everyone who wants to improve their relationships, their health or their lives can take for themselves.

Alchemical Hypnotherapy began in the 1970's, and was the result of a number of serious personal crises within my own life. The most important one was when I was in my early twenties and found myself facing crippling rheumatoid arthritis which left me wheelchair bound.

The doctor suggested that I get comfortable with my invalid state, because he saw little hope for my rapidly worsening condition, which had already affected up to 6 joints in my body. I had to take the doctor's prognosis very seriously, because the condition had stricken other family members in the past.

Yet I am currently in my late fifties and I've been completely free of my arthritis symptoms for the past twenty-five years. In fact, I feel as though I have found the fountain of youth. I am a vigorous hiker, and enjoy taking spirited eleven mile mountain climbing excursions near my home in Santa Rosa, California two or three times a week. Let me share how this came to be.

With no glimmer of hope from the medical community, and no place else to turn, I sought guidance from within. My Inner Guides actually gave me very specific instructions which I followed, and to my amazement they taught me how to heal myself. But there was just one catch. In return for this miracle, they required that I bring the gifts of Spirit Guide therapy, an ancient technology they called "Alchemy," to the world.

Because of that agreement I made with my Guides to share this powerful modality, I have been teaching the art and science of Inner Guide contact with other practitioners since 1979. By 1983 this healing process had morphed into the form of therapy that thousands of graduates now know as Alchemical Hypnotherapy. It was that year that I first had the pleasure of meeting Debbie during her Certification Training at Heartwood College.

Briefly, Alchemical Hypnotherapy is composed of many therapeutic protocols, including the Rescue and Re-Parenting of the Inner Child, Emotional Clearing Therapy, Past Life Regression and Somatic Healing—a specific technology for healing the physical body. At the heart of this process is the technique of Conference Room Therapy, which produces some of the most powerful results of this work. It provides advanced tools which not only allow us to organize the many voices in our heads, but also to tune in directly to the advice from our Inner Guides to help us achieve our life purpose.

Drawing on the experience of the past two and a half decades of her professional career, Debbie Unterman has developed a practical and simplified approach to Conference Room Therapy, which she calls Inner Voice Integration, and introduces here. This breakthrough book explains it, and, in fact, is so perceptive and well articulated, that our Training Institute has now deemed her book, *Talking to My Selves,* to be a required reading textbook for all our entry level students. It's not surprising to me that Debbie would be the perfect person to write the definitive book on this subject. Her expertise in this complex Sub-personality work was evident from the beginning of her practice, and she has used it with immense success with both individual clients and couples.

Have you ever found yourself confused by the prolific and contradictory thoughts running through your head, had trouble controlling certain unwanted behaviors, or had difficulty making clear and timely decisions? Most people have, and if you're one of them, then this book can change your life. All of this confusion is a clue to the non-integrated personalities that we carry with us every day. You'll learn that the voices that know how to alter these less desired behaviors are often drowned out by other more dominant ones. And you can begin your journey immediately by doing the simple exercises at the end of every chapter.

I know you will enjoy traveling the road to self-discovery laid out in the following pages. This book provides you with the tools to change your life as you come to understand and make friends with the many parts of you. With Debbie's help, you will learn how to make peace with the unseen forces that are vying to control your thoughts and destiny, and to work harmoniously toward the achievement of your life goals. And while you practice getting out of your head and into your heart, may you embark on as profound and lasting a relationship with your own Inner Guides as I did.

So, strap on your seatbelt, and get ready for an exciting adventure into the most amazing of all territories—your inner self. I promise you will never see your "selves" the same way again.

—David Quigley
Author, *Alchemical Hypnotherapy: A Manual of Practical Technique*
www.AlchemyInstitute.com
1-800-950-4984

The unexamined life is not worth living.

—Socrates

INTRODUCTION

This book aspires to answer the age old question, "Who am I?" in a whole new way. An epidemic of loneliness, Co-dependency and addiction afflicts much of our current population because so many of us are unaware of our true identity, our purpose, or how to develop a connection with our own inner knowing. Most of us go a whole lifetime being satisfied identifying with our role in a family (a mom), a job (a secretary), or a religion (a Catholic).

According to Gary Zukav, author of *The Seat of the Soul*, "Authentic power is the alignment of your personality with your soul." *Talking to My Selves* explores a larger paradigm than most psychology or self-help books and reaches beyond any religious affiliation to conclude that *we all have the ability to embrace our own unique identity, heal our emotional distress, and find the source of our spiritual guidance* right inside of us. Every chapter teaches how to bridge that mystery in simple, practical ways.

Perhaps the reason we have so much trouble "finding ourselves" when we go soul searching is because we think we're supposed to come up with one answer. The truth is you're a lot of different people at different times and *vive la différence*. Life would be boring if you had to always be the same. The power comes in finding your *many selves*, then getting them all on the same page and in alignment with your Higher Self. That's what this book will help you do.

"There are no limits to what the human will can achieve once the disparate elements of the psyche are united behind a single purpose and external controlling influences are eliminated," according to David Quigley, creator of Alchemical Hypnotherapy, whose principles this book is based on. By discovering the *many parts* of you that make up your individual personality, it will ironically allow you to become *the one* you were truly meant to be. Just do the easy exercises at the end of each chapter to begin this process of Inner Voice Integration.

And don't think these voices are all in your head either. They are actually part of your Mind, Body, Spirit, and Emotions. Keep your eye on the prize and persist until you've learned to discern which of those voices belong to your Guides. They're in there, too, trying to give you your own private messages, like personal Guardian Angels whispering in your ear, speaking through your intuition, urging you toward your life purpose. But you may not be able to hear them over the louder voices who like to dominate your thoughts, giving you their advice all day long. Don't worry. Chapters 11 and 12 will teach you how to get in touch with your own Spirit Guides.

Having trouble with Co-dependency? That's no problem. It's just a matter of tweaking a few characters gone wrong and giving them new jobs as you'll learn in Chapters 7 and 8. By the way, have you ever sabotaged yourself? Be sure to check out Chapter 10 to see what you can do to stop that. And while you're there, find out why it's time to stop being afraid of your own shadow and to start embracing it!

Throughout this book, and especially in the last chapter, I'll share my journey over the last quarter of a century of getting to know all of *my selves*, meeting my Guides and discovering my path. So if you're someone who's ever noticed conversations happening in your head during the day or keeping you up at night, or if you've ever had trouble making a decision because you could hear the argument for both sides, then you should find this book a fascinating look inside the workings of your mind. Follow me.

Talking to My Selves

We can never obtain peace in the outer world
until we make peace with ourselves.

—Dalai Lama

THE WHEEL OF CHARACTERS

Thinking: The talking of the soul with itself.

—Plato

Chapter 1

STARTING WITH THE MAN IN THE MIRROR

I'd like to take you on a journey to begin exploring your inner space: the inside of yourself. All you need is a willingness to open up your mind and see what might be in there. Most of us take the thoughts inside our heads for granted. There was never a class in school where we learned *how to think about thinking*. Nor were we given a guide to the landscape of our mind. Even the stars of the far reaches of the universe have been charted for us to follow as we look up at the night sky, yet when has anyone handed us a map to our mind? This first chapter is an overview to present you with ideas that may be new to you. Then this book will delve deeper and provide you with tools to help you chart the constellation of characters that make up who you are. The end of every chapter will include an exercise to give you more clarity about what goes on inside your head.

You'll learn to identify the various voices that make up the sounds only we hear inside our heads and that we generally define as our thoughts. However, upon closer scrutiny these thoughts can be categorized and eventually recognized as easily as an old friend's voice on the other end of a telephone. In fact, once we learn, shall we say, to put a name and face with a voice, those once seemingly uninvited strangers can become as welcome as special guests around our dinner table. We can even learn to call on them to conference with us when we're looking for advice or wrestling with a decision. So, by the time you finish this book you may never think about thinking in the same way again.

Finding Your Selves

I'm sure most people have had the experience of a conversation going on inside their heads, but when you participate, do you know who you're talking to? In my work over the last two and a half decades of exploring people's subconscious minds, I have consistently found that there is a discordant chorus of voices often causing confusion as they all vie for our attention. Yet I've also realized the rewards gained when those voices are individuated. I've found that as they are untangled they can be taught to work together like members of a team toward a mutual goal. By allowing them to all express themselves individually then teaching them to work together with a vision of the good of the whole, we can become the conductors to get our lives humming like a well-orchestrated symphony.

As we learn to distinguish these voices, we will see them as parts of ourselves with unique, identifiable characteristics. I like to think of them as distinct personalities, more specifically *Sub-personalities* of the whole person. Each one of them holds a little bit of the truth of who we are. How many times have people gone on quests to find themselves? I contend that the best place to start is by knowing yourself from the inside out by knowing your "selves."

One of the major television networks had fun with this concept in the early 1990's on a short-lived sitcom called *Herman's Head*. It followed a 20-something guy through his day at the office and at home, but with a twist. It let the audience in on what was happening inside his head between the words he was saying outwardly. He heard the voices of four different characters, all competing for opposing outcomes depending on what each wanted out of it, on all sorts of matters from going out with women to trying to quit smoking, to meeting with his boss.

One inner character was his Romantic side, another, his more serious Business Go-getter, another was a pure Pleasure Seeker and the last was actually a female side of Herman who held to conservative social values.

The audience saw the four parts hanging out in a setting that looked like a living room where they all lived inside his head, having debates over the decisions he was trying to make. The laughter came from the dilemmas he wrestled with as he tried to satisfy all their desires and stay within his moral boundaries. Although it was simplified (as if those four were the only parts he had)—it very cleverly illustrated what goes on inside all our heads, all the time.

You're Not Losing Your Mind

I'm so often not surprised how difficult it is to achieve peace on earth since most of the people inhabiting it are walking around with battles raging inside them. Thoughts and retorts shoot at us from within, give us advice, then chastise us for not following it. Messages such as, *See, I told you that would happen, you should have listened and you wouldn't be in this mess,* seem to be waiting in the wings ready to say their lines as if on cue whenever something goes wrong. Yet if we wanted to stand and look this enemy in the eye, we would be merely looking at our own reflection. There are many times when we'd prefer they all be quiet, but it is from *listening* to them that they can actually become valuable allies in helping us get what we've always wanted.

I invite you to stretch your imagination and allow yourself as you read this book to construct the cast of characters who may be living in your head. Have fun with it. Let go of any fear you may have about seeming to be a little *off* by talking to yourself. There is a difference being between clinically diagnosed with schizophrenia or dissociative identity disorder (formerly known as multiple personality disorder), and 99% of the population who simply have mindless chatter constantly going on of which they may not even be consciously aware.

This book is not about people who have serious mental disorders that cause them to be plagued by voices in their heads. This is meant to be a guideline for the rest of us with the normal range of "self-talk" that rattles around inside our brains going from sometimes helpful, to basically unnoticed, to somewhat intrusive, or even possibly downright self-destructive if not paid attention to.

Many people have probably wanted to find a way to make that chatter stop, especially in the dark hours of the night when it might keep them awake tossing and turning under the grips of insomnia. Perhaps just like a proven military strategy, the best policy could be to simply *look your enemy straight in the eye.*

Follow the Yellow Brick Road

Reminiscent of the cowardly lion asking the great and powerful Wizard of Oz to come out and fight like a man, how many of us have our own loud and ominous voices bossing us around from the inside? Yet see how much clearer this conversation becomes when the truth behind the booming voice is revealed. As soon as Toto pulls back the curtain, everything changes. Now they're facing an old man with needs of his own who can be reasoned with. He just wants to go home to Kansas as much as Dorothy does.

Just as the Wizard created a persona to make himself seem more menacing than he actually was, it often turns out that the very voices that yell at us in our heads are really on our side. Yet since they've often lost hope of ever getting their needs met, they do whatever they can to sabotage us.

Possibly because we lost our course in life, being turned around by the tornadoes of time, we were distracted by things that took us further away from what our soul was originally urging us toward. By beginning to unravel these voices that tend to all sound alike to the untrained ear, a common thread of truth about our true heart's desire is often revealed. In Chapter 10, we will explore the characters that tend to lurk in the shadows working against us, such as the Saboteur, and how to make them our allies.

Know thyself. Plato urged us to do so millennia ago, yet how many of us can truly take solace in the fact that we have bridged that mystery? One stumbling block may be in the very definition of the self. I'd like you to see yourself as being made up of many different "selves"—once you have this understanding, the potential of truly knowing yourself becomes possible.

You must have noticed that you're not the same person when you're with your mother, for instance, as when you're with your boss or friends or with your husband or wife. You might find yourself using different words and tones of voices at different times, especially with children, animals and babies. Could you imagine someone who always sounded the same no matter what situation he was in? From making a sales presentation to greeting an old friend to speaking to his wife in bed to being at a football game, having the same unwavering voice pattern and language structure would sound stilted, almost robotic or computerized, in short, not real.

It's really very natural for us to change from one personality to another. In English there even is an axiom for this: when someone is very busy multi-tasking we often say they're "putting on a different hat" for each activity. Since we can imagine a person playing the diverse roles of employee, taxi driver, gardener, and cook—wearing a different hat and outfit to fulfill each role—it's not such a stretch to understand that there are parts of you who look and sound different at different times. These compartmentalized sides of you must live somewhere accessible, since it's so natural to flow in and out of them during normal daily activities. This book will teach you how to employ them at will so you can accomplish more with less effort.

Realizing there's more than one "you" can save you from falling into the trap of what I jokingly refer to as "Singular Personality Disorder." Philosophers and psychologists such as Gurdjieff, Ouspensky and Virginia Satir have warned people about identifying too strongly with your name as your only identity and have invited people to have a "parts party." Our identification with who we are as one person signified by our name is part of what keeps us feeling bad about not always being congruous and true to our word, i.e. one part of you may make a statement of intention fully planning on following through with it, but another part of you was not consulted and already had different plans.

Your Own Worst Enemy

For instance, have you ever gotten yourself in trouble by making a promise to be somewhere when you suddenly realized you needed to be somewhere else after it was too late? The people you stood up will now think of you as an unreliable person and you may begin to internalize that belief as well. They may label you as flaky or untrustworthy while you, yourself, may begin thinking that, too.

If we fall prey to the notion that we are just one person who we identify as "I" (or our name), it can become ingrained in our internal dialogue and create negative self-talk such as, *I'm unreliable, I'm a bad person, I'm no good.* For all intents and purposes under this belief system, it seems likely that *I* must *be* bad, since I am the only one in here. Of course, if you say those things to yourself for long enough, the self-fulfilling prophecy kicks in because your thoughts are actually suggesting those negative beliefs and reinforcing them until they become true. Thus, a vicious cycle has occurred starting with something that never needed to happen in the first place if we were more in touch with our "selves."

Rather than succumbing to the self-judgment and shame that ensues, consider going back to the beginning of the scenario based on the Sub-personality Theory that will be explored throughout the book. Let's look at what was playing out internally when your friend first approached you to do something. Maybe you were under a lot of stress from being immersed in a project you were doing all day and when a friend made an offer to do something different it seemed like a welcome relief. You got caught up in the moment and embraced anything that would take you away from the drudgery you were in.

So far I've been simply referring to "you" but let's look at the deeper picture. The first thing to do to shift into this new paradigm is to start dividing *you* up into smaller parts and giving each one their own name. Perhaps you can call the two opposing inner characters involved in this scenario by names, such as your "Social Butterfly" and your "Responsible One." But what if the Responsible One was readily accessible to be consulted with before the Social Butterfly said yes? They could have an inner dialogue that may sound something like:

Social Butterfly: *Wow that sounds great. I'm so sick of working on this. I've got to get out and do something fun with my friends.*

Responsible One: *But remember you already promised your parents you would visit them tonight.*

Social Butterfly: *Oh that's right. I guess I better take a rain check.*

That would be the easiest way to appease that self-punishing voice inside your head ready to label you as flaky. But let's imagine that even after your Responsible One alerted you to the conflict, your Social Butterfly teamed up with another character, such as your "Rebel," and responded that they're going to blatantly blow off your parents and go anyway. Then because of your self-awareness, when a voice starts up inside your head, blaming and judging you for being bad, you can understand that it was not "you" so much as it was a couple of out-of-control Sub-personalities.

Now that we've divided you into some of your component parts, the new self-talk can be much more clarifying. You can now pinpoint the culprits of your transgression and have a talk with them, dialoging until a completion is reached. You can shift the blame from your very *being-ness* (*I am a bad person*) to the *part* or *parts* of you who are doing their own thing. Your thoughts can more accurately reflect your actions, *If I keep listening to my Social Butterfly and Rebel, they're going to get me in trouble.* Then as you become more adept with this new inner conversation, you can begin to find ways for all those diverse characters inside you to get their needs met. For instance, there could have been a negotiation amongst your Sub-personalities for some time off and fun at a more appropriate time.

A Look Ahead

All these voices and characters will be examined in detail in the following chapters, giving you tremendous insight into the workings of your mind. There are four main categories of voices we may meet on this inner journey that can be divided up into the following general groupings. The first category is comprised of those voices we hear inside our heads that don't even belong there and the next chapter will help you discern them.

They are the voices of all the people in our lives who have ever had any influence on us. The loudest will be the voices of our parents, but also included will be teachers, friends, relatives, religious leaders and even television personalities. We call them the voices of our "External Characters" and it's very important to learn to differentiate those from the voices of our "Internal Characters" which most of this book will deal with.

Chapters 3 through 10 will delve into our Internal Characters, whose voices can be divided up into two more categories. First, we have Intellectual Characters who live in our heads where they're constantly barraging us with ideas and telling us what to do. They often miss the present moment, with an eye toward some lofty future goal and a great memory of all our past mistakes.

They will be those Sub-personalities, such as The Judge and The Skeptic, who see the world conceptually in a linear, logical and left-brained fashion. Their voices may be very loud in our heads, where they live virtually cut off from our feelings. They're very goal-oriented and have no qualms about giving us their opinions, unsolicited advice and rationalizations on how they think we've done so far in achieving what they expect of us. Don't look for any compassion or empathy from them. They don't care about how you feel.

Second, on the opposite pole lie our Emotional Characters who live in our bodies. They are connected with both the physical condition of our bodies, as well as how we feel emotionally about what's going on in our lives. They can speak in feeling statements such as, *I'm sick of this. I feel like trying something new*, or may harbor fears that can make us act irrationally. They include such characters as The Inner Child, The Victim and The Rebel. These Emotional Characters live in the present moment, are into sensory gratifications and experience a wide array of feelings. It's as if Emotional Characters and Intellectual Characters are not even speaking the same language.

After finishing up External Characters and the two types of Internal Characters, the fourth and final category will be presented in Chapters 11 and 12. It contains voices that are less connected to our body or mind and more related to the true guidance of our heart and soul. These voices can come more as whispers and urgings that are often attributable to gut feelings and intuitions that we sometimes listen to and other times ignore, but, in retrospect wish we had heeded. Yet amidst all the chatter they may be indistinguishable from our other thoughts and are often drowned out altogether. These voices are not coming from our Sub-personalities at all, but from our Inner Guides, also sometimes called Spirit Guides or Guardian Angels, and are the ones we want to *be sure to pay attention to.*

They can actually be defined as a direct link to our soul. Native Americans attribute them to their ancestors, and modern psychology would call them *transpersonal,* or from beyond our individual personality. Chapters 11 and 12 will be entirely devoted to them. When you learn to differentiate these voices and follow the guidance emanating from their promptings, everything in your life begins to fall into place and you can truly live the life you were destined for.

EXERCISE

To begin to get familiar with the voices in your head practice becoming more conscious and aware of the thoughts you think during the day. If you find you get too busy and forget, then the easiest time to do it is when you're in bed trying to fall asleep at night.

> ➤ Imagine each recurring thought as a "voice."
> ➤ See if you can identify any voices that may speak louder than the other ones.
> ➤ If you can, think up appropriate names to call them based on the words you hear them using. Keep the names fun and personal. Don't worry, you can't do it wrong. The key is in becoming conscious of them.
> ➤ (Optional) If you find it easy and want to try something a little more advanced, then see if you can begin to divide the voices up into the four basic categories below.

Again, the four categories of voices this book will explore are: External Characters, Intellectual Characters, Emotional Characters and Guides, the latter three being connected to our Mind, Body and Spirit. But first, like a gardener getting ready for spring planting, let's weed out the unwanted voices of the External Characters who try to hide inside your head. It's all in the next chapter.

To find yourself, think for yourself.

— Socrates

Chapter 2

EVERYBODY'S TALKING AT ME

It was a beautiful summer day in 1959 in Framingham, Massachusetts, a small suburban town twenty miles west of Boston. I was five years old and ecstatic to have my grandmother, who was visiting from New York, taking care of my three-year-old brother and me while my father was at work and my mother was out shopping. To me the world revolved around my grandmother. When people asked me what I wanted to be when I grew up my answer was always the same, "A Grandma." I was the first grandchild and the apple of her eye, but her three sisters all worried about one thing. They warned her when I was born, "Mary, you have to clean up your language around the baby." Yet as good as her intentions may have been she had many slip-ups.

I followed her around like a shadow, and a lot of the activity of this day revolved around the little silver metal box that sat on our front porch. That was the box the milkman would open to find the empty bottles we left for him every couple of days and replace them with four new bottles of fresh milk covered with red checkered paper caps. The box was a perfect size for me to sit on and the cool metal felt good in the summer heat as we waited there for him much of the day. My grandmother grew more and more aggravated as we returned to that spot repeatedly, hoping to find its prize inside even though we knew we never heard the sound of his milk truck all day.

When my father arrived home from work and found me sitting on my makeshift perch on the front porch, I wanted to greet him with our big news of the day, "The damn milkman never came," I innocently explained. I was shocked to see the anger rise in his face and have him pull me by the arm into the house and start spanking me. He said I was being punished for using bad language. I was just repeating what I heard my grandmother saying all day long. I did not understand what I did wrong.

Whose Voices Are in Your Head?

How easily children assimilate the voices of the adults in their lives as their own. I wasn't trying to swear like a sailor, I just wanted to be like Grandma. My father's reflex reaction could even have been from the External Characters' voices in his head of how his parents spoke to him when he was a child. How many adults who have children become amazed when they hear the same words coming out of their mouths their parents used on them and that they swore they'd never say when they had kids? We all know the lines: "Because I'm the parent – that's why!" "If you don't stop crying, I'll give you something to cry about!" "When you grow up, you'll understand." "This will hurt me more than it hurts you."

It's easy to see children using the same words their parents use on them when they talk to their dolls or stuffed animals. *You are such a bad dolly. Now you go straight up to your room and think about what you've done.* They're already modeling and learning how to be a parent. It's no wonder when they do find themselves in that role that the words come out just the same way, even after a couple of decades. While such a clear connection can be seen between saying things that obviously come from an outside source on an issue such as parenting, imagine the thoughts that never get said aloud that lay dormant in our minds all the time playing those messages like a broken record.

Thus we need to classify these voices, to make you more perceptive as you participate in these inner dialogues. Since, in essence, it all sounds like our own thoughts, to become truly discerning takes practice, but when you can create clarity in your mind out of the jumble of voices it will be truly empowering. Eventually you will be able to and seek your own counsel for answers to dilemmas that may have once caused chaos and confusion.

People are so accustomed to going outside of themselves to find answers—our minds are already so full of other people's voices it's hard to even hear what really are *our own* thoughts. These External Voices may be the most difficult to distinguish from all the Internal Characters you will be meeting in the following chapters.

We are the sum of all of our experiences, so we are intrinsically tied to everything and everyone who made us what we are today. The words that came out of five-year-old Debbie when speaking to Daddy, was really Grandma's voice. That may seem obvious, because those words were actually spoken immediately after hearing them, but let's fast forward twenty, thirty, fifty years. Eventually, you find yourself thinking similar phrases but you've forgotten who they originally came from, or that they came from anyone at all.

So, your mission, if you choose to accept it, is to realize that External Characters often masquerade as parts of us and it is our job to "unmask" them. An old coach, a Sunday school teacher, a favorite movie star may be camping out in your memories without you even knowing it. The thoughts are so ingrained in our minds that we don't see or hear them as different from ourselves any longer. It's like saying that fish don't see water anywhere even though they're swimming in it.

Outside sources have shaped and influenced us in myriad ways. Favorite books we read, teachers all through school, sports heroes, politicians, religious training, friends, relatives, television, comic books, Hollywood, and Madison Avenue have had enormous influence on how we think about the world. If they didn't believe they could sway our thought process, do you think political campaigns or advertisers would spend so much money to buy our vote or sell their brand? They do it with sound bites and campaign jingles guaranteed to stick in our brains. And they know just what they're doing.

As a general rule, however, all the other outside influences pale in comparison to the messages children receive from their parents. The human brain, especially before the age of six, is a virtual sponge, soaking up everything into the vast template of the limbic system of the brain and formulating its world with the input received. Babies are capable of learning the grammar and syntax of any language or languages presented to them and being acculturated into the mores and customs of any culture. There are no filters to weed out the bad from the good. It all gets programmed into the open slate the Creator has provided for the child to fit into the environment he or she was born into.

The best scenario is that the child receives all the unconditional love of an extended family or tribe of supportive voices praising the baby along its adventures of each new discovery in life. Lots of hugs and kudos, gentle corrections, food, baths, tickles and attentiveness can allow children to grow up and build healthy self-esteem. Unfortunately, many families are not able to provide all the parental attention a child needs through its formative years because of any variety of circumstances.

Out of Sight, Out of Mind?

Let me illustrate the deleterious effects of a constant barrage of negative messages during childhood by telling the story of what I discovered in the subconscious mind of a client of mine (let's call her Barbara) during our first session working together. She came to me after having been in traditional therapy for ten years. She and her husband had raised two children but about a year after the youngest left home they agreed their marriage was no longer working. Barbara felt she hadn't been much of a wife due to her childhood abuse issues and the fact that she sublimated much of her energy into her work in the medical field where Barbara devoted close to 80 hours a week. Due to Barbara's people-pleasing personality she willingly gave her husband the house and anything else he wanted in the divorce as she had done during the marriage.

She was glad for the time alone and was devoted to her own healing, including, at her therapist's advice, cutting her work schedule back to only about 50 hours a week to give her more time to nurture herself. She had been on her own for a little over a year when she first came to see me. Barbara wanted to develop friendships, which were missing from her life, but she did not feel capable of expressing herself verbally or emotionally, and had trouble trusting people. She suffered from headaches that plagued her every day for as long as she could remember and admitted she only slept two or three hours a night for the last week before coming to me. Since I knew Barbara was a people-pleaser I wasn't surprised she was also overly concerned about disappointing people who mattered to her, such as her co-workers and supervisor.

Barbara confessed she spent a lot of time beating up on herself when she perceived she had done something wrong. One reason she didn't think people would want to be friends with her was because she believed they would think she was "dumb, stupid, irresponsible and couldn't do anything right." The first thing we needed to do was to trace back those adjectives to where they came from, because they certainly didn't describe her. Some External Character's voice had already become firmly entrenched in her and was coming out as her own Inner Judge (an Internal Character we will explore in the Chapter 3).

Remember that the subconscious mind, which includes the limbic system, is the place that holds the memory of everything that has ever happened to us. There's no need to have it taking up space in our conscious mind, so what's not immediately necessary gets stored away in the vast "hard drive" of our subconscious. Just as you can open a file in a computer by calling it up with the right keystrokes, so, too, can you retrieve old memories from the subconscious that may have been long forgotten – you just need the right key phrases to trigger them. While psychotherapists utilize dream analysis, Rorschach inkblot tests, and even "Freudian slips" to explore their clients' inner worlds, hypnotherapists investigate the subconscious mind head on by direct contact through the modes of suggestion and regression.

The Art and Science of Alchemical Healing

The specific type of hypnotherapy I employ as a practitioner and trainer is called Alchemical Hypnotherapy or Alchemy. It is a system that allows people to regress back to the time in this life or past lives when emotional blocks first formed in order to release them and connect with their Higher Self through a number of unique protocols.

Most of the theories I present in this book come from that process created by David Quigley and the discoveries I've made delving into my own subconscious mind, as well as the minds of thousands of clients. The work often involves the simple strategy of working with the *personifications* of the stuck energies, such as Barbara's Judge, and teaching them to act in the client's best interest. The process of coming to know and understand yourself through discovering and listening to your inner voices is what I call Inner Voice Integration.

Reminiscent of the Barbra Streisand song from *The Way We Were*, sometimes because memories are "too painful to remember, we simply choose to forget" what happened to us. Society often encourages us to "put the past behind us," "pull ourselves up by our bootstraps," "move on" or "get over it." And we willingly comply. Yet the ramifications of brushing our pain under the rug for too long can come back at us in an unfulfilling life, such as my client, Barbara, was experiencing. It takes a courageous soul to undertake the great journey inward to face one's fears in order to turn one's life around.

In order to assure Barbara that her subconscious mind would reveal the memories connected with the negative messages in her head, I directed her, as she closed her eyes and I induced her into a relaxed state, to go back to a time when someone was telling her she was "just dumb, stupid, irresponsible and couldn't do anything right!" She went back to being ten years old with her mother yelling at her to be quiet because her father was drunk again and he would get mad and violent if anyone got in his way.

Barbara's mother told her to go up to her room and not make a sound and if she wasn't totally quiet it was because she couldn't do anything right since she was so stupid and irresponsible. As ridiculous as that might sound to our adult ears, a child being yelled at by a parent will believe what is being said.

While on the outside Barbara had two grown children and a successful career in a hospital, on the inside she was emotionally frozen as a ten-year-old all alone in a dark bedroom, sad and terrorized. Even during her session, she felt the tension in her arms, neck and shoulders of trying to remain still for so long, afraid to talk above a whisper. It was clear she had internalized those fears and the verbal scolding to such an extent that she had metaphorically been locked up for all these years in that scene, and feeling doomed to live there forever. The voices in her head were her jailers keeping her alone and suffering.

Transform The Past, Transform Your Life

Through an Alchemical technique, I helped her transform that scenario in her head to one where her alcoholic abusive father could be removed from the house and the curtains that were always drawn shut were finally opened so the sun could dispel the darkness. I then fed counter-programming suggestions to Barbara's subconscious mind that her mother was wrong and she was actually very smart, competent and took great responsibility for keeping peace at home in a difficult situation, even as a little girl.

It will be Barbara's job now to listen to the voices in her head with a discerning ear in case those old messages creep back in. Then, instead of beating herself up, she can remind herself and her ten-year-old Inner Child that those are her mother's words and they are not true. In time Barbara can teach herself to see her mother's face as the External Character talking every time she hears those words and ask her mother to get out of her head and leave her alone.

There is a good chance her own Inner Judge has become contaminated with the voice of her mother, so she does have her work cut out for her. But in time, she will easily know when she's done something worth judging herself about and when she's fallen back into her old pattern of taking blame for something that's not her fault. The night after that session, Barbara reported sleeping a peaceful and rare six hours straight, which has since become the norm. Making friends can become much easier now that she is free to speak up for herself, as the voices of condemnation inside her die down. Also, her headaches should subside when her mother's voice stops pounding at her from inside her head.

EXERCISE

➤ Look again at the list you made at the end of the last chapter.

➤ Decide if any of the voices you identified are likely to be External Characters, whether or not you tried dividing them up already.

➤ Now go a step further and see if you can hear a person you know or knew saying those words and write that person's name next to those phrases.

➤ You may find that you already gave a new name of an Internal Character to a voice you've now identified and are connecting to an External Character. That's OK. You may have internalized your Aunt Edna into your Inner Cook, or your Uncle Lou into your Inner Comic.

➤ Now that you've read this chapter go ahead and see if you can hear anyone else's voice from your past playing inside your head and add them to list.

You've now just learned that not all the voices you hear in your head are your own. This is not necessarily a bad thing. We may want to keep the words of wisdom we received from our heroes, or people who have inspired us, to help us in times of stress or to reach for greater goals in our lives. The key is in the clarity to know that we have welcomed these messages into our hearts and that they haven't invaded our thoughts accidentally and remained as uninvited guests.

The Triumverate Of The Judge

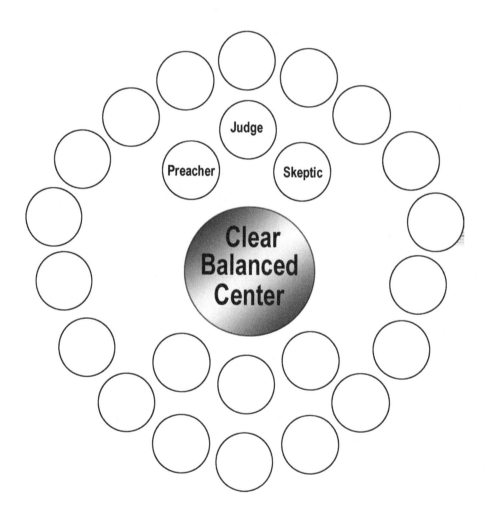

Any fool can criticize, condemn and complain
- and most fools do.

— Benjamin Franklin

Chapter 3

HERE COMES THE JUDGE

Let me introduce the colorful cast of Internal Characters that tend to make up the dialogue in your mind. As you learn the positive and negative (or *toxic*) aspects of each Sub-personality, you will also learn where each character may have come from in the first place and how it could get embedded in your psyche. We start with the Intellectual Characters, and the first three delineated in this chapter are known as The Judge, The Skeptic and The Preacher.

Know that the list I am presenting, which can be seen in its entirety in the chart at the back of the book, is a selection of the major archetypal energies that exist. There could be some that do not pertain to you at all, but might describe someone else you know perfectly. The names I use to describe the personas are generic, so if you think the energy I describe sounds familiar, yet you call them by a different name, that's fine. It's great to personalize them, but it's also helpful to know the "family" (or genus, if we were talking about plants), they belong to.

For instance, the first one, who I mentioned in the last chapter, I will call The Judge, but many people call him The Critic, which is the term used in some schools of thought, such as Voice Dialogue created by Hal Stone, Ph.D. and Sidra Winkleman, Ph.D. You will see it spoken of that way in their first book, *Embracing Our Selves, The Voice Dialogue Manual,* where they introduced their method and described The Critic as "brilliant in its ability to make us feel rotten about ourselves." He could also be given a name such as Mr. Big or The Controller. When you learn about him, you will come to understand that *whatever* you call him, his qualities are what define him, and by any name he remains the same energetically.

In fact, there are different ways to be a judge, and you could say that these first three characters are all judgmental in their own unique ways, which is why we will name and define them distinctively. In his book, *Alchemical Hypnotherapy, A Manual of Practical Techniques*, David Quigley calls The Judge, Skeptic and Preacher the Triumvirate of The Judge. I think of them as "The Big Three" because many people are actually dominated in their personality by one of these Intellectual Characters. They are the filters through which many people view the world that color their perception of almost everything. Far from being rose-colored glasses, which we shall see later, (as are worn by the Emotional Character, The Romantic) these glasses are much darker.

The Judge/Critic

The first one is The Judge himself, whose voice is the loudest one in most people's minds. I believe all the clients I've ever worked with in twenty-five plus years of practice have a judge figure inside them, and for both male and female clients, I find The Judge is generally portrayed as a man. When people first see him in their mind's eye he often looks like a judge in a courtroom complete with a gavel, black robe and perhaps even a white wig. We always address him with respect in a therapy setting, generally with the title of "Your Honor." He likes that.

Although it may seem inconceivable, The Judge is already becoming internalized by age six from things we hear in childhood, just like the little girl mentioned earlier who reprimands her doll with the same words and tones that were used on her. A team of psychologists once did a careful study of the messages a two-year-old receives in a typical day and they came up with a startling finding.

After analyzing the tapes they made following kids around for four consecutive days, there was a huge discrepancy between how many times a child was criticized for something as opposed to how many times he or she was praised. The actual ratio was an incredible 432 vs. 32! Obviously a child in his "terrible two's" has got to come up against the limits of a parent lest he becomes a terror, getting his own way every time he throws a tantrum. However, there could be a way to counterbalance the negativity with a genuine compliment every time he learns his lesson, or at least every two or three times. Not once every thirteen times as this study found.

The effects of being bombarded with different versions of: "Not that way!" "Why can't you learn?" "Weren't you listening?" "You're so stupid!" "Can't you do anything right?" not just at two years old, but continually throughout childhood, has a way of worming its way inside the brain and becoming fixed. Those very phrases start playing inside our heads like a mantra or a broken record. The Judge is the one who personifies all the things anyone has ever told us was wrong with us. The faces and voices of all those relevant External Characters who have ever offended us in our lives are blended into that of our own Inner Judge.

For many of us, this voice is as close to us as the nose on our face, but perhaps more difficult to alter. This voice is often a constant companion, like a cold we can't shake, forever telling us what we should be doing. In fact you could say that the word "should" is The Judge's calling card. It's probably no coincidence that the word *should* is included in the word *shoulders*, as the constant barrage of criticisms can make people feel like they are carrying the weight of the world on their shoulders.

Maybe you've heard phrases such as the following beating you up in your mind? *You just sounded like a complete moron. Why can't you learn to just keep your mouth shut so you don't show your ignorance? Everybody knows what an idiot you are. You're not good enough to get that promotion. You're just no good. You can't do anything right. Well, there you go putting your foot in your mouth again. You're so stupid. No wonder nobody likes you.*

Although, like I said, it's rare to impossible to find anyone without some voice of judgment inside them, there are some people for whom The Judge is such a dominant Sub-personality that it comes through in nearly every sentence they speak. Rather than simply hearing the voice of The Judge criticizing themselves, they find fault with something in everyone around them. Their belief that they always know what's right comes out as self-righteousness. These Judge-dominated people are the ones who always have advice for you, whether you asked for it or not, causing what I call "the unsolicited advice syndrome." You may have heard the phrase that popped up in the '90's: "Stop 'shoulding' all over me." That would be a way to counteract the attacks of someone else's Judge (or even your own).

You may think since these people are always putting everybody else down that they must be very self-centered bordering on narcissistic, however they are not without the self-deprecating voice of The Inner Judge. The irony is that the harshest judgments of many Judge-dominated people are often saved for themselves. If we could read their minds, their thoughts would probably be dripping with self-judgments, but we might think they were talking about someone else because all the sentences of self-condemnation would be said in the second person. Of course, this comes from the way these words were first heard when they were being said to them. For instance, although they might be thinking *I'm so stupid,* in their head they hear it as *You're so stupid* because it was drilled into them that way.

Self-judgment is obviously a problem for many people, due to the ubiquitous presence of The Judge. However what may surprise you is that there are Judge-dominated people who may never speak a harsh word to anyone else out loud. These clandestine conversations occurring inside someone's private thoughts are much more damaging than the blatant ones where someone outwardly shows their contempt and bigotry. Those who make it a point to stuff down any sign of being judgmental, yet never give themselves a break, need to be willing to work on this issue in private within a therapy context, before it negatively impacts their life or self-esteem.

These people are more apt to have a sweet outward disposition and are probably prone to perfectionism, hence the self-judgment of anything about themselves they deem as less than perfect. They may have trouble accepting themselves as they are due to some harsh judgments laid on them by others in their recent or distant past. It was reported that Karen Carpenter's anorexic eating disorder, which eventually killed her, began by reading one review which described her as plump. This kind of a hidden Judge can actually lead to any number of types of self-sabotage which we will go into in Chapter 10.

It's the very insidious and deep-rooted nature of The Judge that makes him so difficult to change. Yet the trick with him, as well as with any Internal Character, is to be able to transform him and utilize the positive aspects of his personality. He may be hard to like, yet that is the only way to stop him from ruling your life. Every Sub-personality has a set of positive qualities which are just as much a part of them as the negative qualities which may be more outwardly apparent. By getting to know your different selves, you can consciously cultivate the more refined traits.

You may wonder what could be good about having a Judge around. Well, who wouldn't want a good, fair judge in our courtroom if we ever were to find ourselves involved in a legal case? As tempting as it may be to condemn the negative qualities and wish to disown them, there are many traps inherent in that kind of thinking. Please believe me that as much as there may be parts of you who you can't stand, the way to win them over is through dialogue and understanding.

In one of my own sessions I came across a very bossy part of me I labeled The Controller. I was very mad at this part because I blamed him for an incident that had occurred just before the session when I had tried to stretch a good time I was having too far and ended up being late for an appointment I'd set up with another friend who then had to cancel. I hated the way this judge character inside of me always played takeover and wanted to be in control of everything to the point of stepping on others.

By dialoging with him in a session, I was able to see that his intentions were not to hurt anyone else, but just to get the most out of life. I was able to take the best qualities of this character and realized that rather than being so controlling, I could be much more effective and have a lot more friends if I could "command" respect for myself and others. I gave him a new name and a new job as The Commander, thanks to my love of *Star Trek* and based on the commanders on those ships, using them as role models.

So remember, just as a tarnished tea set once started out beautiful and shiny, and can be restored with some silver polish and elbow grease, all of our Sub-personalities contain positive qualities which have been toxic and contaminated with negative beliefs and can be *de-contaminated* with the proper strategies. We hear the word "judge" and we may immediately think of being *judgmental* or *pre-judging* people through *prejudice*. But think also of having good or *sound judgment*, or being fair and balanced as in the scales of *justice* which weigh both sides. In fact when we think of the positive qualities of The Judge, keep in mind the "3 D's": Discernment, Discipline, and Decisiveness.

If you are more prone to call this character "The Critic" then we can look at the word "critic" in the same way. We might immediately translate it as someone who is *critical* or likes to *criticize*. On the other hand, there are many times when a clear head and *critical thinking* are vital. And who could ever grow without some *constructive criticism* through an honest *critique* of ourselves or our work?

The Skeptic/Cynic/Guard/Scientist

Just as prejudice is not a naturally occurring state in children, neither is skepticism. Babies are born full of awe and openness to all of life. That's why adults spend so much time looking into their eyes. We know there is no judgment as they look back at us and we enter into their world of wonder and amazement at everything. While they're small, most children are apt to believe in fairy tales and even fairies, and are encouraged to develop their imaginations. Until at some point usually before ten or eleven years old, adults around them stop indulging in their childhood fantasies and expect them to grow up.

Depending on how it is handled, disappointment and disillusionment can set in leading to the early makings of The Skeptic. Skepticism and a wild imagination are pretty much mutually exclusive. Peter, Paul and Mary never told us the ending to the story of Little Johnny Paper after he stopped playing with Puff the Magic Dragon, but we can speculate he didn't tell his friends he knew a dragon when he was growing up. To a kid, being included and fitting in are high on the priority scale along with being accepted and liked. The fear of being laughed at for being different is enough to make children conform to the reality around them which becomes ingrained as one's paradigm of life. Once that point of view of one's corner of the world is learned, it's hard to change.

There's a deep-seated fear inside people about having their reality challenged. That's why it's so difficult to shift whatever paradigm one holds, and generally it remains much aligned with that of one's society and family of origin. When twins are separated at birth and brought back together to be studied, their innate personality quirks are strikingly similar. However, when they are each brought up in different religions, they continue to conform to the rituals they were acculturated into. Just as we know what we do believe in and our faith in that keeps us feeling safe, it makes us very uncomfortable to be confronted with anything that goes against it. In fact, we can literally become threatened by other ways of thinking. It's possible that someday we will look back at the many paradigms we now hold sacred as being as silly as five centuries ago when everyone believed Columbus would fall off the edge of the earth.

Of course we know the lengths to which people will go to defend their religious beliefs, but we'll wait to discuss that with our next Sub-personality of The Preacher, and again, later, with the Emotional Characters of The Warrior and The Martyr. Right now let's take it down to the mundane, because on a much more subconscious level, The Skeptic is ready to come out to defend virtually every opinion and habit we hold dear. When Palmolive wanted women to know that it was tough on grease yet gentle on hands they brought in Marge, the manicurist, to tell her customers that they were soaking in it. Of course their first instinct was to pull their hands out of the water, but Marge was there to soothe their skepticism.

Mr. Whipple was in his store stopping people from squeezing the Charmin to prove to us through reverse psychology how squeezably soft it was. Madison Avenue knows how difficult it is to get past the public's natural skepticism and spends billions of dollars to do just that. And, of course, it works. They say any publicity is good publicity, which is true. Simply having heard of something in print or on TV gives it immediate clout. The huge price discrepancy between a brand-name product and the generic one sitting next to it on the shelf is due to the cost of advertising. Yet, even knowing that, how many of us remain brand loyal?

The Skeptic

The Skeptic is that nagging voice inside urging us to beware and never to expect too much. The Skeptic's scientific bent and need for proof of everything gives him no patience for faith in things he can't touch or know through his own senses. He may not even allow for religious beliefs which can be contested. He's nobody's chump and may be quite materialistic because "money talks" and he believes in the bottom line. He's not just wary of the unknown, but even of well-wishers.

The onslaught of warnings and witticisms come parading through our minds: *Beware of strangers. Never trust friends bearing gifts. Look out for number one. It's a dog-eat-dog world. Everybody's out for something. I'll believe it when I see it. You can't trust anyone but yourself. Don't believe everything you hear. No good deed goes unpunished.* Songs even sing about it: "They smile in your face, all the while trying to take your place – the back stabbers." It's no wonder we remain on guard.

If our skepticism hasn't been drilled into us, it may have been born out of one too many disappointments from broken promises, teaching us that it's less painful to just not believe it until we see it than to have our hopes dashed once again. I have one client who fits that profile. Carolyn grew up with a baby sister who was plagued with life-threatening crises for the first fifteen years of her life right up until Carolyn left home. Time after time family plans had to be cancelled to bring her sister to the Emergency Room. Many a day planned for the movies ended sitting in the ER with her popcorn watching the parade of sick and injured people instead. Her guardedness against disappointment was so ingrained, that when her in-laws took her and the family on a 50th anniversary cruise, Carolyn still didn't believe it would really happen until she was staring out the window of her stateroom watching the shore recede as the ship moved out to sea.

The fact is that there is almost always a Skeptic in the back of everyone's mind, waiting silently to ambush any hope of change before disappointment can set in. It's better for me to draw him out before he sabotages the results of a session. If Steven Spielberg endeared millions of viewers to "E.T." which ends with the dramatic escape from an army of military personnel by making the bicycles fly, then people should be able to dare to dream of an end to their problems.

If I were talking to a sports fan I could tell him the story of John Smoltz, a star pitcher for the Atlanta Braves, who turned around his miserable record of 2 wins and 11 losses through the middle of the 1991 season, with the help of the Sports Psychologist, Jack Llewellyn. By simply going into his mindset around pitching, and leaving it to the coaches to work on his technique, Llewellyn is credited with the fact Smoltz came back during the second half and reversed his record—winning 12 and only losing 2—through the rest of the season.

How did he do it? Smoltz learned to visualize an "imaginary friend" standing on his shoulder during every pitch. He got some ribbing from his teammates for the next few years, but there's nothing like continued success to speak louder than words. This is the kind of ammunition you want to be armed with to give proof and a glimmer of hope to The Skeptic.

The Guard

Another reason to become skeptical, or on guard, is due to having sustained a tremendous amount of trauma and pain, especially betrayal by those you trusted. The wounds inflicted by such deceitfulness are very deep and difficult to heal, childhood sexual abuse probably being the most flagrant example. This is not to say that incest survivors grow up to be skeptics necessarily. There is a good chance, however, that they have built a wall of protection around their hearts, and hired a close cousin to The Skeptic, The Guard, to keep away anyone who may try to hurt them again.

Unfortunately, it can be difficult for any potential romantic interests to stick around long enough to pass through the barrage of tests The Guard sets up for them. One of the most effective therapeutic strategies to open the hearts of these people enough to let love in again is to literally personify

The Guard inside their subconscious minds. Future friends and lovers are not the only ones blockaded from the hearts and minds of these folks. Therapy that probes into the past is a very scary arena for them to enter into, and special techniques are sometimes needed to gain entry.

Rather than engaging in tactics of subterfuge with The Guard, in Alchemy we literally invite people to become the part of them that is the most walled off so we can learn why. Since it's no secret they are, for all intents and purposes, "on guard," we suggest they look inside to literally find their own Inner Guard. This way they can see how this part looks and even imagine themselves *becoming* that guard by wearing the same uniform, such as that of a British Guard, or whatever they see in their mind's eye, thus personifying the core of their resistance.

After The Guard hears that you understand the reason for his presence, he can listen to your arguments for trying something new, since he already knows what he's been doing has stopped working to bring the client any true happiness. Mostly what it's been good for was self-protection, and if people are already seeking therapy, they are looking for healthier alternatives to feeling secure. During the session you can engage The Guard in helping rescue the client from the pain inflicted by the original perpetrator. This method stops the fear of future betrayal and hurt from being projected onto anyone who truly wants to love the client and deserves her trust.

The brilliance of this strategy is that it is built upon the adage that "permission to *resist* is permission to process." Since The Guard is used to being put on the defense, many therapies which are aimed at breaking through those ego constructs will only succeed in building more walls against just such offenses. Better to draw The Guard out from his armament and face him straight on. Once you've gotten him to come out from hiding, much of the battle is won.

Here's a remarkable success story utilizing the "Wall and Guard" technique. Patricia grew up in the deep South after being adopted as an infant by a Christian family. She came to me when she was 34 years old with a literal shoebox full of medicines she was taking. She called herself a guinea pig for her doctors and endocrinologist, because over the course of sixteen years she had so many mysterious symptoms, only some of which could even be diagnosed, that the best her doctors could do was try to prescribe the right medicines to cure them all. Inevitably more symptoms would crop up due to reactions to drugs which then needed more prescriptions to be written to correct them.

She carried an inhaler for her asthma, was about a hundred pounds overweight, had been shaving facial hair since puberty and had stopped getting her period when she was eighteen. When I saw Patricia, she was dealing with polycystic ovary disease and was under doctor's orders to get herself to an Emergency Room ASAP, if she ever felt severe cramping in her abdominal region. To begin the session we asked her subconscious mind to initiate a dialogue with her ovaries to hear what they had to say.

Unfortunately, although she had been successfully hypnotized before, she was completely blocked and unable to see or hear anything. When she got frustrated and apologetically announced that she felt like she was, "up against a wall," I said, "Good! Imagine that there is a wall right next to you and feel yourself walking along it. Describe the wall to me, and keep walking until you reach the gate. When you approach the gate there will be a guard there. When you see him tell me what he looks like."

To make this long story short, Patricia was able to successfully find her Guard who told her he had been standing there a very long time. She saw that beyond the gate was a burned out brown wasteland of dead grass as far as the eye could see. We persuaded The Guard to let Patricia through the gate to find out what may have caused this devastation and told him he could accompany her for protection. Then I directed Patricia to go back to when her ovaries first became diseased.

Her resistance was gone and she was able to go back to an incident at age eighteen when she was very sad because her grandfather, who was the center of her world, had just died. She had found comfort in the arms of a boy she knew, who happened to be black. One day when her father got wind of the developing closeness between her and her boy friend, he confronted her with these words. "I'm so disappointed in you. From the time we adopted you, all I could think about was you giving me a grandbaby. But if you are with *him* I don't even want you to bring a baby into the world. It would be too hard for everyone."

Patricia was devastated. She suddenly realized that rather than taking a chance of disappointing her father, her ovaries simply closed down to the possibility of ever getting pregnant by stopping her menstrual flow. This might seem impossible, yet if we are to remain open to the possibility that her mind was able to affect her body by stopping her period, then we must assume her mind could start it again as well.

That is exactly what happened. After living sixteen years as an adult woman who never got her period after age eighteen, Patricia began cycling normally again within one month of this session, and continued to flow regularly right up until menopause. During the session, Patricia was able to release all the emotions around that incident, including the grief around her lost "womanhood" and the anger at her father for his judgments.

Before I brought her out of trance, I asked Patricia to go back to that desolate landscape behind the gate where she first found The Guard and tell me if it looked different. She reported that it was now full of colors with green grass, trees, flowers and new growth everywhere, like a beautiful garden. Since The Guard was feeling unneeded and superfluous, Patricia gave him the new job of being the gardener! The next time Patricia went to for a check-up on her cysts a few months later, the doctors could no longer locate them on the X-rays.

The Cynic

When bitterness and resentment are sprinkled on top of skepticism, we have the perfect recipe for The Cynic. People tend to lump The Cynic and Skeptic together, but they are distinctive. They say sarcasm is the worst form of humor and I find the sarcasm-based persona of The Cynic the worst form of skepticism. Whereas The Skeptic and The Guard are there for the protection of oneself, which can be valuable, I believe The Cynic can cross boundaries and actually use his words and non-verbal affronts to make others wrong or put them down. A Skeptic might look at you sideways with raised eyebrows, while a Cynic would go so far as to roll his eyes back with contempt and scoff at you. Going way beyond The Skeptic's need to stay safe within his own reality box, The Cynic actually goes on the offensive to cut down any belief system different from his. Archie Bunker would be a good example of the judgmental nature of a Cynic-dominated personality.

Typical statements of The Skeptic would include such common sayings as, *Life's a bitch and then you die; The one with the most toys in the end wins; Show me the money; That's what they all say; Just give me the bottom line*, etc. They are the slogans that bumper stickers are made of, and yes, they are full of cynicism. However, The Cynic would look you in the eye, engage you in conversation, then when you respond, add, "And if you believe that one, there's a bridge I want to sell you." For some reason, this guy isn't happy just having his own cynical view of the world. He's really bugged by people who seem oblivious to the perils and hypocrisy he perceives all around. The Grinch and Ebenezer Scrooge are excellent examples of the extreme end of this archetype. *Bah, Humbug* could be his calling card.

If you could get Cynic-dominated people into therapy, it would probably reveal some unfortunate incidents early in life leading to an adulthood of unfulfilled childhood dreams that are now buried in the dark recesses of their hearts and minds. Every time they see someone whose life is going well it feels like pouring salt in a wound. Since misery loves company they spend the rest of their lives putting other people down and blaming everyone around them for their lot in life. Unfortunately, they are probably the last person who will ever walk through a therapist's door, because therapy is one of those things they don't believe in.

The Scientist

All the aspects of this persona, The Skeptic, Guard and Cynic, have at their basis, The Scientist. Keep in mind when dealing with these types of people, whether they are dominated by skepticism, or just displaying it at the moment, that what they are really asking for is *proof.* Scientists are willing to spend hours, months and sometimes lifetimes in pursuit of data to prove their theories. The ability to thoroughly and tirelessly research a hypothesis, and come up with a solution through logical, deductive reasoning and strict scientific methodology are some of the best traits of The Scientist, who can embody the highest principles of The Skeptic.

For instance, the field of Complimentary and Alternative Medicine (CAM) has been growing over the last fifteen years because of the dedication and research from a handful of M.D.'s, such as Dr. Bernie Siegel (*Love, Medicine and Miracles*, 1986), who have been willing to be pioneers in obtaining empirical evidence of its efficacy. The idea of looking outside the acceptable AMA methods really took off with Dr. Deepak Chopra, who had an outlook which combined his American medical school education with his childhood enculturation into Eastern medicine from growing up in India.

His third book in 1989, *Quantum Healing: Exploring the Frontiers of Mind/Body Medicine*, was based on Quantum Physics, a scientific basis which could be used to prove the role that consciousness has on the prevention and treatment of illness. He then enrolled Candace Pert, a neuroscientist, who in 1972, as a graduate student at Johns Hopkins University, had helped discover the brain's opiate receptor-molecules that unlock the cells in the brain so that pharmaceutical opiates, as well as the natural opiate chemicals which the brain produces, endorphins, can enter. She then went on to help develop the exciting new field of psychoneuroimmunology (PNI) where she was able to prove the huge role that our emotions have over our bodies and immune system, which was evident in the case of Patricia's ovaries.

However, there is a detriment to The Scientist's rational and logical mind. People who spend all day balancing spread sheets, programming computers, in a laboratory looking for scientific validation, or anyone trained to discount hearsay as insignificant and irrelevant, have trouble looking inside their own subconscious minds for answers to their problems. Mr. Spock might say, "It is illogical."

Interestingly, some so-called scientists, actually a large number of doctors, who have been trained in the scientific method, can even have problems believing empirical evidence that is put right in front of them if it does not support their predisposed beliefs. Dr. Larry Dossey, M.D. is fascinated with the data he's seen in over 150 studies about the power surrounding intercessory prayer (where someone prays for someone else to be healed, without the sick person knowing it). In a December 1996 interview in Spectrum Magazine, he said, "I happen to believe that physicians, as a process of going through the educational programs of medical school and postgraduate training, undergo some sort of collective hypnosis about this issue of consciousness… It has always astonished me that you can present data about the potency of consciousness, the importance of meaning and value to people's health, and physicians engage in some sort of selective blindness. They can view the data, and not see it."

This relates back to the aversion to religious beliefs The Skeptic holds, as well as the inability to shift paradigms easily. The following year, Dr. Dossey repeated the same message in a special issue of *Body Mind Spirit Magazine* devoted to visionaries of health care into the 21st century. He warned, "To our great detriment, we forget that it takes a recognition that there are both physical and spiritual components to healing, and that's what I mean by the term *holistic* – bringing these together into a harmonious point of view. The research documenting the effects of intentionality and intercessory prayer is very abundant… We've never acknowledged that our thoughts can act outside ourselves – outside of our own brains and bodies. But this is what we're faced with. This will lead to the respiritualization of the practice of medicine… We're going to have to deal with it, and it will find an honored place in medicine of the future."

We see that The Scientist, which is the best part of The Skeptic, can still have a down side, but conversely, The Skeptic also has a positive side. Who doesn't need a dose of healthy skepticism with advertisers, salesmen and telemarketers trying to sell us everything under the sun? Folks these days without any radar up tend to be very gullible and may get in trouble by being taken advantage of. Con men can sniff them out in a minute and if they want to stop being an easy mark, they have to learn to develop a part of themselves that knows how to be more wary.

A healthy Inner Skeptic can develop out of necessity from being burned one too many times, in order to sniff out potential danger. Telemarketers recently have made us ready to wield our sword every time the phone rings, warding off strangers trying to sell us something. Seniors have become vulnerable targets and some are losing their life savings. However, for every client I need to teach how to ward off potential shysters, I have many more whose skepticism could prevent any therapeutic progress. There needs to be a healthy balance between being savvy and becoming too hardened and closed down.

Of course, the therapy I use is very much based on the power of the imagination to help create change and we know that the imagination is not familiar territory for The Skeptic. This does not preclude my being able to work on a Skeptic-dominant personality necessarily, but it certainly demands that I win over their Inner Skeptic with some sort of proof to get him to give it a go in the first place or at least to allow the results of a session to work.

In much the same way as Hollywood asks us to "suspend disbelief" for two to three hours while we watch a movie, I ask the Inner Skeptic to give the work we do a 30-day trial period while the client tries it out. In fact, the best bet is to give The Skeptic the very important job of watching the client's life closely for the next week or month between our sessions and reporting back to me any changes he notices. When we're together again I often have to probe with questions that can help measure any progress in sleeping or eating habits or whatever issues we were working on. Often this will bring to light the fact that changes have actually occurred, which will enroll The Skeptic to become an ally in our work together.

Working with a Skeptic-Dominant Client

There are plenty of techniques, such as the 30-day trial period, the Wall and The Guard technique and telling true stories of success with others such as John Smoltz, which make it possible to work with the *Sub-personality* of The Skeptic in a session. It's a different story when a client is *dominated* in their personality by The Skeptic, Scientist or Cynic. I actually pre-qualify all my clients before working with them to make sure they are willing to try a methodology where having an active imagination is a vital pre-requisite.

You never know how a Skeptic-dominant client will do with this kind of therapy. Here's an example of a client with this profile, whom I'll call Bill, where I was not able to obtain the results I would have liked. Bill was a married man whose skepticism was bordering on cynicism, but it was softened by his determination to get help and change. His very existence was in question before he ever took his first breath. Many women might be able to say that they are totally unprepared for motherhood, but with Bill's mother, that would be an understatement. She actually thought she was going into the hospital to have a tumor removed from her stomach and she ended up taking home a baby boy. His parents were young and basically in shock at what fate had handed them. Through the years, he was shown over and over that his mother was not capable of caring for him and his father wasn't much help either.

His only happy memories were before the age of six, living in the South, where he remembers having friends to play with. Unfortunately, his British mother was constantly depressed; she blamed it on living in America and convinced her husband to move the family to India. Bill had to undergo three grueling days of injections before the move, which still didn't save him from coming down with a serious case of hepatitis once he got there. The following year his mother gave birth to his baby brother who died during infancy.

He never saw his mother grieve, but she was slowly becoming dependent on prescription medications. She retreated into obsessive house cleaning as a way to stay occupied, while his father made Jack Daniels his best friend. He realizes he grew up not only as an Adult Child of an Alcoholic (ACOA), but completely touch-deprived as well. His father believed money was the way to show love, and spent most of his time working.

Bill has no recollection of the time between seven and nine years old, but is told that he threw uncontrollable temper tantrums (most likely as his only means of getting attention). His parents' answer was to distance themselves even more by sending him off to boarding school in Great Britain. His time there was full of loneliness and angst. He remembers one time when he was so fed up at being taunted by a couple of boys he simply pushed them off their bicycles and kept walking.

At sixteen, he was reunited with his parents, but his mother's depression was worsening. One day Bill was forced to ride in the back of their car with his mother while his father brought her to the hospital after she had overdosed during a suicide attempt. Bill's father's instructions to him were to make sure his mother didn't pass out before they got there by whatever means necessary. She survived.

As an adult Bill was full of anger, yet incapable of expressing it appropriately which often got him into trouble in social situations. Much like that boy at boarding school, he was known to blow up at both his close acquaintances as well as complete strangers. He never really learned how to make friends, but he craved the idea of being surrounded by a community of like-minded people. He and his wife recognized the need for both of them to receive therapy, as they were enabling each other to remain emotionally stuck.

Bill had been diagnosed with generalized anxiety disorder three years earlier, but had stopped taking his medicine. While I was seeing him he reported sometimes becoming immobilized and bedridden for up to two days at a time. When he could get out of bed he would wander around feeling disconnected from his body that would literally be trembling—full of fear, anxiety, tension, as well as overwhelm and hopelessness. His Inner Skeptic would continually be asking, "What's the point of getting up?"

His head was filled with voices of self-condemnation from his Judge, mixed with the despair of his Victim and the sarcasm of the Cynic. As angry as he was at other people he really was aiming most of it at himself. When I tried to point out the sad truth of his childhood, his Skeptic immediately took over saying it was nothing other people hadn't gone through, too. Minimizing the effects of childhood abuse or neglect is typical for many men who believe they should have been strong enough for it not to bother them.

The idea of "pulling yourself up by your bootstraps" is a way for a Skeptic-dominant person to keep themselves walled off from their emotions. The banter in his head would continually include The Judge adding insult to the injury of his childhood trauma by releasing a tirade at Bill with words such as: *You ought to be able to do it yourself, but you can't do anything! You're a loser! You're useless! You'll never get it right.* At some point his Skeptic would surrender with his favorite saying: *What's the point?*

During the four sessions I saw him for, my goal was to give him some sort of proof that things could change and I had to continually remind him of every difference in him between sessions. One way we had of proving the effectiveness of the work to his Skeptic was to give Bill back the chance to have a dream. He felt like that had been taken from him when his father had forced him into one profession when Bill had his heart set on something else. We set his long held dream as a realistic goal: for him to have a loving circle of family and friends, as well as a new profession that feeds his soul.

The first step in accomplishing that goal was for him to stop treating his Inner Child with the same emotional disregard his parents had for him. His Inner Child was very clear about what he needed. He wanted to be out in nature more, to start exercising and to experience being loved. His wife was willing to help with the latter by promising to hold him once a week for ten minutes while Bill accessed the memories of being little and having a loving mother's arms around him. He also promised his child he would run four mornings a week and garden at least once weekly.

His ability to follow through with those tasks would make the difference to the success of the work we did. The most I can do with any client is lay out a plan and hope he takes the initiative to put it into action. Then The Skeptic has a chance to make an informed decision as to whether change is possible. Of course, if a client refuses to do the work, The Skeptic and Judge can then say with certainty as Bill's both believed, "It's useless. There's no point. You can't follow through with anything. You have no will power. Just give up."

Another detriment to working with a Skeptic or Cynic-dominated client is the fact they want results now. Unfortunately, in typical Skeptic fashion, every time Bill showed up for a session, and I asked him if he was doing his homework, he told me he had not and came up with all sorts of excuses of why it wasn't really that important. When he did not take the time to follow through with the wishes of his Inner Child and the promises he made to him, it served to reinforce his Judge's belief that it was useless. Eventually he stopped coming. However, all's well that ends well.

As a therapist, I must remain detached to the results my clients achieve with me. I am happy for them to receive help wherever they can find it. The spark of hope that was ignited during Bill's journey with me into his sad past did not go out. When I spoke to him two years later, his Skeptic was still strong in the belief that our work together was not the cause of his success, yet he had accomplished the goals we set for him. He was visibly happy, and was busy with new friends he and his wife had made. And most importantly he had found the profession that made his heart sing and was proud to tell me he had started a new career.

The Preacher/Guru/Seeker/Believer

The third type of judge archetype is almost the opposite of The Skeptic whose scientific bent and need for proof leaves little room for religious beliefs and may even lean toward atheism. The Preacher, in contrast, builds his world around his spirituality. In choosing the word "Preacher" to define this Sub-personality I'm using it as a verb denoting "one who preaches," not necessarily connoting a preacher of any particular denomination. In fact, if any religious Western connotation to this word makes you feel uncomfortable, try on a more Eastern name, The Guru.

It matters not which brand of spirituality one adheres to, the gist of this character is displayed through any sort of religious fanaticism or dogmatic zeal. It's evident in a self-righteous, arrogant, moralistic attitude which can be seen in Christians, Jews, Muslims, Hindus, Buddhists, New Age circles and even cult members. It typically comes out in a closed-minded adherence to the belief that "my way is the only way." The Preacher doesn't need to stand on a soap box for his or her nose to be in the air. Its holier-than-thou attitude, especially when allying with the Emotional Characters of the Warrior and *especially* The Martyr, has caused this not-so-subtle saintly judge figure to be responsible for most of the bloodshed on the earth. The inherent hypocrisy of killing for God is obviously lost on The Preacher, probably due to the deep religious programming that often leads to its development.

If a couple's adult daughter has been kidnapped by the Moonies, they can immediately see the need for religious de-programming from the ideas she's been fed. However, if the ideas of an entire community are instilled into a child's head from birth, and corroborated by everyone who's been living there for generations, they are seldom questioned. When I first went to college in upstate New York my roommate was from a town where the only Jewish person she ever knew was the local dentist. I must have matter of factly brought up my own Jewish heritage at some point, and one day I found her staring at me until she finally admitted she was looking for my horns. My roommate was not endowed with a personality which displayed The Preacher in any noticeable way; she was just an 18-year-old away from home for the first time. But this is an example of how easily people can be programmed with subconscious beliefs that may lay dormant yet are quite ingrained.

Of course The Preacher Sub-personality does not always come from indoctrination since childhood. It can also have adult onset as in the lyrics of the famous hymn, "Amazing Grace." Those words, "I once was lost, but now I'm found," were written by a slave ship captain on one of his voyages where he had an epiphany—a moment of realization and revelation that turned his life around. It's now sung in many churches and is the adage of people in 12-Step programs who testify, or you could say, preach, to others that they, too, can change. This "born-again" attitude need not be a negative one if it's not accompanied by a constant need to proselytize to others. You know how preachy an ex-smoker can get about the dangers of cigarettes.

Because The Preacher is opposed to all "sins of the flesh" it is no wonder that many people adopt this Sub-personality to help them overcome a life of drugs, alcohol, promiscuity or prostitution. It's a perfect fit. That's why President Bush pushed through the faith-based initiative his first week in office in 2000, while the bill was still stalled in Congress. He believed that a conversion to religion, by its very nature, leads to sobriety, which is valid. Faith in a higher power can curtail people from engaging in dangerous and life-threatening activities. In addition, having the support of a group of like-minded people is often necessary to keep addicts from keeping company with their old crowd and being tempted back into their self-destructive habits.

Another positive quality of The Preacher is the ability to let one's deeply held spiritual beliefs pull one through the difficult times in life even if the answers may not seem clear in the moment. A sense of detachment can be a wonderful attribute that The Preacher can instill, as well as an air of transcendence. Whereas The Skeptic will act myopic and mopey, The Preacher/Guru can take in the big picture, realizing that *this, too, shall pass.* He or she can also endow someone with the fortitude of spiritual discipline. This can help people in many ways from making lifestyle and dietary changes necessary to heal from life-threatening illnesses or addictions to practicing meditation or doing yoga.

In my practice I do not see the same pervasiveness of this character as I do with The Judge and Skeptic. It could be that their presence is just as prevalent in the world, but the very definition of this Sub-personality keeps most of those people who are Preacher-dominated out of my office. Because their belief system conforms to a certain set of precepts, generally religious, it's common for them to seek friendship and counsel with others who share their same beliefs. The reality box in which a Preacher-dominated person lives would be even smaller than that of a Skeptic/Cynic. Much of the thoughts in their heads as well as the words that come out of their mouths might be memorized lines that they read in their version of the holy book.

Conversationally, they would be less apt to engage in discourse based on their own opinions and more apt to come out with a Bible verse, one of the Ten Commandments, a line from the Koran, or a page from *The Book of Miracles*. It's as if their ability to have their own thoughts has been suppressed and replaced by that of The Inner Preacher/Guru inside their heads.

There are many times in life, especially during crises, when it's a blessing and a comfort to have a whole system of thought in place to help you through. Yet it's important to remain open to any contrary feelings coming from your gut or intuition. That could be the voice of your Inner Guide whispering to you and one which The Preacher is negating. I'll speak more about Inner Guides in Chapters 11 and 12. The most important thing is to make sure people aren't ever disempowered from thinking for themselves.

Some ways The Preacher/Guru, in its toxic state, may talk to you would include any of the following statements in your head. *If you keep using birth control you'll go to hell. It's not spiritual to be rich. God loves the ones who suffer most. You created your own reality so it's your own fault these bad things are happening to you now. God is punishing you for your sins. Money is the root of all evil. It's your lot in life to suffer. God is on our side. Sex is dirty if it's not for procreation. It's not right to be angry. You should go home and meditate instead of going out with your friends.*

Working with The Preacher

I had a male client, Jerry, whom I saw for years while he was in the grip of a stubborn Inner Preacher who was forever wreaking havoc with his sex life. Each session brought to light more pieces of the whole puzzle. Jerry had geared himself from childhood for a monastic life. He had been a choir boy at his Catholic church and by age twelve had read the biographies of every saint. In ninth grade he was already enrolled and determined to go into a monastery. That is until puberty and hormones kicked in.

To complicate matters Jerry was having homosexual urges that brought on guilt due to religious conflicts, as well as trauma from being beaten up by bullies who detected as much. He ended up marrying a woman who knew about his bisexuality. They had three children, but were divorced when she fell in love with another man and Jerry took custody of their small children until she remarried. He was devastated by the loss of what he saw as the love of his life and withdrew into celibacy for seven years. It was during that time he was seeing me for sessions.

While working with Jerry, I instructed him to go back to the origin of his guilt over sex, which, I could hear from talking to him, was the crux of his issue. This is the same technique I use with all my clients, just as I explained in the previous chapter about Barbara, when I fed back the very words she heard in her head so she could learn where they came from. I always honor the ultimate wisdom of the subconscious mind and the fact that it holds all the answers.

The way I serve people is through my ability to circumnavigate the mind, following the clues it gives me like a scavenger hunt, since the mind stores memories *in association* to other things. One interesting note about the subconscious mind is that it always perceives time in the present, as if everything is happening *now*, which means it is *timeless*. You may be able to relate to the feeling of some very joyous or very frightening event, which you can think of and experience "as if it were yesterday." The more a strong emotion is associated with a memory, the more likely those memories are *seared* into the cells of the body and the mind.

Because of the timeless nature of the subconscious, you may have heard of individuals who have been able to go into hypnosis and experience their own birth or even the time while they were in the womb. In the same way, clients often slip back into previous lifetimes, just as easily as they can explore any incident during this life, if that is where the association leads them. One can truly appreciate this phenomenon more fully when it is experienced in a session.

What was uncovered when I asked Jerry to go back to his guilt over sex was that The Preacher Sub-personality inside him was actually one he came into this life with, who got even stronger due to his Catholic upbringing. It became obvious through inner exploration that this was by no means Jerry's first lifetime in which religion played such an integral role or his first time wrestling with his attraction to other men. Through past life regression he got in touch with one particular lifetime that stored many memories of repressing his sexual feelings for men. It also shed light on his comfort level with celibacy and his desire to join a monastery.

Although he actually uncovered three other lifetimes as a Buddhist monk where he took vows of celibacy as a small boy in the traditional way, it was his past life in a Christian monastery that was causing most of his problems. He had a clear memory of a peaceful, religious life which he shared with the other men in his order who all engaged in daily activities of working and praying while "living in the body of Christ." He could recall the joy of being immersed in a deep intimacy with all the other monks from prayerful, quiet times they shared living together for decades almost as a family.

He knew that the love he had felt for some of his brothers had sexual overtones, but he saw himself squelching those urges through extra prayer and the constant sound of the voice in his head telling him, *You can't possibly do **that**. We're living in the body of Christ. You've given up your physical body.* Then he saw a picture in his mind's eye of lying in his room in the monastery staring up at the crucifix on the wall and praying for the strength to resist. In this life, every time Jerry had an attraction to another man, those same words plagued his thoughts, *You can't possibly do **that**.* That voice in his head is why it was easier for him to live celibate for all those years than to live with the guilt of giving in to his desires.

Finally, during a breakthrough session, he went back to the contract he had made in all those lives to be celibate and broke the contract. He was no longer willing to live the old programmed belief and assumption that he couldn't trust his own body. Jerry explained during the session to the monk he once was that he understood it was his old belief that the only way he could find God was by denying his body. But he let him know he was ready now to find God by exploring his body instead. He was no longer willing to suppress what his body was telling him, and wanted to start seeking God through the bliss of sexual energy in his body *as the source* of his spirituality.

Once he made that decision to stop splitting his mind and spirit from his body and sexuality, everything in his life changed. The voice of his Inner Preacher gave way to the voice of his own body's wisdom and inner guidance. Within weeks Jerry got a clear message that a man would soon be coming into his life that he would be having a relationship with. He was shown a very clear picture of some of the man's physical features and knew immediately when he met him. That day began what has now been a period of seven years of what Jerry describes as "a deep abiding compassionate love, rooted in my love of God, and including a passion for the physical world and a love for my own body."

The Seeker/Believer

Now there is another side to this character which is more aptly described by giving it a different name; yet notice how it is still of the same energy, almost the flip side of the same coin. It comes out more subtly, and is more appropriately labeled The Seeker or The Believer. While some are preaching, there are always those who quietly listen to their words and take them in. Often they willingly give up their power to someone they consider more knowledgeable in the ways of the spirit. Some of the most difficult sessions I've ever done are on people who have believed someone else's instructions of what to do with their life rather than making their own decisions. It usually has to do with the areas of life which The Preacher has the most opinions about and likes to exert the most control over – sex and money.

I had one female client who was told point blank by a well known spiritual leader to move 2000 miles away and marry a particular man. I saw both the husband and wife two years into their marriage for sessions separately and together. I saw no cohesiveness or common interests between them except for the direct orders of their "guru" to marry each other, which they had done out of blind obedience. I was particularly perturbed by the way I saw the man treating the woman during our time together and I told her so in private.

Years later she thanked me for my words of warning which she obviously heeded. In the case of that couple, his Preacher Sub-personality displayed guilt-inducing arrogance and dogmatism which her Seeker/Believer bought into out of a sense of duty and helplessness. Luckily there was still enough of a small voice of intuition inside her which my words must have resonated with. Since the relationship was already leaning toward a propensity for violence, I worry about where it would have ended up if I hadn't been called to intervene.

It was almost as if the sessions were able to break a spell she was under by giving her someone else's voice (outside of herself) to present another viable opinion rather than that of her External Guru. People who are used to depending on the opinions of others are particularly vulnerable to succumbing to the loud voice of someone else's Preacher/Guru. Science fiction gives us Darth Vader as a good example of the worst qualities of this character being used to go out and actively seduce others into following him, in *Star Wars*, a modern myth of the battle between good and evil.

The Conference Room

In Alchemical Hypnotherapy, the way we utilize Sub-personality work in its most advanced form is in the use of "Conference Room" therapy. That is where we get all the disparate parts of a client, who have any opinion on a particular issue being worked on, to sit together around a table and talk among themselves. It gives everyone a chance to speak and be heard and the goal of the session is to reach consensus among them.

As you meet more and more of the possible cast of characters, remember that you may not have the voice of every one of these Sub-personalities speaking inside of you. In fact what they have to say at any given moment is completely dependent on the issue you're dealing with. The best way to know which characters are conversing in your brain is to *give them something to talk about.* It helps if it's controversial and juicy. Especially if you have a dilemma over a decision you're trying to make or a habit you're trying to break. If you can hear yourself talking about something by starting with the words, "On the one hand," and then in the next breath adding, "But on the other hand," then you've got opposing Sub-personalities talking to you.

All three Sub-personalities: The Judge, The Skeptic and The Preacher, are all Know-it-All's in their respective fields, with a good and a bad side to each of them. In your life, you can expect to get dragged into a pretty heated argument if your opinion differs with a person who is dominated by one of them. In your own head, if you hear a disagreement over a hot topic in your life, it's likely that one of the loudest voices with a convincing argument is coming from one of these characters. There's a good chance their side is the one of existing social and moral values with a great deal of logic to it. There may be another side of you with a much more emotionally weighted opposing point of view – which you'll see when we start exploring the Emotional Characters inside you in Chapter 5.

Utilizing the Intellectual and Emotional Character Tables

If you haven't already done so, this would be a good time to turn to the back of the book where you will find the tables of characters. You can get a quick portrait of all the Sub-personalities discussed in this book at a glance—their strengths, their weaknesses, jobs that would suit them and words they might say.

Since the mind works in pictures and associations, I have taken the liberty of drawing parallels between well-known people—some living, some dead and some fictional—to help portray each archetype. I've attempted to find people to exemplify both the best and the worst in each character, with the bottom of the list generally describing the latter.

You may disagree with some of my choices. Just know that they are not meant to be taken too seriously, but are for illustration purposes only. Obviously we are all multi-faceted beings, however I have chosen people I believe are good representatives of the categories into which they have been placed. My hope is that you have fun with the compiled tables, as you see aspects of yourself and your friends in them.

EXERCISE

To practice getting to know The Judge, The Skeptic and The Preacher, try this exercise by yourself or with a friend to help you. First come up with a charged issue you are dealing with currently in your life. If you want to do it with a partner, you can let them read you each of the following steps, answering one at a time while they help you bring out the voices with probing questions. Or you could do it alone by writing the answers down. Even if you are working with a partner, it would still be good to have some paper handy to write down what comes up.

➤ Take your issue and make it into a question starting with the words, "Should I?" The question could be, *Should I leave my job and start working for myself?* or *Should I go out with the guy I just met?* or anything else you're in a quandary about.

➤ Listen to see if there's a Judge inside you who wants to tell you what it is you *should* do according to traditional social mores. Become The Judge and speak in the voice of "His Honor" to yourself.

➤ Listen for a Skeptical or Cynical voice that's not so sure that would be such a good idea and why not?! How does he or she feel about the issue? Become that part of you that questions everything.

➤ Listen to hear if there are any moral sides to the issue which The Preacher would like you to think about. If you're not sure what kinds of words to use, first listen for them to come from within, or else try speaking like a well-known preacher on a pulpit, imagining yourself as the subject of the sermon.

➤ Listen for the helpful, positive suggestions each character comes up with and write them down in one column.

➤ Take all the negative, toxic things that are said and list them in a separate column.

➤ Notice, when you look down the list of phrases you hear from the toxic side of the characters, whether those statements are things you heard from anyone in your life growing up or even presently.

➢ Begin a list of which people in your life may be External Characters who are posing as your Inner Judge, Skeptic or Preacher.

➢ (Optional) If any other messages begin to voice their sides of the issue and they don't fit these profiles, write them down anyway and see if you can find out whose voices those belong to in upcoming chapters.

In reading this book you will hopefully be able to discern which side of any argument that goes on in your mind, is "right" for you. Sometimes our emotions can sway us to do things before we've really had a chance to think them through, and in that case, the solid down-to-earth ability to discern right from wrong can be a valuable asset of The Judge, Skeptic or Preacher.

However, sticking to the tried and true may not be serving the needs of your soul's journey and listening to the ideas that may sound a little crazy to these guys may be just what you need to do to follow your destiny. The ultimate goal is to learn to come to an agreement that makes all the parts of you happy with the Inner Voice Integration of your *body, mind, spirit and emotions.*

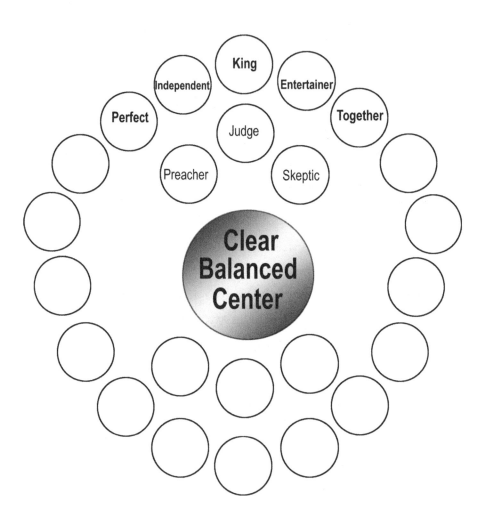

Knowledge of the self
is the mother of all knowledge.

— Kahlil Gibran

Chapter 4

GETTING TO KNOW YOUR SELVES

Now let's meet the rest of our cast of Intellectual Characters. There's a good chance that out of this next group, only a few directly apply to you. In fact, other than actors who may play these roles at one time or another in their career, there probably aren't many people who actually embody all of them at once.

To be able to give you a better feel for some of these following voices who may be difficult to relate to personally, I suggest a famous person whose very being exemplifies a particular character. For instance, when Johnny Carson died in early 2005, his peers piled on praises, time and again reaching the same conclusion: he was the consummate entertainer. I'll explain in this chapter why "Johnny" is such a classic example of The Entertainer/Comic persona. The other Intellectual Characters we'll explore here are (in their masculine gender for now): Mr. Together, Mr. Perfect, Mr. Independent and The King.

Mr. & Ms. Together

Examples of Mr. or Ms. Together abound in the world. You're probably able to tap into this archetype rather easily every time you get ready for work or a date, especially if you're out to dress to impress, or as the saying goes, "dress for success." Our "Mr. T," as I sometimes call him, is apt to be seen strutting his stuff around the office wearing his new power suit and tie.

Every functional adult has at least some aspect of a Mr. or Ms. Together who can take care of business no matter what's going on around them. It's the part that shops, pays the bills, balances the checkbook, keeps track of the kids' soccer games and carpool days, while getting you to work on time every morning so you can bring home the bacon. If you have trouble juggling all of those elements in your life, it's time to ask for help from your Mr. or Ms. Together.

This character is organized, confident, attractive and smooth talking. People strongly endowed with this character know just what to say and just how to look saying it. They're go-getters and jet setters. If you give them a job, you can expect they'll get it done and then some. They want their piece of the pie and their eyes are set on the sky. They're driven and will work hard to get what they want. If they don't have a lot of money yet, they will soon. *How to Succeed in Business, Without Really Trying* is a classic example of the rise of a Mr. Together-dominated person.

The problem with people who are out of balance with this energy is the price they may have to pay for their success. Because of their tendency to be workaholics there is a good chance of missing personal time with loved ones, yet the highest price one might expect is the toll it takes on the body in terms of lost sleep, which of course, can lead to its own consequences. Sleep deprivation isn't the only way this archetype has of wreaking havoc with the body. While it's true that all work and no play can make Jack a dull boy, it's also true it can lead to ulcers, heart attacks, high blood pressure, headaches, anxiety and a host of other ailments, including a few drinks or too many sleeping pills to help them slow down.

Speaking of the body, it is an area of great concern to our Mr. and Ms. Togethers, but not necessarily in terms of keeping it healthy. They're more interested in how it looks, because to them, appearance is everything.

We can see how prevalent this archetype is by the popularity of invasive and non-invasive ways to change your looks. From basic make-up and hairstyles, to toupees and hair transplants, steroids and weight lifting, chemical peels and Botox, liposuction, facelifts, and tummy tucks, breast enhancements and penis enlargements to nose jobs and designer hair colors, there's no end to how you can make yourself over. The plastic surgery industry in America will continue to thrive as long as Americans continue to put such tremendous importance on the more superficial and materialistic values of this Sub-personality.

This is not meant as a judgment on people's right to choose to look better, but more of a reality-check as to how much is too much or when enough is enough. I had one client who had a strong Mr. Together, who was newly married to an even stronger Ms. Together. This is a short story because there wasn't much I could do to help him, and his wife was not interested in any help at all. In fact, I never heard from him again after our first session.

The story he told me was that his wife would never let him see her without her make-up on. They had to sleep and make love in total darkness. She got up hours before him so she could prepare herself to be socially presentable, even to her own husband. He was working long hours and she was spending their money on interior decorators and designer furniture. When I asked if maybe they needed to sort out their priorities, he got very offended and insisted that they would not be accepted by their social circle if their house wasn't perfectly furnished. For people to benefit from any form of transformational therapy, there has to be at least an openness to change, and they cannot come hoping to change someone else.

This is an extreme example, I know, but it does illustrate the potential traps of putting too much emphasis on being "Together," and I don't mean as a couple. The boost in confidence a Mr. T. can give you to "fake it 'til you make it" in a new job is one thing, but having to continually act as if you're someone you're not is something else. The risk here is of being too concerned with how and whom *you believe people want you to be.* This character is one you need to be able to put on and take off just like your power suit.

We all need to exude an air of professionalism which may entail putting up a confident front or wearing a bit of a mask at times. That's part of the versatility of being human and exhibiting appropriate boundaries to separate our home life from our work life. However, the danger comes when we are afraid to ever step outside of the degree of safety our mask provides for us.

A common occurrence, rather than being dominated by the characteristics of only one Sub-personality, is the more complex personality profile where people utilize a combination of the energies of at least two characters in tandem to produce potentially powerful or sometimes toxic results. Things can get sticky when a Ms. Together is in alliance with a strongly developed Ms. Perfect, which was most likely the case with the wife of my client. Let's take a look at that character next, followed by a few more that Ms. or Mr. Together often teams up with.

Mr. & Ms. Perfect

The path to perfection is a slippery slope. The problem with perfection is that even when one reaches it, that moment lasts for only a brief period. It's usually the pinnacle of some project that came to a successful fruition. However, before long, life continues on with its ups and downs. When a person is ruled by the need for perfection, Mr. or Ms. Perfect will demand it in every moment—a totally unrealistic goal—and can make that person a regular pain in the neck to everyone else around.

The house can never be clean enough, the car cannot remain ding-free, the children can't be expected to get straight A's, and the dog will not stay out of every mud hole. Life's imperfections will drive a perfectionist crazy. If Ms. Perfect has a strong Ms. Together she can hire plenty of help to keep the house clean, the car shined and the dog washed, but she still can't control the kids' grades. If she does not have her life so together, she will probably have a strong Inner Judge which continually tells her it's all her fault things aren't perfect and that may send her into a depression or a feeling of just giving up, because she'll think, *what's the use of even trying?*

There are a couple of ways to make a Mr. or Ms. Perfect see things a little differently to get what they really want. First of all, the striving for *perfection* can be reframed—instead strive for *excellence* as illustrated in the book, *In Search of Excellence*. The author, Tom Peters, makes the point that seeking excellence leads to success whereas seeking perfection leads only to frustration and failure.

Another method I employ with clients—it works every time because the logic is so impeccable—is to let them realize there is only one thing they can do absolutely perfectly and no one but them can do it. The fact is that they are the only ones who can be perfect at being their own individual selves. *You can absolutely be perfect at being you* and The Inner Perfectionist has to agree. Every person is a unique spark of creation and there is nobody in the world that can play the role of you better than you!

Another concept I would like to bring up briefly is the concept that everything *is already* perfect. That's a hard one for some people to wrap their minds around, and we may not always agree with God's plan, but if we can truly have faith that everything happens as it should, we can let go of a lot of grief, frustration and anger.

Sometimes it takes looking back to see the reason that accepting what appeared to be bad news, such as getting fired from a job or having a heart attack, turned out to have positive consequences. You may have gotten a new job that was even more satisfying and the heart attack may have started you on a whole new healthier lifestyle. The ability to accept what is, as perfect, is a learned behavior, and a good one for Mr. or Ms. Perfect to be able to embrace.

Mr. & Ms. Independent

The underlying sentiment of a person dominated by this character is summed up well by the lyrics of the old Simon and Garfunkel song, "I am a rock; I am an island. And a rock feels no pain, and an island never cries." Luckily very few people take it to that extreme. Generally the agenda of a Mr. Independent is a positive one. He is willing to push forward despite the odds until he succeeds.

He and Mr. Together can actually make quite a winning entrepreneurial team. A person who possesses both can be destined for greatness. These people are the ones who may have ground-breaking lateral thoughts such as Steve Jobs and his partner, Steve Wozniak, who together started Apple Computers. Even Bill Gates who developed an operating system that made personal computers available to anybody displayed the spirit of a Mr. Independent. Sylvester Stallone persisted in producing *Rocky* independent of the big movie studios that turned him down. Obviously Mr. Independent is willing to take risks and also to endure failures, yet try again and again.

However, without a strong alliance with an Inner Mr. Together, a Mr. or Ms. Independent may wind up outside of mainstream society and possibly even alone. He might exhibit the strong, rugged individualism of a John Wayne type. Aside from being a cowboy, there are other ways to withdraw from society. While a great deal of money can give someone the ability to live independently, so can not caring about money at all. Homeless people can become islands unto themselves. We'll be talking more about the starving artist who may live on the fringes of society when we get to the Emotional Characters. But artists are a prime example of people who display independent thought. Because of the passion that usually accompanies it, however, they are not the classic Intellectual Character of a Mr. or Ms. Independent.

This character is more of a loner who protects himself emotionally by putting up a tough exterior of not needing anyone. He could end up alone and even homeless because of his inability to ask for or receive help graciously. If he tries being in a relationship, it may not last long once his partner wants to really get to know him. If he does get a job in a company where he's working with others, his boss may find him insubordinate and his co-workers may find he's not willing to be a team player.

He would be better off in a position where he can work independently and come and go as he pleases. He can still be a wonderful asset to an organization because of his innovative ideas and ingenuity. Something like a traveling salesman, a videographer or a cable guy might suit him well. But he's more apt to go the entrepreneurial route as something like an independent contractor. As far as being in a relationship, actually a Mr. Independent does well with a Ms. Independent. That way they can get space without hurting the other person's feelings and neither one has to worry about feeling smothered.

I know one couple who exemplifies that. The husband is a very successful business consultant and the wife is a Medical Doctor who loves training for and running marathons during her time off. This couple has been happily married without children for over thirty years spending much of their time independent of each other. They often meet in Switzerland to go skiing together.

On the other hand, most Mr. and Ms. Independents may prefer the experience of having a variety of sexual partners since they feel no qualms about going against what people may think. Mr. Together may have fantasies of that kind of lifestyle, yet be unable to retain it for long, since he has to look proper in the eyes of others.

The Entertainer/Comic

For entertainment in medieval times there was the court jester, and if you were lucky, a traveling minstrel show. Today we have our MTV, Hollywood, Broadway, movie stars, news anchors, talk show hosts, Las Vegas revues, rock legends, "American Idols" and more. Everywhere we turn there's someone available to help us forget our problems and be happy, just a click away.

If they are really good at it, we are collectively more than willing to repay them with fame and fortune, and why wouldn't we be? The Entertainer/Comic stands out from the crowd as a pleasant diversion, often an escape. In contrast to our everyday life experiences which tend to be routine, this archetypal character is talented, extroverted, engaging, charming, popular, charismatic, funny and dramatic.

And when you have the powerful combination of this character with a Mr. or Ms. Together, it has been demonstrated to be the easiest and most efficient way to raise millions of dollars fast. The first one to show us how to do it was Jerry Lewis with his annual Muscular Dystrophy telethons. But the entertainment industry has been responsible for bringing financial aid to deserving causes like nothing else ever did or could have, beginning with Farm Aid in the 1980's and continuing right through the 9/11 tragedy in New York.

On a smaller scale, you may have noticed how local organizations, schools, churches, public television, etc. will often have a very passionate, charismatic speaker or entertainer onstage just before asking for donations. The growing industry of Multi-Level Marketing (MLM) structured businesses, such as Amway, has learned to enroll people through extravagant stage performances to which they urge distributors to bring their hot prospects. Before they know it audience members are swept away in the excitement of the moment and reaching into their wallets or signing on the dotted line.

In looking for a classic example of The Entertainer/Comic, who doesn't remember their class clown from school? Just when you thought you would die of boredom, a joke from their lips could wake up the whole room. That ability to hold the attention of an audience and have them waiting with baited breath for every word is both a gift and a curse. People love you, but do they ever really know you? Those famous song lyrics of Smokey Robinson sum it up so well, "The tears of a clown, when there's no one around."

Let's examine two different reasons why the tears could be there. The first reason could literally be because, when alone, the person dominated by this persona feels lost and lonely when he or she is not being surrounded by adoring fans. The desire to be up in front of an audience becomes almost a need, like an addiction, or you could say, a Co-dependency. That was depicted brilliantly by Bette Midler in *The Rose,* the movie based on the life of Janis Joplin.

The second reason for tears when a Comic or Clown is alone has more to do with the face he or she must wear in public. Often these people have spent years using humor as a cover-up for the painful feelings they've learned to suppress. Everyone expects these types to be funny and "on" all the time, and generally they expect the same of themselves. Whether or not they literally perform as a clown, they often plaster the mask of a smile on their faces without make-up, as something they can hide behind.

I mentioned at the beginning of this chapter that Johnny Carson was a classic example of The Entertainer/Comic. He worked hard to protect his private life and keep it out of the media as he made America laugh every night for twenty years and he succeeded. However, he was eventually defeated by his nicotine addiction, which he could never conquer and tried to keep under wraps because he was embarrassed that he continued to smoke. It's common for Entertainer/Comic-dominated people to carry around some monkey on their back.

If anyone gets close to discovering the emotional scars being covered up, The Comics' best defense mechanism kicks in and a joke pops out of their mouths to quickly divert attention away from their pain. In fact it could have been because of some pain they were running from that this character developed in their personality. I have seen this up close and personal because I have a father who is dominated by it. His apprenticeship in the comedy clubs in New York ended prematurely when his mother begged him to get a real job and he finally complied, not due to any lack of talent, but because he wanted to be a good son.

In fact, when my parents were on their honeymoon in Niagara Falls, the scheduled comic couldn't get there due to a bad blizzard. My father offered to take his place onstage and the resort liked him so much they contracted to bring him and my mother back every year on their anniversary for Dad to perform there. Unfortunately, the hotel burned down a few years later. He did, however, continue throughout his life and to this day, to perform for charity events, sales conventions and reunions, and he does a fantastic job. I've seen him break up a room of a hundred people for forty-five minutes non-stop. All my life, people have told me that my father is the funniest man they ever met.

Although he doesn't talk about the painful memories from his childhood much, I know that his parents split up when he was young, during the Great Depression, and it was very difficult for his mother to make ends meet, even after she remarried when he was ten. When my grandmother died, and I was going through her old photos and cards, I found a poem he wrote on Valentines' Day when he was 12 years old that she had saved for sixty years.

The paper it was typed on in 1938 has yellowed, but it serves as a wonderful insight into the psyche of an Entertainer/Comic-dominated person. It's called "Trouble" and is written in the style and pentameter of a poem, but it starts out like a play by setting the scene as a "house with a poor dressed man and lady entering, and the boy downstairs thinking who it could be, saying:

> Sounds like his walk,
> Sounds like his sigh,
> Sounds like her talk,
> Sounds like her cry.
>
> Boy, things are bad,
> Just listen to that,
> My father just sold
> His very best hat.
>
> Gee, but they're worried,
> Guess I'll go see,
> If I can't cheer them up.
> Please God, Help me."

The King & Queen

The preceding three characters have been written about so they can be understood on their own or in conjunction with Mr. or Ms. Together. In contrast, The King or Queen archetype is more of a comparison to it. For simplicity's sake, let me use the masculine gender for a minute. The most important comparison to make is that whereas Mr. Together feels like *I've got to do it all myself or else nothing will get done right*, The King understands the idea of *delegating* tasks. Therefore while a Mr. Together is staying up all night working himself ragged to accomplish it all, a King is resting peacefully knowing the work is in good hands.

We can look at past monarchies to understand more about this archetype, in both its positive and negative consequences. There have been Kings and Queens who were very beloved and ruled their subjects with love and compassion. They understood what it meant to live up to the position they were born into, or *noblesse oblige,* and did it with grace, benevolence and social responsibility, empowering those around them, and making sure their subjects thrived.

Then there were those who patronized their people and treated them with condescension. There were even some who took advantage of the power their position afforded them and misused it, perhaps ruling with an iron fist. Those Kings and Queens were despotic, tyrannical and cruel. They were out of touch with those they ruled and repressed rather than empowered anybody. They may even have subjected them to cruelty and controlled them in ways ranging all the way to imprisonment, torture and death.

Rather than working from a sense of obligation to their birthright, they instead used their position for narcissistic and selfish ends. Marie Antoinette showed how out of touch royalty can be from their subjects when she was told the people had no bread to eat, and she allegedly said, "Let them eat cake." We can see from visiting castles all over Europe and anywhere that monarchies existed, the opulence and decadence that some rulers blithely lived in while their people were starving. So often, throughout history it's been the basis for revolution.

To understand this archetype in modern times we can look at examples in our culture of people who would be dominated by The King or Queen archetype. The classic example is Donald Trump who has built an empire out of his family name. He is even called, "The Donald" in reference to "The Don," which the head of the Corleone family was called in *The Godfather.* In fact, all real-life Mafia Dons are King-dominated people.

Along with the obvious examples of Bill Gates, Richard Branson and Oprah Winfrey, perhaps you can think of some people *in your life* who display the qualities of this character, both in its highest and lowest form. Maybe there's a matriarch in your family who acts and is treated by everyone as The Queen. She may rightly deserve the respect of everyone around her, or maybe she's self-appointed and actually more of a "royal bitch." At least this archetypal character usually commands respect and displays some healthy self-respect which is, unfortunately, lacking in too many people. If your self-esteem is low, it could benefit you to embrace the positive characteristics of The King or Queen.

Also remember, if you want to truly be great, it's important to take great people with you and entrust them with tasks you may falsely believe nobody can do as well as you. By allowing The King or Queen inside of you to rise to power you can begin to delegate authority to others. Then, sit royally on your throne enjoying the respect of your position, while you guide the people you've empowered to help you take care of business. Enjoy the synergistic results of your team's efforts under your leadership. Then you can get a good night sleep knowing all is well in your kingdom.

EXERCISE

I purposely did not put many direct quotes of what the characters in this chapter would say. That is because for this exercise, I want you to find the ways that you hear the characters inside you talking in your head. The chart in the back of the book gives some examples of what a quote of theirs might sound like, so feel free to look at it if that will help you get started.

There may be cases where it's more appropriate to connect with someone you know who epitomizes a character that you don't really have inside yourself very strongly. On the other hand, don't assume that because you haven't built an empire you don't have a King or Queen inside you. You can still have an inner Oprah or Trump waiting to come out. What words might that character say?

As for The Entertainer/Comic, in my case, as much as I wish I were as funny as my father, I just was not gifted with his timing or his ability to tell a joke. In fact, I even sometimes have the right lines, but not the delivery. I was the one who would say something funny at my desk in school, but no one would laugh until the class clown would repeat what I said, then he would get a laugh for it. Yet even though I am not dominated in my personality by that character, I can nevertheless identify my Inner Entertainer/Comic—it expresses itself most often through storytelling.

> ➤ Make a list of the last five Intellectual Characters we explored in this chapter: Mr. or Ms. Together, Mr. or Ms. Perfect, Mr. or Ms. Independent, The Entertainer/Comic and The King or Queen. Leave space in between each one or better yet, use a separate piece of paper for each one.

➢ Under each heading write down someone you know who epitomizes that character. It could be someone you really know, someone who is famous or historical, or even someone fictional. For instance, you might write down Martha Stewart as an example of a Ms. Perfect. That's a good way for you to begin to notice the traits of someone who is dominated by that Sub-personality.

➢ Begin listing some of the classic things that person might do or say that epitomize the traits of that character. This will help to personalize what you learned in this chapter. So maybe Martha Stewart would say something like, "Life is too complicated not to be orderly."

➢ Now find out if there is a part of you that resonates with that person you wrote down. For instance if you thought Martha Stewart made a good example of a Ms. Perfect, is there some way that you act like her in your life? You can give her your own personalized name, like "Ms. Picky" or whatever feels right.

➢ Alright, now it's time for you to shut your eyes and imagine what you say to yourself or others when you are displaying your Inner Martha Stewart, or Ms. Perfect or Ms. Picky? Maybe it would sound something like, "My hair looks so bad today I better wear a hat." There may be some characters you just do not relate to. That's OK.

➢ If you tried answering the optional question in the last chapter, look back at your previous list to see if any voices you wrote down are starting to be identified.

➤ (Optional) Notice if you have any combinations of two or more characters who work together to your benefit or detriment. For instance, Ms Perfect may combine with your Inner Judge and become a fashion critic saying something like, "Look at her. Those colors just don't match at all!"

Although we haven't exhausted all the possible Intellectual Characters who may exist inside of us, we have covered the major archetypal personalities. Know that if you learn the energies inherent in our generic list of characters, you'll find that even though you use different names for yours, they will generally fall into one of these categories. Yet, please feel free to acknowledge any more Intellectual Characters you may know are part of your inner world, such as The Teacher or The Student whom we haven't described here.

Now let's move on to some of the other voices who may be ruling your life more than you realize and who are members of the family of Emotional Characters.

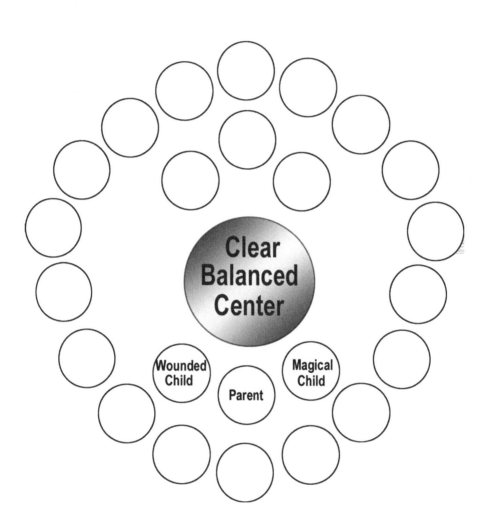

Western cultures place great importance on filling the human "brain" with knowledge, but no one seems to care about filling the human "heart" with compassion.

— Dalai Lama

Chapter 5

THE GREATEST LOVE OF ALL

As their name implies, Emotional Characters are connected to our feelings, even though we can still hear their voices in our heads. However, these voices are the ones that let you "listen to your heart" when you hear what they are saying to you. In fact, while the Intellectual Characters remain cerebral and are essentially located in the grey matter of your brain, these Emotional Characters speak not only for your heart, but also for the whole rest of your body.

In our society we tend to define most things as being either good or bad, black or white, right or wrong; which, within ourselves, creates a prominent partition between the mind and body. People with medical issues are sent to specialists who divide you into your component parts and see you as an arm or a lung or an ear, depending on their field of expertise. If none of them can help you, they may even dismiss you by telling you it's "all in your head" (which is actually being proven to be true through more and more studies, if doctors would only take notice). Of course, what they mean by that is that you should change your mind so you won't hurt anymore. It seems to be a more logical answer to them than the idea of looking at you as a whole body/mind continuum.

In our polarized and dualistic world, the mind is seen as superior to the body. Admonitions such as, "Be rational" and "Don't be so emotional" abound. Being logical is considered a more acceptable way of solving a problem than by intuition or gut feelings. We know that in the medical and scientific worlds, only hard evidence through investigative substantiation is given any credence. In the judicial arena proof is required while speculation and hearsay are totally dismissed. Commonly reduced to a binary system, witnesses in a trial are often allowed to answer only "yes" or "no."

It's no wonder we're trained to spend most of our time in our heads, often completely cut off from the signals our body might be giving us. We're content with the advice we receive from within from The Skeptic/Scientist, The Preacher and The Judge to the questions we have in our life. Yet the real truth is that the Emotional Characters actually tend to *rule us* on a much more hidden and subconscious level, even going so far as to give us pains and illnesses for which no cause can be found. As we explore the Inner Child and the rest of the Emotional Characters we will be gaining insight into the messages our bodies are sending to us.

We can look at what happens in the realm of relationships when we combine logic (men) with emotions (women). Even though men tend to be the head of the household, when it comes to making decisions on major purchases, Madison Avenue has had to rethink its strategies, because it discovered that it's generally the wife who has the final say. They learned their lesson well and today are careful to pay special attention to the color schemes women want in order to sell more cars, for example.

To bring it down to the intrapersonal level, have you ever thought you really wanted to do something, yet as hard as you tried your body just felt frozen and nothing you did made a difference? It could be that you were experiencing a debate between an Intellectual Character, such as Mr. Together, telling you something like, *Today's the day to ask your boss for a raise*, and an Emotional Character, such as The Victim, having the final word of, *I'm afraid he'll turn me down.*

In Search of The Inner Child

As we enter the realm of the Emotional Characters, the first stop has to be a visit to the Inner Child. The Inner Child is the child *you once were*. It is the most well known Sub-personality among this colorful selection of voices we will be meeting, which include the Victim, Rebel, Adventurer, Lover/Romantic, Artist and more. Just like with the Intellectual Characters, there may be some that do not pertain to everyone. Except for the Inner Child, whose voice is present inside every adult, yet sadly, is seldom acknowledged or even heard.

It's not a matter of people being purposely neglectful to the needs of the Inner Child. It just seems to be a commonly held belief that somewhere along the path to adulthood, the child we once were disappeared. If pressed to come up with that moment in time when an adult took over the body of the child who had possessed it, perhaps most people would say it happened when they turned eighteen. Or maybe it was a moment when their world changed, such as living through a divorce or the death of a parent or even the birth of their own child. Some will even say they never felt like a child because they were too busy being saddled with adult responsibilities, such as taking care of younger siblings. Psychologists may point out it is simply a matter of reaching maturity from having completed their developmental tasks and putting childish things behind them.

Once again we are seeing things in dualistic terms by declaring a clear split between being a child and being an adult. But is there really such a well-defined division? Don't we all know a very precocious twelve-year-old, and conversely, some twenty-something's who don't have the maturity to be on their own yet? I suggest that we imagine a continuum rather than drawing such a solid line, so we can allow ourselves to keep a foot in both worlds and be able to travel seamlessly between them. Even as much as we adore children and rush to defend their innocence, we still clearly value being "grown up" over being "little," and kids are first in line to vie for that privilege. It is not until retirement that we afford citizens the right to enjoy a "second childhood."

If you asked any parent of a youngster what they would do in order to protect their child, they would probably tell you they would do anything including giving up their own life to save that of their child's. An equally valiant effort would be put forth to protect a cherished possession of monetary or nostalgic value. Therefore, why are people so unconcerned about the welfare of their own Inner Child? Does the value of life go down as we grow up?

Why are we collectively in such a rush to walk away from childhood for the rewards of adulthood? Most of us are unwilling to be seen acting silly or childish, yet how many wish we could go back to enjoy the freedom and carefree days of our youth again? If you are on a soul-searching mission for your life's purpose, the things you liked to do as a kid are always a big clue. Doesn't it make sense that the true nature of your heart's desire was present in you as a child? If you've ever felt that the adult world is a bit drab and stilted and wanted to be able to go back to that childlike world of whimsy and fantasy you enjoyed when you were young, a connection with your Inner Child is the key.

For me it was also the key to relating to kids again. In a way, it is true that children and adults live in two different worlds. Children's worlds are full of wonder, magic and imagination until some nebulous moment in time when we seem to reach that point of no return. The door shuts and we find ourselves in the formal adult world of propriety and responsibilities. From personal experience, I remember that when my brother and I were kids, we would sooner have gone to the dentist than to have had to go to the Bronx to visit our great aunt and uncle. We sat in the stiff chairs and endured boring conversation and the smell of mothballs until we asked to be excused to go into the back bedroom to play cards or whatever we had brought to entertain ourselves until it was time to leave.

Then in our twenties when we thought we were "all grown up," I can remember how completely foreign children suddenly seemed to us. It was almost as if they were a different species with which we could not communicate. When I found myself around kids, I had no clue what to say to them. I confess to having felt completely disconnected from my own Inner Child, as if the baby really had been thrown out with the bath water.

Hearing The Inner Child

So let's look at what I've discovered life can be like if we could grow up and still keep our connection to that little person we once were. We could live in a world where the duality between being big or small can be bridged. The great humanistic psychologist, Abraham Maslow, puts the ability to "transcend dichotomies" high on his list of the ten qualities of self-actualization. We can create a world where we don't need to keep secrets from ourselves by pretending our Inner Child doesn't exist, and also by truly valuing all the things kids have to say and really listening to them.

Children are constantly admonished to "grow up!" and to not "be such a baby," or to "shut up and just listen." It doesn't surprise me, but it still disturbs me, when I have male clients who go back to incidents as children when they were told not to cry. One man, who was fighting an addiction to painkillers, had grown up in England, and went back into the humiliation he felt at his boarding school where he was made fun of for crying when he was only six years old and lost a karate match. Even worse was a case I had when a client's father had punished him and called him "a baby" for soiling his diapers which he was wearing because he was a baby!

We have moved beyond the belief so prevalent at the beginning of the 20th century that "children should be seen and not heard," but not completely. I once had a client who grew up around that time and was constantly fed that line. After two hours of trying to cajole his inner child out of his hiding places, he was finally able to say one word, "Hello." It was a breakthrough for that seventy-year-old man who began to weep with joy.

When will we have a world that truly honors the wisdom that comes "out of the mouths of babes"? The first thing we need to do is to learn to understand the way children communicate. For instance, in my work with adult survivors of childhood sexual abuse, I continually hear the Inner Child as having given very clear clues to the adults who could have stepped in to help. However, it was never by saying per se that someone was doing something to them. The way they told was in statements such as, *I don't like visiting Grandpa anymore. Do you have to leave me with him? Can't I go with you? I don't want to sleep in that room. I'm scared to go to sleep. Am I going to die tonight?*

I was quite lucky that my parents knew how to hear me when I was about four years old and said something that raised a red flag for them. Luckily, my babysitter had not yet hurt me when he "played a game" with me of getting naked and laying on the bed together after we had put my baby brother to sleep. The next morning I went into my parents' room and proudly announced, "I have a secret and I can't tell you what it is," just like my teenaged babysitter had instructed me. Of course, I'm sure the boy had expected me to keep the fact I *had* a secret to myself. If I had, he would have had the opportunity to go a little further the next time, as child molesters admit to doing, which I was saved from because of my father's perceptive listening skills.

I found out later in life, (actually my father and I had never discussed this incident until he read the first draft of this book), that on that very day in 1957, he went to that teenager's house and confronted the boy's father, exposing the secret. My dad insisted that the father send his son to therapy immediately or else he would take the next step and report it to the police. My father then followed up to make sure the family had taken the responsibility to get their son help, which they did. That action may have saved many children from sexual abuse since most offenders are known to have multiple victims.

Sometimes the way a child tells is not with words at all. Often the symptoms of the body are speaking for them instead. Obviously, with children who are being sexually abused, the tell-tale signs can come in the form of bladder or vaginal infections which are normally very rare in small children. Sometimes the mouth or throat area is affected. There may even be a marked decrease in the amount of talking a child does, because of the secretive nature of the act. The child may begin to cover his or her mouth more or make contortions with their lips as if they are being "buttoned up." In other words, the "telling" is being done through a child's silence.

It is not only children who are being abused who develop symptoms to let their bodies speak for them. When I was nine or ten years old, my body started talking to me in a painful way in the form of excruciating stomachaches. After the first of many barrages of tests over a ten-year period, which began at Massachusetts General Hospital in sixth grade, I was given a nebulous diagnosis of pre-ulcer. I believe today I would be diagnosed with Irritable Bowel Syndrome (IBS), since I was treated with anti-spasmodic medication. It wasn't until I began working on my issues in my thirties that I realized my Inner Child was speaking to me in a way I had not been able to hear.

I learned that my stomachaches were a response to the emotional repression caused by my desire to fit into my parents' and society's expectations of me in the 1960's. I was so eager to please, it was as if I was trying to squeeze myself into a smaller space than my soul required, and had to hold my breath most of the time in order to do it. Later in therapy I learned to breathe all of my "Debbie-ness" right into my solar plexus where I used to be riddled with pain, letting Little Debbie know I loved her just the way she was.

It makes sense that the first relief from the pain I ever achieved, that allowed me to stop carrying medicine around with me all the time, was when I started doing Transcendental Meditation (TM) in college. Interestingly, Deepak Chopra says that no drugs including anti-spasm drugs, opiates, anti-depressants, tranquilizers or bulk-forming agents have been found effective with healing IBS, which has no structural cause. Yet mind/body approaches and relaxation techniques, such as hypnotherapy, have had a near 100% success rate at reducing the classical symptoms.

Some of you may still be wondering why you should care whether or not you ever get in touch with your Inner Child, if such a thing exists? This is how I like to answer that question. Think of all the beautiful, wonderful things about children. The list of their positive qualities might include being *fun, intuitive, playful, happy, spontaneous, innocent, loving, curious, creative* and *authentic*. Now think about the things about kids that might drive you a little crazy. Their negative traits might include being *spoiled, bratty, loud, dependent, ungrateful, demanding, selfish, messy, mean* and *needy*.

Now think of adults you know. Do you know any adults who still have those negative traits of children? Those are people who have not developed a healthy relationship with their Inner Child. In fact, the truth is that for many of them, their bodies may be fully grown, but their emotional maturity may never have gone beyond that of being big kids disguised in adult bodies. They've simply sprouted into *spoiled, bratty, loud, dependent, ungrateful, demanding, selfish, messy, mean* and *needy* adults.

The Magical Child

Let's examine what happens when people consciously embrace and nurture their own Inner Child. They can mature gracefully into *fun, intuitive, playful, happy, spontaneous, innocent, loving, curious, creative* and *authentic* adults. By working through the physical and emotional pain that numbs us from enjoying the vibrancy the world has to offer, we are able to emerge healed and feeling whole again.

In Alchemical Hypnotherapy we do this through the technique of *Running and Changing* our past incidents that have festered and created emotional complexes in our psyches. We saw a good example of this with Barbara in Chapter 2 and her trauma as a child over trying not to upset her alcoholic father.

Let me give you another example of a simple "run and change" I did with a woman I'll call Anna who came to me feeling unhappy inside. She used words like "awful, unpleasant, inadequate, weak and undeserving" to describe herself and the lack of joy in her life. To get to the root of Anna's emotional complex we used the strategy of going back to the first time she felt that all her joy had been taken away.

During the session her subconscious mind immediately went to the memory of a time when Anna was little and her parents woke her up to drive to the mountains in the middle of the night in order to see snow and make snowmen. The only problem was when they got there the snow had melted and she felt that her parents had lied to her. To make matters worse, in her child's mind she actually believed the snowmen were *dead*. Anna had no idea that incident had devastated her Inner Child so much.

To make her feel better, her father's answer had been to tell her to look up at the stars and see the angels in the sky. In an amazing turn of events, during the session the angels told little Anna that the snowmen went up to be with them, and then, when it snowed, they went back down to be snowmen again. This delighted her child so much that we changed the incident by having little Anna imagine playing with what she was now calling the "snow angels" and she said there were even little ones she called "snow children." Anna came back from that session feeling renewed and ready to embrace life with joy again.

The way this works scientifically can best be understood through the exciting field of quantum physics. It tells us that every experience we have is colored through the perception of all our past experiences, which live in every cell of our body. Deepak Chopra, in his Mind Body Medicine course available to doctors, nurses, and other healthcare professionals, lays out a new perception of the body using the Quantum Mechanical Framework.

A "quantum" is the smallest indivisible unit of energy, and quantum physicists see a thought as a unit of information and energy, which is what they say the universe is made up of. They know that 98 percent of the atoms of the human body are replaced once a year and the DNA of an atom changes every two months. They say we need to reinterpret the body as a field of changing patterns that each person controls. Quantum physics sees the body as a river of energy and intelligence, since we are a part of a thinking, conscious universe.

Another way of looking at it is that our physical bodies are where our memories and dreams call home for awhile, and our minds house a field of information and energy that we experience subjectively. According to the research of quantum physics, *changing the perception of the body changes its physical constitution*. It shows that the way we experience the physical body is a direct result of all the concepts, ideas and beliefs we have held about it up to the present time.

I once had a chance to see that truth in action when I was a child away at summer camp. I went to a YMCA camp, and one night after dinner a camper at my table remarked how much she enjoyed dinner. Another girl at the table said, "I'm surprised. I thought you were kosher and didn't eat pork." Upon hearing those words, the same girl who had just finished telling us how much she liked the food, turned around and vomited. It obviously was the word "pork" and its association to her body/mind, and not the food itself, that resulted in that physical reaction.

Through her research with the neurotransmitters, Candace Pert has helped quantum physics prove that our mind is in every cell of our body. Our consciousness conceives, governs, constructs and becomes matter. Neuro-associated conditioning fixes us into a view of reality that is hard to break out of. So if you want to create a new healthy body, step out of the collection of memories and conditioned associations, and see the world as if for the first time, as my client, Anna, did with her snow angels. Use your memories, but don't let them use you. Know that you *have* thoughts, but you *are* the space between the thoughts.

Through therapeutic emotional clearing processes, such as Running and Changing Incidents and other techniques we use in Alchemy, we literally make our cells new again. It occurs through peeling off the layers of protection we wear in order to go on with our lives, and letting go of old worn out assumptions we've made about the world around us by re-examining them. When we talk about getting in touch with our Inner Child, we can see that this gives us the ability to perceive anew again in our adult body, through the eyes of a child. When we reach this state of clarity with our past we can begin to live fully in the present, and we can call this healed child who accompanies us now, our Magical Child.

One woman named Susan, who has done years of therapy to work through many painful childhood issues, both in traditional counseling and through Alchemy sessions, puts it this way:

If you really embrace that child, it will spring forth in you as a garden of wealth from which you can harvest happiness, joy and treasures that you would never expect. Carrying that child with you in your heart is a gift you can give yourself. To accept that child will keep you young at heart even though your body may be 50, 60 or 100, because you can see with the eyes of a child. You can be happy when you see leaves change and snow fall, or see a thunderbolt, even though your adult self may be tainted, having seen them so many times before. It's just like the reflection of that magical world we see when we look into the eyes of an infant.

The Adapted Child

Isn't it interesting the way nearly everybody adores babies until some point when that fascination ends? We can stare at anyone's baby all day long while they eat, crawl, learn to walk, sleep, gurgle, laugh, cry, even have their diapers changed. When is it that the love affair between babies and grown-ups stops? Could it be when they begin to talk and really assert themselves, usually around the "terrible two's," which we saw can bring up our Judges? Suddenly what was cute as pie becomes challenging and sometimes downright annoying, especially when we don't want to hear what they have to say.

Luckily, unless kids go into complete rebellion when they get older, as we'll explore next chapter, children are usually moldable and adaptable to their parents' wishes. In the same way a plant bends toward the sun, kids will intuitively comply in the direction of love and approval. This creates an array of Sub-personalities who stem from one's Adapted Child, including, but by no means limited to, the Inner Judge.

So many people miss the wisdom they could receive from their Inner Child because just as people tend to ignore a lot of the ramblings of children, they similarly dismiss the messages coming to them from their *Inner* Child. They either have no clue that one exists or they don't realize the gifts it could bring once they would tune in. Keisha came to me because she felt completely blocked from being able to take her real estate brokers license exam. She had even tried to trick herself by paying for it first, but she still could not get herself to study and actually lost her money instead of showing up for the test, due to her emotional shutdown over it.

When I began to dialogue with her parts in a session, her Ms. Independent was the one who was determined to take it and pass it, to prove that she could do anything, like she always had to, growing up with five brothers. The fact that Keisha was simultaneously pursuing careers in three different fields and starting a non-profit foundation to help support cancer patients didn't faze Ms. Independent. After all, she had told me her father never slept and never let the children rest. If he saw them doing nothing, he made their mother give them a chore to do. During the session Keisha saw that she was being just like her father and heard the inner guidance that to counteract that tendency, she needed to play more.

Even though her father had been dead for years (which is no obstacle for communication to take place on the inner plane), Keisha found him more than eager to have a chance to give her some post mortem fatherly advice. In her mind she heard her dad give her Inner Child a very clear message for Keisha to pass on to all of his kids to "go have fun!" He even apologized for making her feel so overly responsible, and for giving her the message that it was irresponsible to rest.

That opened up a chance to dialogue with her child who began listing all the ways she knew how to play and have *lots* of fun. Then little Keisha told her that after playing they would be able to concentrate on studying. She actually gave her advice in a way only a child can by advising her to wear pink the day she goes to take her exam and to, "Give a little love to the test. Stop thinking of it like the big, bad grizzly bear."

This is an example of how children intuitively learn what pleases their parents and what displeases them and how they learn to adapt. It is simply an instinctive matter of survival that kicks in at an unconscious level, just as surely as it would if we were drowning and fighting to breathe. Survival of the human species can only exist if there are parents to bring up children, who need their care longer than any other mammal on the planet. By becoming conscious of these behaviors we can change them to become the person we want to be, rather than the one we needed to be in order to fit in growing up.

The truth is that although we may be instilled with certain inherent behavioral traits, every character we are delineating in this book could have been born out of an adaptation we made in our personality in order to conform to our environment. We may have needed to be funny or skeptical or people-pleasing or perfect. In this case, the Intellectual Character of Ms. Independent, who is dominant in this client's life, illustrates the development of an Adapted Child. She learned in her session she can still utilize the strengths of Ms. Independent, within the new parameters of balance she'll find as her Inner Child teaches her to play and rest more. And enjoy life.

The Wounded Child

Since the adaptations we make in order to survive manifest as Sub-personalities, and obviously the descriptions of all the characters have a positive and a negative side to them, you now realize that the contamination inherent in their weaknesses stems from a deep subconscious wound and not a conscious desire to be bad. Those unhealed places inside are responsible, as well, for the fact that we have so many adults walking around acting like big spoiled children.

It is as tempting to simply, "Say no" to that behavior, as it would be to say it to a pesky child who's trying to get our attention. However, we know that ignoring kids tends to induce even louder and more aggravated attempts to get us to listen. Similarly, the longer we put off listening to our wounded Inner Child, the more he and she will act out. That is why the "Just Say No" to drugs, alcohol or sex approach cannot be successful in and of itself, without addressing the underlying causes of the behaviors.

By remaining oblivious we are actually hurting ourselves, by not seeing our inappropriate conduct as a symptom of deeper issues begging to be addressed.

The majority of people choose the path of least resistance and never decide to delve within to see what is there. Just as with a leaky faucet, or any other problem we choose to ignore, it does not go away. Instead, the human organism has a myriad of ways to spring a leak. Apart from addictive behaviors, it can manifest internally in psychological ways such as depression, anxiety, dementia, or any number of mental illnesses, or physically as ulcers, tumors, allergies, cancer, headaches, chronic pain or degenerative diseases. Many relaxation techniques such as bio-feedback, meditation, deep breathing and yoga have already been scientifically proven to be helpful for many of these symptoms.

What dialoguing with the Inner Child does that is different, is that it gets to the root of the problem. Perhaps this account of a dream a woman had and wrote down will illustrate how the subconscious mind actually sees the Inner Child as a living, breathing entity inside us, and urges us toward reconciliation with ours. Her words are both an accurate re-telling of her experience and an insightful analysis of its meaning to her:

I travel a long way, and then on the street I meet a child. It's a girl. She appears as a stuck-up little snob. She's answering back and she's not behaving very nice. I am telling her off for being such a naughty, spoiled little brat, and somehow, instead of answering me back, she appears to be on the edge of tears, saying, "Just wait 'til my dad comes. He'll tell you off for shouting at me."

Then I feel sorry for her and say, "Let's go to bed and sleep and be good girls," and as we lay down I feel calm and I notice that there's no little girl around; that it's always been only me, my scared to death inner child, knowing myself, frightened by life, by being alone, by possibilities that something could go wrong. And I was shouting at her and being so sharp to that poor little bird inside me!

All of a sudden, the grown-up me, finds myself at some familiar place. There are some marble pillars around and a fountain. In the fountain there's a small half-broken wooden toy, the hedgehog, my toy from a childhood, that now, after all these years looks more like a shabby brush for cleaning wooden floors. I am touched and delighted to see it, and somewhere from the background I can hear music. It's a song from a long time forgotten; an ad [jingle] that I loved as a child.

I feel tears on my cheeks. I am stretching my arms toward the hedgehog, trying to get a hold of it, but it all disappears. I awake sobbing and cry loudly without any shame. I cry for my inner child I treated so harshly, not having understood that its naughtiness was just an answer to the enormous fear of being left alone.

As brazenly as our adult mind is so quick to disconnect from our past pain, this dream depicts the nebulous boundaries our subconscious asserts between who we were then and now; and how it works toward reconciliation and integration. Of course, in this example, we don't even need to dig for any interpretation. It's actually much closer to the way I work with the subconscious mind in sessions, than the way it usually presents to us in our dreams. Metaphorically speaking, David Quigley claims that there is a Wounded Inner Child present inside us for every developmental stage of our life that we did not get a chance to finish up during childhood.

The Parent/Adult

To conclude the discussion of The Child we'll delve into the Sub-personality of The Parent or Adult inside of us whose function it is to take care of children, including one's Inner Child. This is not to be confused with the spiritual archetype of an Inner Parent which emerges as a Guide from within and will be discussed at length in Chapter 12 along with other types of Inner Guides. This Sub-personality, as we shall define it, is strictly the part of a person who plays the role of parent—and may or may not do it very well.

This often overlooked Sub-personality became evident to me a few years into my practice. Going into sessions I automatically expected to find the solution to people's dilemmas by tracing back to the causative incident in childhood to discover and rescue the associated Wounded Child. However, more and more I began to detect an interesting anomaly.

What I was assessing in some clients as *resistance* to being able to find their Inner Child, I came to realize was actually the case of there being *no adult* present. The Inner Child was running the show! I had to rethink the course of therapy we needed to take, and change directions to instead go in search of the client's Adult or The Parent part of them. It became evident that as my much as my eyes told me I was gazing at an adult, the fact was that there was really a big child sitting in front of me who had taken over and was in charge.

These are often clients who didn't have a good example of healthy parenting modeled to them as they were growing up. There are many reasons for this including, but by no means limited to, being orphaned. The death of one parent, divorce, poverty, as well as a parent's physical or mental illness are all possible causes for people to grow up without an understanding of what it's like to have their parents' unconditional love. Most of the time, however, it's simply a matter of one's parents having received inadequate parenting during their childhood.

I've even found clients from very wealthy families where the parents were literally absent or otherwise pre-occupied because of work or social obligations, and the children were placed in the care of nannies or other hired help to receive most of their emotional needs. In these cases money and gifts often took the place of love. In other instances parental emotional, physical or mental abuse blurred the perception of what parenting looked like. Sometimes parents were simply too busy working to make ends meet, unable to perform all their parental duties due to time constraints and no fault of their own.

In such cases the work I do revolves around letting a client see how their Child made the necessary adaptations in order to survive, constantly searching for the fulfillment of their basic needs for love and nurturance any way they could. They might have substituted eating or other addictive behaviors to fill the void and seek comfort; or never felt completely fulfilled, even within seemingly happy marriages, and didn't understand why. The most important thing to do with these clients is to teach them that they deserved more—without any need to place blame or judgment—and that it's not too late for them to find that Parent or Adult within themselves to give the love they always desired to their Inner Child.

YESSSS! (margin annotation)

As far as the traits of The Parent/Adult Sub-personality, some of the positive ones would include being understanding, extroverted, giving, generous and caring. These qualities can be so evident in some people who are dominated by this persona that all the kids in the neighborhood (and sometimes even the other adults) might call him or her "Mama" or "Gramps" because the desire to nurture everyone around them exudes from them.

Mom - take care of LR (margin annotation)

On the toxic side we may know parents who are smothering, Co-dependent and overly protective. Taken to an extreme it can leak out onto their children who might be known as "Mama's boys" or are sheltered from the world and may not even be allowed to go out and play. Another toxic trait of The Parent could be the proverbial stage mother who pushes their children into beauty pageants or talent shows, even if they may be obviously untalented or disinterested. Gypsy Rose Lee's mother is a good example.

Betsy B. came to see me because she realized she had a history of getting into unhealthy relationships. We discovered a contaminated part of her we named "Mom" that kept picking the wrong kind of guys in the past because this part liked to mother them. She suddenly realized this was why all her previous boy friends had elements of being little boys in them. The sadness at losing her last boy friend quickly went away when she realized it was that Mom character who was the one who couldn't let go. Betsy was then freed up to change that pattern and find a mature man to love, while Mom was redirected to the more appropriate job of taking care of Little Betsy.

At this point I should mention that in Transactional Analysis (T.A.) they use the terms Parent, Adult and Child (P-A-C) in a very specific way that is a bit different and may be confusing for those of you who are familiar with that school of psychology and personality theory. Let me take a moment to compare the connotations of these three words to make the distinction clear.

In his classic book from 1967, *I'm OK—You're OK: a Practical Guide to Transactional Analysis,* this is how Dr. Thomas Harris defines the Parent: "The Parent is a huge collection of recordings *in the brain* of unquestioned or imposed *external events* (italics added)." According to our definition that would cover all the *External Characters* and *Intellectual Characters* we've met in the previous chapters (especially The Judge), whose messages were internalized from childhood—most specifically the ways we were told we were bad (or "not OK").

Harris defines the Child as the one who records all the transactions of *internal events* early in life and as he says, "Since the little person has no vocabulary during the most critical of his early experiences, most of his reactions are *feelings*." Thus the Child, as perceived in Transactional Analysis, would be synonymous with the way we have presented all aspects of The Child here, and would include as well, any or all of the *Emotional Characters* in the following chapters.

Now the Adult, as delineated in T.A., is seen as the "data-processing computer." Harris puts it all together this way, "Through the Adult the little person can begin to tell the difference between life as it was taught and demonstrated to him (Parent), life as he felt it or wished it or fantasized it (Child), and life as he figures it out by himself (Adult)." Their definition of the Adult relates to the positive traits of The Parent/Adult that I listed above.

In its highest form The Adult persona would coincide with what I call the "Clear Balanced Center" in my Wheel of Characters diagram. When we have truly achieved the state of Inner Voice Integration, this is the clear part of us who can observe all of our Sub-personalities as they act their various roles around the spokes of the wheel, yet can remain centered, watching it all and processing it from the central hub without judgment.

Summary

This chapter began our exploration of the Emotional Characters by introducing The Inner Child who can be found in many forms. We learned that the way we grew up and survived as best we could was by adapting into any number of the various Sub-personalities delineated in this book, each one of which can actually be defined as an Adapted Child. Yet even as the constellation of these adapted traits have formed our adult personality, there is always the voice of our Inner Child self, who has often been silenced, squelched and repressed beneath the louder voices.

When we are fully in touch with our Magical Child we can be inspired to new heights of creativity and joy because we are really listening to what our heart desires. Yet, before we can achieve that connection it is necessary to first heal the traumas of our Wounded Child, who can otherwise stew inside of us and cause toxic symptoms in our body or emotions.

We looked at some of the unique ways in which the child can speak, such as through silence or bodily symptoms. Ignoring the cries of our child can clearly block us from fulfilling ourselves and finding our bliss, and may result in illness and pain. It is the job of our Parent or Adult to listen, understand and love our Child.

The true goal of getting in touch with the voices of all of our Sub-personalities, including our Inner Child, is to allow them to become integrated into a connected body/mind/spirit. In reality, there has been so much research annotating the physiological impact of the mind/body connection that you could say, they are one and the same system—what Candace Pert simply calls the *bodymind*. The powerful fabric that holds it all together is *love*. The purpose of learning which persona is beneath the voices we hear in our heads is to learn to hear what they are telling us and embrace each one as a unique, lovable part of ourselves.

We have the choice to separate our "Selves," even from ourselves, in the unconscious way most of us do in our western society through the negative, disparate voices inside us. Or we can choose to feel the deep interconnectedness within ourselves first, so that we can then expand it into a feeling of oneness with everyone and everything else. As much as your Inner Judge may object, you have the final power to embrace each part of you, including that child you once were, and begin the process of truly accepting and loving yourself (and selves) unconditionally.

EXERCISE

This exercise may stretch you out of your comfort zone more than any other so far. I urge you to bend as much as you can—it's for your ultimate benefit.

> ➤ Begin to formulate the characteristics of your Inner Child by making a list of some of the positive (perhaps even childlike) and negative (childish) traits you believe he or she displays in your personality. For instance, you might not know if it comes from your Inner Child, but if you have a short attention span and a quick temper, write those in the list of negative qualities. You can even use bodily ailments you'd like to be rid of in this list. If you are a loving person and like to lend a hand to a friend in need, put those down as positive qualities.

> ➤ See if you can get the list to include at least ten traits for each side. If you have a problem coming up with them, ask a close friend or relative for their perception of you.

> ➤ Know that the list of negative traits represents an opportunity. You can now decide whether to keep displaying them, or to transform them by beginning a journey to heal from the experiences of your life that left these scars, by listening to this child and possibly starting a path of therapy.

> ➤ (Optional steps) Find a stuffed animal that is somehow meaningful to you. Maybe you already have one in the house, or you may need to borrow or buy one. Make sure it is visually attractive to you and soft and cuddly to the touch.

➢ Hold the stuffed animal out in front of you and look it in the eyes. Read your list of positive traits, as if the stuffed animal is your Inner Child beginning with, "I love you, little (your name), because you are …"

➢ Now read your list of negative traits, beginning with the phrase, "I don't like it when you…"

➢ Put your list down and now hug the stuffed animal as if it is your Inner Child and listen to hear if he or she has anything to say back to you.

➢ Journal any insights you receive.

THE EMOTIONAL CHARACTERS

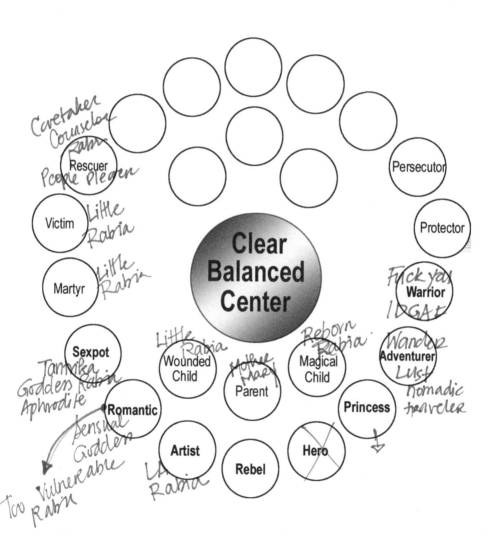

Clear Balanced Center

Rescuer · Victim · Martyr · Sexpot · Romantic · Artist · Wounded Child · Parent · Rebel · Hero · Magical Child · Princess · Adventurer · Warrior · Protector · Persecutor

Handwritten annotations:
Caretaker Counselor Rabia
People Pleaser
Little Rabia
Little Rabia
Tamika Goddess Rabia Aphrodite
Sensual Goddess
Too Vulnerable Rabia
Little Rabia
Mother Mary
Little Rabia
Reborn Rabia
Fuck you IDGAF
Wander Lust
nomadic traveler

Do what you feel to be right,
for you'll be criticized anyway.

— Eleanor Roosevelt

Chapter 6

WHAT GOES ON IN YOUR HEART?

In the Chapter 5, we explored the three aspects of the Inner Child, the first of our Emotional Characters. The Magical Child and Wounded Child would correlate to the positive and negative qualities of all the characters we are delineating and the Adapted Child can be understood to manifest, potentially, as any of our list of characters. These next two chapters will continue to introduce you to an array of Emotional Characters you should be readily able to relate to either in yourself or others.

The Prince/Princess

We met the archetype of The King and Queen as Intellectual Characters. Here we have a less mature, younger and more emotional version. It could also be seen as an older, perhaps teenaged, Inner Child. The most important quality this Sub-personality has to offer is a deep sense of deservingness. There are so many people with a wounded Inner Child and fragile egos whose sense of self-worth is low. In fact, I would say that the most common issue that threads through the histories of most of my clients is a self-proclaimed lack of self-esteem.

Connecting with their Inner Prince or Princess can instantly add value to their self worth because this character knows how to receive all the gifts and compliments the universe brings to them. It's like second nature for some people to be set to rebut every nice thing anyone tells them with an instant negation or apology. Maybe you've even caught yourself replying to a comment of how nice you look with a retort such as, "Oh, this old thing," or "No way, I didn't even put on any makeup today."

I have had several clients who were so self-deprecating, that I've had to give them homework to graciously accept all compliments by simply saying, "Thank you" for at least one whole day. You would have thought by their objections that I was torturing them. In cases such as that, which are not so uncommon, it is invaluable for them to be able to get in touch with this part in themselves. Another assignment I might give would be to start pampering themselves in luxurious ways such as long bubble baths, a massage, or aromatherapy. The Inner Princess or Prince can be cajoled out through such indulgences.

Of course, it is also possible for a person to be endowed with an over-inflated sense of self importance by a contaminated Prince or Princess. These people expect to be waited on hand and foot. You might say they act like they were born with a silver spoon. It could be a matter of their birth position, such as Paris Hilton or Nicole Ritchie, or they may be living in a fantasy. A typical secret hope they may be harboring would be, *Someday my Prince will come.*

Some children who don't feel appreciated in their present circumstances even retreat into the daydream that, *My real parents are a king and queen and one day they'll come back for me.* That notion could be a saving grace for them, or it could lead them into feelings of superiority and being above the mundane tasks of picking up their toys and cleaning their rooms. They may start acting like prima donnas or spoiled brats demanding special treatment and feeling above the rules that apply to everyone else.

As they get older, crying over a broken nail or refusing to go out in anything less than an Armani suit can become quite tiresome to others, although there are plenty of spas and fashion houses to cater to their whims. A healthy balance of deservingness with a dose of humility is a winning combination. I believe both Princess Diana and John Kennedy, Jr. exemplified the best of this archetype. Sarah Ferguson and Michelle Kwan continue to model gracefully the best of a modern-day Princess.

When I started having my own Alchemical work done, and was healing from a string of damaging Co-dependent relationships, I relied heavily on my Inner Princess to boost my self-esteem. I went back to the comfort I felt when I was little and my grandfather would call me "Princess" and I brought that resource back with me. One of my students, who is a recovering alcoholic and has learned to put up healthy boundaries, has an Inner Princess whose sense of merit is summed up in the phrase she uses as a motto with men, *What part of treating me like a Goddess don't you understand?*

The Rebel

Part of the maturing process includes developing an identification of oneself as separate from one's parents. This usually happens around puberty and involves a period of rebellion against the status quo while the teenager explores and pushes against the boundaries of his or her world. Since virtually all of us experience this phase of defining ourselves in the world, most of us can relate to this Sub-personality, at least to some extent.

The rebelliousness does not have to be against your parents; it can be against an institution such as school, a religion, or even the government. The Sixties was a time when a whole generation, defining itself by the slogan, "sex, drugs, rock & roll," began to rebel against the social structure, which had never been questioned before. Even the gender lines were being bent for the first time as boys grew their hair long and girls began to wear pants and burn their bras.

I had one client who was doing a Conference Room session on the issue of making money. Her Rebel came to the Conference Room table and sat down right next to her Inner Preacher, who was contaminated with the programming from her early days at her parochial school. When he gave his very strong opinion that she should tithe all her extra money to the church, her Rebel started blasting him with all the hypocrisy she saw growing up.

It brought her right back to when her whole class used to rebel against their "No Dancing" policy by wearing their corsages to church on Sunday after the Saturday night dance they had defiantly attended. Through lots of dialogue we were able to utilize The Rebel's righteous anger to break the Inner Preacher's subconscious hold on her that kept telling her she didn't deserve money for herself. This ability to take a stand and say "No!" to things that don't feel right is one of the main strengths of The Rebel.

There is one interesting oxymoron around the concept of teenage rebellion. Often built into the need to be different from the given "enemy" is a deeper need to conform to the peer group the teen is now affiliating with. It may have been by piling into phone booths in the '50's, smoking pot in the '60's and vowing virginity until marriage in the '90's. Proving oneself as part of the crowd can even take rebelling to dangerous or life-threatening ends, such as we see in gang or fraternity hazing rituals.

The Rebel archetype includes all of the above characteristics and assumes an autonomous identity within almost all of us, coming forth to display itself as needed by our individual life circumstances. A bit of a Rebel could be just the right spice your life needs to keep it from becoming too humdrum. The Rebel is the one who whispers in your ear, *Go ahead and take a chance; Splurge on yourself; Play hooky from work and go fishing; Who cares what anybody thinks! Try it—you'll like it.*

Without the spirit of the Rebel, we would all be conformists to exactly what we were taught, without ever venturing outside the box. Of course, like anything, it can be taken too far and it's important to seek the proper balance. A contaminated out-of-control Rebel might sound a lot ruder in our ears. In fact he'd probably speak with a lot of expletives and four-letter words, which make them difficult to list here in their entirety, so you can fill in the blanks for yourself.

The basic thread of an unhappy Rebel's inner discourse would basically sound like: *Who the Hell does he think he is? (Blank) him if he can't take a joke. I'm outta here! If she thinks I'm doing that just because she says so, she's crazy. Don't mess with me. That driver just cut me off; he can't get away with that!* Obviously there are many people in the outside world to clash with, but often the outrage our Rebel is responding to is against one of our own Intellectual Characters. We saw the above example of rebelling against The Preacher, but the most common is against our Inner Judge. The Judge/Rebel feud is older than that of the Hatfields and McCoys.

The more out of touch the demands of our Judge are with our heart's desire, the louder the retaliatory tactics of our Inner Rebel. In fact it is rare to have a session where I only hear from someone's Judge. That would be like having a debate where only one of the parties shows up. The Rebel is the polar opposite of The Judge, where The Judge will always side with reason and social acceptance, and The Rebel will always come back with how the person feels about things, despite what The Judge thinks he or she "should" do. The goal, of course, is for those to be the same thing. Then we live in a state of peaceful detente. Otherwise it can lead to a Rebel-dominated personality, such as the stereotypical "Rebel Without a Cause."

The Adventurer and The Hero/Heroine

The best way to get a good feel for these two characters and to learn the distinction between them is to illustrate them through two well-known *Star Wars* characters, Hans Solo and Luke Skywalker. Think about the difference between these two. Even though we see Luke go through many adventures, he would, nevertheless, depict the archetype of The Hero. He is out to avenge the death of his aunt and uncle with selfless, altruistic motives.

Hans Solo, on the other hand, is the captain of a fast ship and will risk his life running from the star fighters because he needs the money Luke will pay him so he can get the bounty hunters off his back. Throughout most of the first movie, his motives are purely self-serving and he admits he has no desire to get involved fighting someone else's battle. It's all a big adventure for him, even though in the end, he does move into a hero role himself.

People whose personalities are dominated by The Adventurer value their freedom above all else. As the vehicle to take them exploring all the great adventures the world has to offer, their body is also valued very highly, and they work hard to take care of it. They may be athletes or at least on a regimen of physical fitness and healthy eating habits. Because of the many wonderful experiences they have had, they are generally quite entertaining, gregarious and good storytellers.

Their physical fitness and entertainment value tend to make them very attractive, but beware of getting into a relationship with someone with a strong Adventurer (unless you are one, too), because settling down is incompatible with their nature. Their relationship with you will probably become just one more of their adventures. They may even spice it up with a bit of high drama because they tend to attract a lot of that, and it could make a better story. Speaking of stories, you may not want to believe everything they have to say—that fish they caught may get a little bit bigger every time they talk about it.

By the way, while you're busy working for a living, it's best not to trust them with that rent money you're tempted to give them to drop off at the landlord's. It may never get there, but they'll have a great excuse for why not. It could serve as the perfect segue for the exit to their next big escapade. Otherwise something else will, because the routine of settling down quickly becomes too mundane and the road will call once more. Adventurers make much better friends or lovers than mates or roommates, as the boredom factor sets in quickly for them. Just like the rolling stone that gathers no moss, it's very difficult for The Adventurer to put down roots.

However, if your own life is too mundane, you may want to listen for the voice of your Inner Adventurer urging you to book that trip you've always wanted to take to Tahiti, or pursue whatever personal goal you never seem to have time to fulfill. Whether it's trying out for a part in a play, going whitewater rafting, or visiting a friend far away, allow The Adventurer to lead you out of any ruts you have fallen into. When my father's best friend dropped dead of a heart attack at forty-two before he had gotten to take his family on any vacations due to his heavy workload, my father vowed never to let opportunities for fun to slip by. Too bad it was too late to impart that wisdom to his friend.

The Hero label is one that often comes to people through outside circumstances. It could be from running into a burning building, or stepping out in front of a car to save a child. It could be from stopping a purse-snatcher or anything else that puts them at the right place at the right time, to which they respond by doing the right thing. Usually when these people are interviewed, we see other people calling them a hero, while they downplay what they did.

Captain "Sully" Sullenberger, who safely landed US Airways Flight 1549 in the Hudson River in the winter of 2009, is a perfect example. In the eyes of the 155 people on board, who all walked away from that near-disaster, their loved ones, and the rest of the world, he personifies The Hero. Yet when interviewed just days later and asked how he feels about being labeled with that moniker, he replied, "I don't feel comfortable with it; but I don't want to make them wrong." He further admitted "I'm beginning to understand why they may feel that way." From his perspective he was just doing what all his training up to that moment in his life had prepared him to do.

Although that story obviously received widespread attention for the heroics involved, similar cases of everyday heroes sprinkle the local news every year. On any given day, an athlete can become a hero to his or her fans, by making a certain play that wins a game or a championship. However this role is not an easy one to assume.

Even Charlie Brown knows that it is a slippery slope from Hero to Goat—a lesson many political and sports heroes learn the hard way. Just ask Michael Vick who was a star quarterback with the Atlanta Falcons until he was caught running a dog-fighting operation. Similarly, baseball legends in their own time Alex "A-Rod" Rodriguez and Barry Bonds, as well as Olympic gold medalist Marion Jones, to name just a few, all faced steroid accusations that disappointed their adoring fans.

During the 2008 U.S. Presidential election, "Joe the Plumber" was in fact called "the hero to conservatives" by many including a NY Times blog site, and he rode that train all the way to a book deal. Of course the very question he asked Obama about higher taxes during a campaign stop, which shot Joe into the limelight, also resulted in him being investigated and found to be delinquent in paying his own taxes. We will explore the dynamic behind the ubiquitous scandals that plague so many prominent figures when we delve into our dark side in Chapter 10.

Unlike the high number of Rebel-dominant people, it's unusual to find many Hero-dominated personalities. Those individuals are likely to be people who purposely choose the kind of pursuits that put them in harm's way knowingly, as in our example of Luke Skywalker. This would include the noble ranks of firefighters and law enforcement officers. It's interesting that so many fictional superheroes have an alter ego who is very plain, such as Superman, Batman and Spiderman, since it would be very difficult to live in The Hero persona all day every day.

Of course, those who choose The Hero's path already have personality traits that lead them there. Even though he may have many adventures along the way and even get caught up in the dramatics, The Hero is basically altruistic, while The Adventurer, like Hans Solo, is much more out for his own personal thrills. The fictional last name may have been chosen by design, since Adventurers tend to be more solitary and may not do so well as part of a team. The Hero is more likely to get drawn into what he does because he believes in a cause or a higher calling, which is all the personal satisfaction he needs.

Based on the numerous references to heroes in the media, especially post-9/11, in songs, in the news, in the military, in sports, in the movies, in space, on reality TV shows, at schools, and everywhere you look, it seems apparent that society needs them today. Instead of always seeking the hero worship of our idols, however, perhaps it's time to begin the archetypal hero's journey in ourselves that Joseph Campbell wrote about. Mariah Carey's song, *Hero*, describes it beautifully: "and when you feel that hope is gone, look inside you and be strong. And you'll finally see the truth: that a Hero lies in you."

I don't believe a better case for it can be made than the one depicted in *Spiderman 2* when Peter Parker begins to merge with the superhero persona as he gets unmasked and reveals himself. He goes through periods where his powers fail him, and struggles with his belief system that tells him he can't maintain both a fulfilling personal life and his superhero status. Yet he discovers in the end, he can have it all. His allegorical journey can be seen as our journey: Finding out what our own inner strengths and gifts are, and utilizing them to fulfill our destiny.

Before we leave this character, it's important to look at the possible pitfalls contained here, as we already touched on above. The notice a hero attracts gives more of an impetus to some people with weak egos to want to become one, especially after having tasted the thrill of the adoration of the masses or the media attention. This brings us to the contaminated aspects of The Hero. We've all heard of those sad cases where a tragic fire was found to be started by the very same person who was first touted as a hero for discovering it. Sometimes the one responsible was even a firefighter who was actually injured putting it out.

One downside to The Hero is the potential to become addicted to the feeling of being adored, admired, even emulated. Of course since we tend to grant hero status to people who rescue others from danger, the Co-dependent relationship set up for a contaminated Hero is the need to find victims to rescue. Thus this need for adulation can actually lead to the disempowerment of others to play the victim role for him. Other personality flaws can ensue, also, including delusions of grandeur and becoming glory-mongers. Or they may continue to revel in their moment of fame, such as a high school football hero, never able to recapture that feeling, leading to them to live in their glory days of the past forever.

The Warrior Ryan

The Warrior combines a bit of The Hero and The Adventurer, but more in the context of battle. The battle does not necessarily mean on the battlefield, as we can infer from the term, "spiritual warrior," as used in the ancient Celtic divination tool of Rune stones, it could simply indicate a stance some people assume as they go through life. It's in their posturing and attitude of "don't mess with me" that they seem to exude. You see it in students and masters of the martial arts. They don't go around picking fights, but they know if someone picks one with them, they are fully equipped and prepared to defend themselves.

They are also prepared to fight for anyone they see who is being mistreated, but they do so without any thought of being singled out as a hero. They would simply see it as something that needs to be done. Since Warriors are defenders and protectors of the innocent, we know that the military is full of them. In fact, the military is a Warrior-creating machine. This archetype can actually be, and literally is, drilled into people from the moment they enter basic training. The military mentality that needs to be implanted in the mind of every soldier is best expressed in the words of the poem, *The Charge of the Light Brigade*: "Yours is not to question why, yours is but to do and die."

Remembering that we are placing The Warrior in the category of Emotional, rather than Intellectual Characters may be a bit confusing. Let's examine why it fits here. The Warrior's emotions may not be so apparent, because, for the sake of being prepared to face warfare, the softer emotions of soldiers need to be drilled out of them. However, other very powerful emotions run deep, such as patriotism, loyalty, rage, and the willingness to die for a cause. The marine slogan of, "no man left behind" is a very intense emotion. The passion you hear from men in the field as they put themselves in danger to save a member of their unit is apparent and emotionally charged.

One Vietnam vet explained it to me as a reflex action that happens before the brain has even had time to engage. He said if there were a group of soldiers together and one saw a grenade nearby, he would automatically fling his body on top of it without ever thinking about the act and its consequences to him. It would not strike him as having been heroic, but strategic, although he would be lauded as a hero by those around him whom he saved, and honored as one by governmental medals.

Of course, as with all our characters there is a potentially negative side to The Warrior. One danger is the mindset to see warfare as a solution for everything. This mentality says things such as: *shoot first, ask questions later; might makes right; I was just following orders;* and *kill for peace.* If we combine the mindset of The Martyr, whom we'll meet in Chapter 9, with that of The Warrior we come up with kamikaze pilots and suicide bombers. The same would be true of Samurai warriors who committed hari kari as an honorable end.

Other negative trappings could include being insensitive, heartless, cruel, domineering, and intimidating. All through history, including in our current events, we see the results of this shadow side of The Warrior including such catastrophes as the genocide of Native Americans, the Mei Lai massacre, Tiananmen Square and the Nazi concentration camps. When you combine the contaminated mentalities of The Warrior with The Preacher you get such events as the Crusades, the Holy Inquisition, the Taliban, abortion clinic bombings, and September 11th.

Let's come back to the usefulness of this character in our everyday lives. The greatest gift of The Warrior, which I work to impart especially to my female clients, is the ability to draw a line in the sand and stand behind it. It can help us feel strength and courage in our convictions and an ability to stand up for them. From the time boys are little they are being trained and encouraged to "put up their dukes and fight like a man" while girls are taught to back away from confrontations and be the peacemakers. (More about this in the chapters on Co-dependency.)

Of course, that is a generalization based on sex-role stereotypes. In reality we have some very formidable women and some very wimpy men. Regardless of one's gender, the danger of being without a strong internalized Warrior (or the female counterpart could be called The Amazon) to stand up for ourselves, is the potential of being pushed around, victimized, and hopelessly Co-dependent.

The Sexpot

The Sexpot side of us is one that many people may work hard to hide or disown. It generally doesn't work, which can get people into boatloads of trouble (as we shall see in Chapter 10 when we explore The Shadow). So unless you have committed yourself to a life of celibacy, you may as well have some fun exploring this part of you.

I urge you again to be creative with these different parts of yourself, by giving them personalized and meaningful names. Of course we know many men are already prone to giving this side of themselves pet names. Perhaps, we could say it is the way guys have always owned up to and expressed the fact that they are not alone in there. Most of them would even admit that sometimes that part of them has a mind of its own. However, that's not exactly what I mean. It would be better to be able to name the whole side of you that is your Sexpot, rather than delegating it to only one particular body part.

For instance, I did a session with a man who was happily married to the same woman for many years, but the marriage was being put in jeopardy by his professed addiction to surfing pornographic sites on the Internet. I commended him for his courage to face this issue in therapy. Who knows how many men he represents who continue to act out in secrecy and shame? He certainly was not alone in supporting this $57 billion a year worldwide industry. In the United States, $2.5 billion is spent on Internet porn alone.

These recent statistics from Family Safe Media also contend that pornography revenue is larger than the combined revenues of all professional football, baseball and basketball franchises. It looks like my client, who for fun we can call Peter, is in the company of 40 million American adults (28 percent of whom are women) who admit to regularly looking at pornographic websites. Ten percent consider themselves addicted. Interestingly, 53 percent of men in Promise Keepers said they looked at a site in the last week, and 47 percent of Christians claimed pornography is a major problem in the home.

Turning our attention back to Peter, he gave the name of "Dirty Old Guy" to his Sexpot, or maybe the contaminated aspect of this Sub-personality could be more appropriately labeled, The Lecher. By doing an Alchemical process with him, called the Addicted Personality Technique (APT) we came to understand what it was he really desired. It turned out it was something we can't print here, but suffice it to say it was definitely something he would never be able to get out of his computer.

However, by discovering his Inner Woman, (an archetype we will explore in the chapters on Guides), he found he could have all his wishes fulfilled. He no longer felt like a Lecher or a Dirty Old Guy when he was with his Inner Woman, whom we'll call Isis, so he gave his Inner Sexpot a new name to match, Antonio. As he embodied Antonio, Isis was much more appealing than that "empty feeling" he had admitted to experiencing after his Internet exploits, whenever he compared being on the computer to being with her. After all, we know the biggest sex organ is the human brain.

Whether a person is sitting in front of a keyboard and a computer screen with images on it, or shutting his eyes with beautiful visions being created by his imagination, is there that much difference? It's a matter of first choosing one fantasy over another, and secondly, deciding which one is healthier. Who wouldn't choose Antonio over a Dirty Old Guy? We might even call the highest vibration of The Sexpot a Sex God or Goddess. Best of all, this session had a positive effect on his marriage and his sex life with his wife.

As we've heard so many times in the metaphysical community, *we are not human beings having a spiritual experience, but spiritual beings having a human experience.* Well, as physical beings it is important to enjoy the privileges of the body. In fact there is even a Yoga practice that is a branch of Buddhism called Tantra, which espouses the discipline of sexual practices, such as those found in the Kama Sutra, as a way to enlightenment. The Tantric practitioner (or Tanrika in the feminine form), finds God in the eyes of his or her beloved, unlike the contaminated side of this character that looks for love in all the wrong places.

Whether or not a person is practicing Tantra, the positive qualities of The Sexpot include a healthy sexual expression and an uninhibited relationship with his or her own body. This may need to be honed through years of experience with one's own partners and oneself in the realm of sexuality where practice makes perfect. Of course, in order for some people to do this, it may be necessary to first deal with any objections from The Judge or Preacher. Then if the shoe fits, feel free to don yourself with the title of Sex God or Goddess.

The Artist

There have been two books published over the last twenty or so years that have come a long way in allowing people to get in touch with their own Inner Artist. First came *Drawing on the Right Side of Your Brain* by Betty Edwards in the 1980s which helped right-handed people put the pen in their non-dominant left hand to help free themselves to just do it and not care what it looks like. Vice-versa for lefties who may be naturally more artistic since their hand-dominance comes from the more artistic right side of the brain already.

The second book became a phenomenon in the '90s and sprouted play groups and morning pages of journaling. Called *The Artist's Way*, by Julia Cameron, it went a step further to say that everyone has an Inner Artist who is connected with your Inner Child and your capacity to play. Hopefully, many of you have read one or both of these excellent self-help books — both speak the truth.

Obviously, everyone has an Inner Artist that can be coaxed out through awareness and practice. Yet some people live a life dominated by The Artist. The dedication to the pursuit of art has driven the life of many great and talented people throughout history. Some enjoy the rewards of their efforts during their lifetime and others die penniless, only to be discovered posthumously, or maybe not at all. There is a thread of similarity that seems to run through all of their lives which defines the qualities of The Artist archetype.

Whether you are one of these people, or you know one, these characteristics are probably very evident. If you do not define yourself as an artist, or don't even feel that you have an artistic bone in your body, there may be an Inner Artist waiting to come out of you, but it is very important first of all, to keep your Judge in check. Remember that art is more than simply being able to draw well. It can be writing, flower arranging, cooking, decorating, gardening, acting, photography, video, music, sewing, and more. Even in baseball, when a pitcher throws a strike, they sometimes describe it as "painting the corner" of the strike zone.

One of the most important things The Artist is able to accomplish is to have a vision and bring it to life. Generally there is a drive to share the vision with others, but that is not necessary. In fact one reason for not sharing could be because of the sensitive nature of The Artist. The idea of having his or her creation critiqued by others may be more than a sensitive soul can bear. Whether or not artists wish to share their art, the overwhelming urge to create is what drives them. Artist-dominant people are dripping with creative juices and despite the reception they are given, they remain driven to keep on doing more. Often these visionaries leave legacies that speak for the sentiments of whole nations or generations. Society rewards them by letting them be a bit eccentric.

Of course, as always, eccentricity can turn toxic in the contaminated aspect of this character, just as with all the rest. In this negative state, The Artist may become forgetful of real world commitments, not only to others, but also to himself. Then we also have the potential scenario of the proverbial "starving artist" on a monetary level. As much as The Artist is driven to continue onward to completion in the frenzy of his creation, he may be simply doing *art for art's sake*. Whether The Artist is working for money or not, while obsessed with a project, he may neglect more worldly things, such as paying the bills, showering, changing clothes, cleaning the house, even eating.

If you attempt to help, you may meet his temperamental side, to put it nicely. He may be completely out of touch with the things going on in the outside world, such as what day it is, as the creative fever continues to entrance him. The best idea is probably to bring him some food and his body will finally tell him he's hungry. The fact is he may not be at all grounded or in touch with his body while he's in the throes of this state.

For those of us who are not Artist-dominated, the most important aspects of this archetype to be aware of for our own enrichment are the peaceful and colorful vibrations it brings to our lives. We can let our Inner Artist help us express our individuality in so many areas from how we dress and wear our hair, to how we decorate our house, set our table and cook our food. Don't let the voice of your Inner Judge or Skeptic stop you from following the ideas your Inner Artist has for ways to enhance your life.

Even with as little space as a cubicle at work, our Artist can still help you to hang pictures and arrange your desk creatively to allow your personality to shine through. Forget about dressing for success all the time; for fun let your Artist *Dress to Express* sometimes. Listen to the advice coming from your Inner Artist as you go shopping or look in your closet for an outfit to wear. Don't let the fashions of the day stop you from shining your light out to the world with your very being-ness.

The Lover/Romantic

Now, unless you've been living a monastic life since birth, you have definitely experienced your own Lover/Romantic. The next chapter will go in depth about the trouble you may have gotten into because of it. Ah, yes, love is a many splendored thing; however, it is just as true that in both its positive and negative connotations, the slogan of this character most certainly has to be that *Love is Blind.*

We've all experienced the bliss of a new relationship when everything our partner does is wonderful—for the first three to six months, at least. Those same traits, after a few years, could be sending you to counseling or worse—divorce court. But let's rewind back to the moment when your eyes met across a crowded room. Suddenly it's as if you are experiencing a new sense of aliveness inside every cell of your being.

You've just been hit with one of the most powerful drugs known to man—endorphins. If you've ever put on rose-colored glasses you know what it's like to look through the eyes of The Lover/Romantic. But sight isn't the only sense titillated. If your fingers should brush against each other you feel fireworks going off in your nervous system.

Every rose smells sweeter, every bird's song sounds new. Who needs chocolate?

You have just seen your salvation in the eyes of your beloved. You have projected all your hopes and dreams for your perfect partner onto his or her face and perhaps he or she has done the same with you. Unfortunately it is difficult, or more realistically, impossible, for anyone to live up to those ideals of perfection. Sooner or later both of you will be squirming to get down off those pedestals. If the love is real it will endure the reality check that will surely follow as you let each other come out from behind the projector screens that have been placed in front of you both.

Of course the game of love is not always played by two and the voice of your Lover/Romantic may be one of the most active ones inside your head even while you're alone. How many hours of idle fantasy do we spend with ideas of love and romance floating around in our imaginations? The memories of past romantic evenings or the fantasies of future ones drift through our minds and invade our thoughts probably more often than any other. Waiting for the phone to ring, daydreaming of flowers arriving, fantasizing about the babies we'd make together, help to wile away the hours.

This character surely gets us in touch with our softer side. Lines on our faces lift and tensions melt as we meld with our Lover/Romantic. Barriers we've erected around ourselves come down as we find common ground with another and move into a space of intimacy. The walls that our Skeptic, Cynic and Guard have built to keep us safe can finally open to make room for our lover and may crumble altogether. The physical changes a person in love displays are evident for all to see. In a world filled with such a pervading fear of intimacy, getting in touch with your Lover/Romantic is the path to connecting with others.

Leticia wanted a Conference Room session on the subject of finding a man in her life. The only problem was that she was still feeling very betrayed by her first husband, who she said tricked her into marrying him. She described how she was done caretaking men the way she did all the time for her ex-husband, who later admitted to having lied to her about having a sprained ankle when they first met. There was no part of her subconscious that was available to even let a man approach her. Leticia was consciously unaware that her Skeptic was teamed up and in cahoots with her Cynic (yes, you can have one of each), whom she called Ms. Aloof, to keep men out.

Believe it or not, even her Judge was telling Leticia that not all men are bad, but judges are not very appealing to the opposite sex. I had to help her find her Romantic, who could be the one to open her heart to love again, since Ms. Aloof and her Guard/Protector were keeping it locked tight. Without a Romantic, there was no way this woman would ever have another man in her life no matter how many sessions she had about it.

In the end I was able to make a deal with all her parts for The Romantic to be accompanied by The Skeptic, who together could open the door through which a man could enter. The Protector would be standing guard right behind them in case the guy was no good. If that was the case, after those checkpoints, Ms. Aloof could then take over with the big guns.

Leticia got a chance to try it out in trance through a mental rehearsal with prospective suitors. First I presented a scenario of a man who would play on her sympathies with a broken ankle. Ms. Aloof jumped right in and told him to call 9-1-1! Next we tried again with a vision of a more appropriate type. Ms. Romantic and The Skeptic gave him the thumbs up and she imagined setting up a first date with him where they would go to church together and then out for Sunday brunch. The system worked. I often find myself teaching women how to say "no," but in this case I had to teach Leticia how to say "yes" to love.

A good depiction of the way a Romantic gets stuffed and replaced with The Cynic of all cynics is in the movie, *Casablanca*. It happens when the character, Rick, played by Humphrey Bogart thought he had been shafted by the woman he loved, played by Ingrid Bergman. Of course all those feelings he had worked so hard to forget came rushing back when he heard Sam playing their song, "As Time Goes By" and found himself staring into his lover's eyes. The closing scene at the airport is a classic depiction of the unconditional devotion of a Romantic. Unfortunately, he didn't get the girl, perhaps because his Romantic was in an alliance with his Martyr, who we'll be speaking about in depth in Chapter 9.

The positive qualities of The Lover/Romantic shine a spotlight on all the goodness our hearts have to give. Other than the ability to share intimacy with our beloved, this character is able to see the best in people, be empathetic, expressive and even poetic. We may believe our muse is outside of ourselves, but it can be tapped into by getting in touch with our own Inner Romantic. Just look at the litany of love songs, poems, and pieces of art that gush out of those who have been smitten by Cupid's arrow. A helpful hint for keeping a marriage loving and passionate is for both partners to tap into their Inner Romantics every day and allow them to connect for even a minute or two.

However, the contaminated side of this character suffers from the desperate pangs of unrequited love and the unrealistic illusions that can accompany it. The measures to which some people will stoop in order to cling to something that once was, but is no longer healthy, is often more painful for friends to watch than to endure oneself. A toxic Lover/Romantic may be willing to remain in the embers of a relationship that died a long time ago rather than to face their fear of abandonment. This "hopeless romantic" can remain addicted to the memory of that endorphin rush that wore off so long ago, stuck in his or her own daytime melodrama and caught up in the cycle of Co-dependency.

EXERCISE

This chapter has described eight Emotional Characters who contribute a tremendous amount to your personality. They ranged from the regal Prince or Princess to the more active Rebel, Hero and Adventurer to the colorful Sexpot and Artist to the dreaminess of the Lover/Romantic. Remember these names are only generic in nature to give you the idea of the archetypal pattern your own Sub-personalities may fall under. As always, the idea is to personalize them.

For instance, in my inner world I have a Sexpot, but that's not what I call her. Remember my client who calls his Antonio; well, I have no idea why, but I have given mine the name of Suzie the Floozy. Do you see how much more dimension that adds? You don't need to think too much about it, just play with a name that feels right. A name I have given to my Magical Child is Lucky because of all the fortuitous situations I find myself in. I'm so good at finding great parking spaces that my family actually calls it "pulling a Debbie."

My Rebel got her name from a picture I have of myself from my flower-child days with my face painted with a daisy across one cheek. I think of her as "Daisy" but sometimes I make plays on words and she becomes the "Flow-er"—the one who knows how to go with the flow. Because of the controlling nature of my Judge/Controller, I had the homework assignment after one of my sessions to not wear my watch for a week and be led by the intuition of my Inner Rebel. That was a great learning experience but it was tough since I got my first watch as a graduation present from kindergarten and have been wearing one ever since.

It may turn out that you already have a pet name you call a part of yourself, or perhaps your friends have given you a handle that actually describes a particular Sub-personality. Because of my love for fast driving, a friend of mine gave me a nickname in my early twenties of "Rhonda

Racer," who I now know is an aspect of my Adventurer. After paying too many speeding tickets, I learned to give her more healthy outlets than the highway, such as go-cart racetracks and roller-coasters.

> ➢ Just for fun, write down any nicknames you've ever had that might relate to any of these characters you met so far, especially these last eight Emotional Characters.

> ➢ Identify which character that name might belong to. You may need to go back to the chapters on the Intellectual Characters, if you have not given them personalized names already. Refer to the chart in the back of the book for a quick summary of traits.

> ➢ Whether or not you have any nicknames, look at the characters in this chapter again in terms of your own life and if you strongly relate to any of them, make up a name for that part of you. Maybe you have a Hero inside you like to call Superman or a Warrior who feels like a Zorro or a Xena. Maybe you would call your Inner Princess, Ariel. Try a name on for size to see if it fits. You can always change it.

> ➢ (Optional) Go back to the issue you were working with in Chapter 3 and involve all the characters you've met since then, who would be relevant to the issue, to express their opinions. Not every character will have something to contribute. For instance, The Sexpot would not be of any use to help you to decide whether to leave a job, if that was your issue.

> ➢ Pay particular attention to the last step in that exercise to see if you had already identified characters that you now

have more understanding of so you can place them into the category where they belong.

➤ Notice how much more colorful the conversation becomes when you add the voices of the rest of the Intellectual and Emotional Characters to those of the "Big Three" who may have been drowning everyone else out.

THE CO-DEPENDENCY CHARACTERS

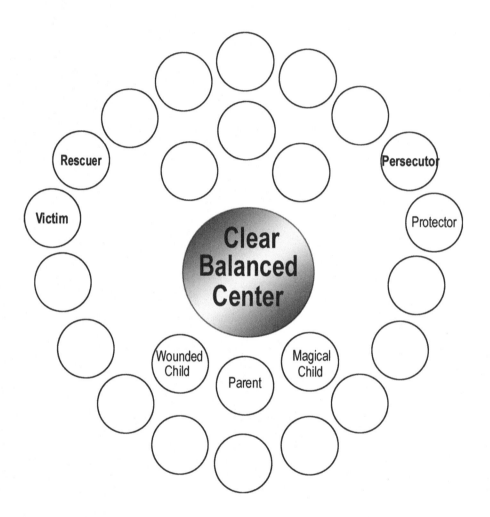

Authentic human interactions become impossible when you lose yourself in a role.

— Eckhart Tolle, *A New Earth*

Chapter 7

CO-DEPENDENCY—WHAT A TANGLED WEB WE WEAVE

I would like to introduce you to a special set of Sub-personalities that combine to form a well-documented phenomenon commonly referred to as Co-dependency. The complicity involves three very specific players, namely: The Rescuer, The Victim, and The Persecutor/Protector. We will continue our discussion of the Emotional Characters by delving deeper into the matters of the heart, (which we started with the Lover/Romantic), and some of the fine messes these next three characters can get us into.

As opposed to The Judge and Rebel, who we can imagine on two opposite ends of a magnetic pole repelled by each other, these three can be seen more as running in a circle chasing each other's tails. Picture a merry-go-round fixed with three horses going up and down and round and round endlessly (if left on their own). It's almost with mathematical precision that these energies are drawn to each other, as if there is an unwritten law of nature that demands that this sequence of Rescuer—Victim—Persecutor perpetuates itself in a damaging, yet predictable cycle.

Luckily, just as we developed a support system for Leticia's Romantic who was being smothered by her Protector and Ms. Aloof, there is a strategy that can keep everybody out of that Co-dependent loop forever. Since this is such a complex phenomena, we will begin to discuss the problem in this chapter, and offer the solution in the next one. Rather than the traditional set of exercises that has ended each chapter so far, there will be a special "Co-dependency Quiz" at the end of Chapter 8 that will allow you to see how you deal with this matter in your own life plus serve as a review of both chapters.

Please understand that there are many more people we can be in Co-dependency with, than just our lovers. The invisible force of this dynamic can be seen with members of a family, between parents and children or with siblings, as well as with co-workers, friends, bosses, even your pets. "Co-operative Dependency" can actually be played out with virtually anyone in your life. A more healthy solution to seek would be a state of "Inter-Dependency" or "Co-Creativity" and this chapter will show you how. Let's start with a good friend of The Lover/Romantic—The Rescuer.

The Rescuer

This is the part of you that is always finding a way to lend a helping hand, often putting your own needs last. The Rescuer is always looking outside, rather than within, for where to give and who to help. It happens with love interests constantly, especially if The Lover/Romantic is still wearing rose-colored glasses, because when teamed up with The Rescuer, these two characters can be quite intense. But again, there's no shortage of people and things that need rescuing other than one's present partner.

Every day in your mailbox you'll find some worthy cause begging your Inner Rescuer to help. Whether it's orphaned children, people devastated by natural disasters, or a species on the brink of extinction, there will always be those less fortunate than ourselves. That can keep our Rescuer very busy. It's lucky for all those causes that busy-ness on behalf of others is the business of The Rescuer. Common responses for this character are: *Oh, you poor thing. What can I do for you? Here, let me help you. How much do you need? I'll do it! Let me pay for this, get that, be there.*

4 637 3405

Frequently called The Caretaker or The Pleaser, these names reveal the underlying energy of this person. Other descriptions are The Good Son, The "Yes" Man, The Dutiful Daughter or The Good Neighbor. As always, you're welcome to make up your own name for the part of you that tends to rescue, please or caretake others.

There does seem to be an abundance of female Rescuers, although it's by no means a club that excludes men. Society conditions girls this way from the time they are very young. Little girls are taught domestic skills at home and at school, daughters, primarily, babysit for younger siblings, and girls are encouraged to play with dolls (in order for manufacturers to sell a doll to boys, they needed to call it GI Joe).

In the first half of the twentieth century the only jobs women were channeled into were secretaries, teachers, and nurses, all involving taking care of others. They were expected to quit their job as soon as they got married and invariably became pregnant with their first child. So it's quite logical that women would naturally fall into this role. Perhaps there is even an instinctual or biological basis for it, but that's irrelevant for the purpose of this discussion.

To help delineate the three characters involved in the cycle of Co-dependency, let's view them each playing out a role in the basic family unit of Mother, Father and Child. As you might already notice, The Rescuer is very mommy-like. We know there are many "Mr. Moms" out there with more maternal instincts than some women. Yet as nice as it is to stay away from gender-based stereotypes, for the sake of simplicity, I will use female pronouns to describe this character, which can and, as mentioned above, does go by many names.

As you can imagine, being a "W-O-M-A-N" who can "bring home the bacon, fry it up in the pan and never let him forget he's a man" can be a lot of work, and get very tiring. But that doesn't stop this Wonder Woman-esque character. Most people who are Rescuer-dominated have much of their identity tied up in the qualities connected with caretaking others.

All those poor victims out there who need rescuing certainly fuel the fire of Co-dependency. This is why women with this caretaking tendency are often aptly labeled "Co-dependents," but The Rescuer can't do it all by herself. The Rescuer *needs* someone to rescue. It's the same way we explained that a contaminated Hero *needs* someone to save and The Entertainer/Comic *needs* an audience, which is what makes all of these characters vulnerable to a form of Co-dependency.

The difference between The Hero and The Rescuer, however, is that there are very few glory-mongers around who are out there *seeking* the limelight. I've never heard of a "Heroes Anonymous" group; whereas Co-dependency is an epidemic, and you can find at least one 12-Step group of Co-dependents Anonymous (CODA) in every major city in America.

It's hard to fault The Rescuer, though, since the only thing she's truly guilty of is having too big a heart. She firmly believes that since she has so much love to give she's just being a good person by doing what she does. Of course, she's not thinking about the consequences of her actions, such as potential burn-out or danger. This noble desire to help everyone is among the strengths of this character. Other positive traits include being empathetic, dependable, selfless, and giving.

She feels capable of helping because there are so many people out there needier than herself. Yet The Rescuer has one huge blind spot: she is unable to admit to having any needs of her own. She may be exhausting herself physically and emotionally by constantly giving, but when you ask her how she is, she'll always respond, "Just fine, thank you."

It is literally impossible and would be completely out of character for Rescuers to have any needs, because by definition The Rescuer *cannot be* needy. As soon as they feel needy, they are no longer accessing The Rescuer persona; they have just become The Victim, who we will see, can make a career out of being needy.

Before we get into The Victim, though, there is one big secret connected to Rescuers that's important to understand. There is a huge subconscious hidden agenda motivating their outward behavior. It is: *the more I love you (or give to you), the more you'll love me (or give to me)*. This sheds light on an important psychological factor that goes into making someone so interested in pleasing and caretaking others.

They were conditioned as children to be rewarded for being good, caring, loving and helpful. The positive reinforcement they received made this role very hard to ever give up, similar to the kudos The Entertainer received in childhood. Two more traits of The Rescuer to be aware of: One is the way they can induce guilt in those close to them, which can border on martyrdom. Another is how they may enable others to continue dysfunctional and addictive behaviors. This disempowering trait is the one that gets them labeled as "enablers."

The Victim

The Victim is a sad sack who holds the feelings that are impossible for The Rescuer to have or admit to. It is the part of us who feels hurt, needy, neglected, scapegoated, and seeks sympathy, sometimes even by developing physical or psychological symptoms. The voice of The Victim is often a loud, whiney one inside our head that many people are familiar with and most ignore.

Other negative traits of this character are that it tends to feel picked on, abandoned, taken advantage of, misunderstood and all alone in the world, sometimes even depressed, while it's busy blaming others for its lot in life. Like a tumbleweed being blown around by the wind, this character wallows in self-pity, feeling a victim of circumstances, generally unwilling to take any responsibility for its "victimization."

Its slogan is the familiar lament, *Poor me*, and it asks the burning million dollar question, *Why me, Lord?* Some other things The Victim might whisper in your ear include: *I can't do anything right. I shouldn't have even gotten out of bed today. Good things only happen to everybody else. Oh, no, here we go again. Why do these things always happen to me? I'm so miserable.* There are many self-help books which would direct you to disown this pitiful part, yet I ask you to embrace and transform it with love and understanding, just as with every other toxic or contaminated Inner Character that is a part of you.

Once again, socially speaking, it is more permissible for women to be seen in the role of Victim, although in actuality, the position is open to all equally. The "pity parties" that women can indulge in openly give them an edge in being able to use the battle cry of The Victim: "Help!" to readily seek aid or healing. This could shed some light on one reason it's so difficult for men to merely ask for directions. They would rather suffer the consequences of getting lost than the apparent humiliation of asking for help.

Although most people would like their own Victim to get lost or just go away, this ability to ask for help is actually one of the most wonderful gifts the positive aspect of this character brings to us. It allows us to let down our guard and accept our vulnerability. Two other blessings The Victim bestows are: knowing when to slow down and how to rest.

The fact is that boys are socialized to be tough and aren't given as much freedom to cry and complain. This often forces men to sublimate their pain into anger, which is why many men are so comfortable with The Persecutor part of themselves. But simply because they don't show their emotions as easily doesn't give men a free pass from victimization. It just means their Inner Victims may have to go underground and present themselves in different ways. This is also true for women who feel invulnerable.

Some people know this as the "two-by-four" or the "sledgehammer" approach, often coming in the form of an illness that forces them to slow down. And it brings us to an important point about The Victim. Unlike every other character except for The Inner Child, The Victim is more than just a Sub-personality whose voice can be heard in our head. It actually uses the *whole body* to speak for it, if it's not acknowledged in any other way. And whether or not you choose to listen, it will get its point across.

Statistics bear witness to the fact that women literally tend to give until it hurts, when you connect the organs associated with giving and loving, to the diseases that kill women. The most obvious organ connected with giving is the breast since a baby lives on the milk that comes from it. Therefore breast cancer is more dreaded than the disease of the other organ associated with giving—the heart—which is actually the number one killer of women in America.

In fact, nine times more women die of heart disease than breast cancer—it kills more women that the next six leading causes of death combined. In the "Go Red Campaign" alerting people to this dangerous silent killer, they elucidate: "If women want to keep taking care of everyone else, they need to take care of themselves first."

The Victim and Wounded Child have something in common. Their suppressed emotions have nowhere to go, so they erupt out of the body like a boil. They often have the same thing to say, and thankfully their voices eventually get heard. Many people owe a complete 180-degree turn in their lives to a "healing crisis," such as cancer or a heart attack that got their attention. After such an experience they can begin to live the life they always wanted because they know what it means to live each day as if it's their last.

Jessica had broken out in hives all over her body a few weeks before her wedding day. During our session we tried to find out the message her skin was delivering externally: There was a part of her that believed she was jumping into marriage too quickly, thus making a "rash decision." With all the social pressure Jessica was under, her rational mind didn't feel she could even entertain the thought of putting off the wedding, but her body was not going to let her go through with it and it did what it had to do to stop her.

You can see that because of her Inner Victim, Jessica may have been saved from making a big mistake. Through her misery came resolution and clarity. If she had chosen to ignore the voice of her Victim, which spoke through her body, she may have never gotten over her rash and remained a Victim for years to come. Remember our Intellectual Characters can keep us rationalizing our life circumstances with any spin they want to put on them, but an Emotional Character, such as The Victim, is so viscerally honest that it can force us to face a truth we may not *want* to hear, but *need* to hear.

Another engaged client, Ellen, needed to deal with the anger she was feeling toward her fiancé. She had given up her house to move in with him, before realizing that he had a drinking problem. When she called me to cancel her appointment because she was sick, I decided since I had worked with her many times before, to do a session right then over the phone.

This gave Ellen, who is the president of a large organization and a Ms. Together-dominant personality, the perfect opportunity needed to do her inner work. Because her illness brought her in touch with the vulnerability of her Inner Victim, Ellen was able to get beyond the walls she usually keeps in place. We went back to when someone she loved had lied to her before. It brought her back to when she was very little and her big brother, who was much older and she saw as her protector, moved away from home after he graduated from high school.

Of course he had no idea how much of a betrayal that felt like to his six-year-old sister who had felt abandoned. As Ellen communicated to him in trance, she reminded him that even after he left home, she would still have the school nurse call him, instead of her mother, to pick her up at school when she got sick. She related how special it made her feel when he came to get her, just to have that time alone with him and receive his undivided attention.

Because people call a therapist when they need help and don't know where else to turn, you could say it is always The Victim who brings a client to therapy. In Ellen's case, the act of getting sick was the pattern she had developed as a child to get attention and feel loved. Inevitably, examining the way a person is feeling victimized today, allows an old dysfunctional behavior to be healed.

While she was still in trance and in touch with her subconscious mind, I made sure Ellen let her Inner Child know she didn't need to get sick anymore in order to get love and attention from a man. She was already feeling better by the time we finished the session. As you may suspect, there was much more involved in the complete resolution than I've gone into here. We will re-visit Ellen in the next chapter where I will discuss some of the specific techniques I used.

Remember, when The Victim's positive traits of asking for help and slowing down are unavailable, seemingly unrelated symptoms often appear to let The Victim emerge in a disguised and much more painful way. This is true of Mr. or Ms. Together-dominated people and Rescuers especially, because they tend to be very busy and in total denial of their own emotional needs—usually completely lacking a connection with their Inner Victim.

If we say that The Rescuer is playing the role of the "Mommy" in the Co-dependency cycle, we can see that The Victim is certainly playing the role of the helpless Little Child. Let's look now at how the "Daddy" role plays out.

The Persecutor/Protector

Who is my inner dad? DAD ROLE

So far in this chapter we've looked at characters with a more socially accepted feminine slant to them. Now we come to the character who almost always personifies maleness in the traditional sense. First of all, let's look at why we call this character by two names. By definition, it would be impossible to find positive qualities for a Persecutor, so we instead describe its positive energies with a totally different name that maintains the integrity of the archetype.

Imagine a guy standing with his hands balled up in a fist, like a boxer without gloves. Now consider two very different scenarios that might warrant such behavior. The first would be one of a bully picking a fight with someone for no good reason and often with someone smaller than he is. The second would be a fellow that might even stand up in reaction to the first guy, raising his own fists and responding with a retort such as, "Hey, why don't you pick on someone your own size?!"

The posturing of both is the same, although the intention behind each is very different. The first would obviously be playing out the role of Persecutor, whereas the second is displaying the characteristics of The Protector. While The Persecutor abuses his power through bullying, violence, revenge, abuse, blame and shame, The Protector displays his strength and courage in order to protect himself and others, by clearly defining his boundaries, drawing a proverbial line in the sand, and saying, "No!"

The Persecutor may harbor a chip on his shoulder and basically throw his weight around for no reason at all, whereas The Protector displays good personal boundaries and harnesses his ability to respond appropriately to a situation that warrants righteous anger. He would only engage in violence as a last resort while The Persecutor might go around raging for his own pleasure or merely because he feels he has a right to. One is out of control, manipulative and hurts other people; the other is in control of his emotions and acts with a similar sense of bravery as The Warrior.

Despite many opinions to the contrary, anger in and of itself is not bad when used correctly and stops before it reaches the point of uncontrollable rage. It is an emotion just like joy and sadness, but it is often condemned because of how it can be abused. If used correctly, it is the key to standing up for ourselves and our rights. Even people like Martin Luther King, who follow the path of non-violence, can still feel and express anger at their targets of injustice; yet through social conditioning most of us, and especially women, have been taught to suppress their anger and channel it into tolerance, forgiveness, and politeness (traits such as those we see in The Rescuer).

Generally, this makes the world a nicer place for people to get along. However, it also takes away our ability to respond appropriately in certain situations that warrant setting our limits, and results in being taken advantage of and letting people cross our boundaries. These situations can lead to acquiescing to things we don't always agree with, which often result in resentments, misunderstandings, and getting bullied, blamed and shamed (traits such as those we see in The Victim).

What ends up happening with women who were never taught to stand up to people who hurt them, rather than ever learning to protect themselves, they instead look to fall in love with a big strong man to protect them. In the same way, traditionally, men find women who are soft, open and vulnerable, rather than developing those strengths in themselves. We see the markings for Co-dependency here when we start looking for someone else to compensate for the traits we lack in order to make us whole, without taking full responsibility for ourselves.

This will lead to The Lover/Romantic teaming up with The Victim to hone in on this compensatory set of traits in another when searching for a partner, just like a hound dog sniffs down a scent, which can lead to falling in love for the wrong reason. Plus the main problem with leaning on someone else, of course, is the fact that he or she will not always be there to count on. Even if the love is true, they can still die and leave you alone, so it's like building a house of cards that can collapse in on itself. Of course, The Victim could use those misfortunes as more ammunition to prove her point, and create a bigger self-fulfilling prophecy without ever finding a new way.

All around us the culture encourages this behavior as normal. Emotionally it seems totally natural and romantic, and it feels like the perfect partnership to find someone with traits that are complementary to our own. However, this is how the Lover/Romantic opens the door to Co-dependency, which these three characters then play out, substituting partner after partner in the same script. This scenario that sounds so benign and is supposed to lead us into "happily ever after" is instead the insidiousness that is at the root of situations from divorce and depression to date rape and domestic violence.

It is the reason that some people get victimized over and over again and that so many battered women cannot get out, no matter how much they want to, until they can break this vicious cycle. Without healing first, battered women will even leave a shelter just to find another man who will abuse them, and the cycle starts all over again. Many people know that they're stuck in a repeat pattern with relationships, but usually don't have a clue as to how to change anything.

People think these women are stupid to let it happen at all, but without any intervention, that pattern is as inevitable to repeat as night follows day. And it's not just battered women who fall prey to The Persecutors out there. Without the "response ability" to say no and steer clear of danger, many women without an alert Inner Protector can and do become victims every year. And it's not always The Lover/Romantic who puts someone at risk; it can also be the big heart of The Rescuer.

Shannon LaForge, a courtroom deputy has this piece of advice she's been sharing with women over the web (www.thelpa.com/lpa/protection-advice.html). "As women, we are always trying to be sympathetic: Stop! It may get you raped, or killed. Ted Bundy, the serial killer, was a good-looking, well-educated man, who *always* played on the sympathies of unsuspecting women. He walked with a cane, or a limp, and often asked 'for help' into his vehicle or with his vehicle, which is when he abducted his next victim."

LaForge made another safety point to protect women from what *America's Most Wanted* TV show called "The Crying Baby Theory" when profiling a serial killer. He had a baby's cry recorded and used it to coax women out of their houses when they were alone at night by making them think that someone left a baby at their front door. The advice police have for women who this might happen to is, "Whatever you do, *do not* open the door."

That is a difficult boundary for women—all the instincts of The Rescuer are screaming to rescue that crying baby, which is the exact sentiment the External Persecutor is counting on to snag his next victim. The Protector archetype that knows how to set limits and boundaries for you, is a vital one in order to say "No!" to the people and things that don't belong in your life. Sometimes called the Warrior/Protector, since The Warrior also knows how to draw a line in the sand, this archetype plays out the role of a caring father in our metaphor of the family.

Although it is a quality that is more often assigned to men, it can be even more important for women to empower themselves to say no since they are more at risk of being taken advantage of. Once women can own this part of themselves, they can help teach their children to keep their boundaries strong so as not to fall victim to abductions, child molesters, or the bullying from young persecutors on the playground. For someone of either gender, without access to an Inner Protector, a person's boundaries can be violated as easily as a ghost can walk through walls.

Focusing in on Co-dependency

We've taken an in-depth look at each of the characters in this Co-dependency "triangle" (see Illustration 1 on page 143) first, because it is vital to know how each part exists on its own in order to untangle the individual players from the whole dynamic that performs like a carefully choreographed dance. I'm sure you're beginning to catch on, but let's continue by taking a detailed look at how this Co-dependency merry-go-round is constructed.

It has an autonomous existence inside a person, but it takes on a more holographic or three-dimensional quality, as it plays out between two or more people. Different scenarios of it play out all around us, so by having a thorough understanding of how it works, you can begin to take control over whether or not you let it trap you in its web.

Most people think of Co-dependency as involving two people, so that's primarily how it's been presented here so far, but it can get even more complicated than that. Since the carousel is carrying three energies, it can triangulate very easily when there are three people involved. It's as if each person involved jumps on one of those horses and plays out one of the characters. This process of triangulation can and does occur in family, social, and business situations where any three people keep switching the role they're playing as easily as they could jump on a different horse.

For instance, a husband is doing something his wife doesn't like that makes her feel Victimized. In the blink of an eye she gets mad at him, making her the Persecutor while he now becomes the perceived Victim. Then his friend comes over and the husband rants and raves about what a witch his wife is, and becomes The Persecutor himself. But when his buddy chimes in trying to play The Rescuer to appease him, he inadvertently has jumped on the Persecuting bandwagon.

The husband hearing this suddenly changes his tune and comes to his wife's defense, becoming her Rescuer, as soon as he hears her being Victimized. He might even turn around and begin persecuting his friend, making him the new Victim. This is how the Co-dependency cycle keeps us riding the merry-go-round. It's so ubiquitous that it goes right past us without thinking anything of it.

It sounds like a contradiction in terms to say that we can be Co-dependent all by ourselves, but that's actually *the place where it originates*. The trap for it is set right inside us. If we have not cleared the tendency toward it, we can allow it to permeate all our interactions because it is literally rooted in the workings of our psyches and our lives. When the earmarks of a Co-dependent person remain unconscious and unchecked, individuals automatically seek others to play out the cycle with. Conversely, once you've learned to recognize it, you can refuse to ever get sucked in again.

Without any stop-gap measure, however, Co-dependency can spread quickly. Just as gardeners learn when trying to rid a yard of thorny bramble bushes, if you just clip the branches, they will grow back and continue to invade everything around them, and the longer you let them go, the bigger and more dangerous the thorns become. When you trace them down to their roots, you find the roots have spread in all directions and it can hurt your back to attempt to pull them out by hand, thus an impossible task. However, if you dig a little deeper and concentrate on pulling out one lateral root at a time, the job becomes easy, and in a short while, the pesky plant can be eliminated forever.

Since the 1980's Melodie Beatty, the author of *Codependent No More* and *Beyond Codependency*, as well as Robin Norwood who wrote *Women Who Love Too Much*, have been leaders in bringing this widespread problem to light and explaining how it affects women (especially) in their relationships. Readers are enlightened with tremendous psychological and emotional understanding of this vicious cycle and asked to own it in themselves as their first step to ending it. Yet they fall short in specifically outlining a clear model for reversing the perpetuation of the cycle, and helping people untangle from it forever.

It's as if they're showing you the depth of the roots of the pervasive weed, and warning you of the danger of its thorns, but recommending that you just keep clipping the branches whenever you find them growing back. Their solutions for ending it amount to suggestions of long-term therapy and practically a lifetime commitment to a 12-step program for group support—the same course of healing that is used for eating, drinking and sexual addictions, which is what they see Co-dependency as. Instead of labeling most of the world as addicts, it's time to give people the tools to untangle themselves from this web, which catches everyone in its grip at one time or another.

This can be done by giving new jobs to the contaminated aspects of the infamous threesome of characters that perpetuate this dysfunctional pattern: The Rescuer, Victim and Persecutor. We can then resolve it by turning them around and getting them to act in the highest aspect of their characteristics, which includes but is not limited to, The Persecutor becoming The Protector. But first, let's dig a little deeper in to look at how those roots got planted in the first place by our family of origin. At the end of Chapter 8 you can see how Co-dependency may be affecting you by taking a simple quiz.

A family is a place where minds
come in contact with one another.
If these minds love one another
the home will be as beautiful
as a flower garden.
But if these minds
get out of harmony
with one another
it is like a storm
that plays havoc
with the garden.

— Buddha

Chapter 8

CO-DEPENDENCY—THE TENDER TRAP

This chapter will make a clear break from the disempowering, yet widely held paradigm of Co-dependency as an addiction, and present it as an easily recognizable problem of Sub-personalities gone awry—complete with a solution that can be followed like a roadmap to healing. Note that the formatting of this section will be slightly different than the rest of the book.

In the last chapter we described each of the three characters involved in Co-dependency. We will now watch how these three parts interact to see how the interplay weaves through them, entangling them and binding them to one another in this tender trap. And we will go deeper into the comparisons of these three to members of a family—The Rescuer as mother, The Victim as child, and The Protector as father. Most importantly you will see how emulating a healthy family unit *within yourself* can set you free from Co-dependency.

How it All Begins

We know how hard it is to break away from our well established patterns of doing things simply because it's the way we have always done them. It's evident every holiday season how much difficulty two families can have blending the unique rituals of each spouse. They're all infused with meaning and have been passed on through many generations, but some may clash with others. Both spouses often get uncomfortable at the thought of giving up any of the holiday traditions they grew up with.

In the same way, it is not uncommon to seek the comfort of *familiarity* when choosing a relationship to settle into. People can feel that sense of fitting, like a hand in a glove, when they choose someone to love, not necessarily because it serves them in the healthiest way, but simply because it feels like home. We've heard that women often choose to marry someone just like their father and men find women who remind them of their mother.

That is because there is no greater influence on a person's development than what is learned on all levels from our parents. It is natural for people to attempt to recreate the template of their family of origin when it comes time for them to leave home. Let's take a look at another important way our early home environment may have influenced us much more deeply than merely our attachment to traditional family customs.

One thing everyone agrees on about the origins of Co-dependency is that people prone to it generally come from dysfunctional families where their emotional needs were not met. Instead, members of theses families were forced to play roles by taking on different *personas* (Latin for "mask"), that worked within the set of family rules, i.e. "Because I'm the father and I said so, end of discussion." or "We don't talk about things like that in this household."

For the survival of the family, the children in these dysfunctional families frequently and innocently end up acting out a variation of one of these three roles we're calling Rescuer, Victim and Persecutor (out of dozens of possible roles). As they mature, what started out as a role they took on to fit in or survive then becomes the dominant aspect of their personality. Remember to think about the energy of a character. For instance, someone who might call herself "The Cinderella" in her family would be carrying the energy of The Victim and as an adult would likely be Victim-dominant.

John Bradshaw first described this dynamic and demonstrated the delicate balance of family roles in 1988 in his ten-part public television series called *The Family* by setting up a mobile and showing how *any* changes in one person's role disrupted the whole balance of the family. He used different names, such as The Hero, The Lost Child, and The Scapegoat, who all fit within the parameters of our three Co-dependency characters.

The main idea he wanted to make people aware of was that in a dysfunctional family, each person's *unconscious* participation in playing out a role is vital to maintaining the equilibrium of the family unit. If you are wondering whether this pertains to you or not, the chances are good, since Bradshaw claims 96% of all families are emotionally impaired to some extent.

In his later books, he came to realize that all families must go through this balancing act: that it is actually the normal way every family functions. The key difference is that when healthy parents see it happening in their children they adjust accordingly. The dysfunction exists when families are not aware and conscious of this dynamic. The devastating result is that parents end up violating the natural development of their children's own true identity as they are forced into exhibiting false personas to keep peace in the family. This excerpt from his book, *The Family*, explains how:

In themselves roles are not bad and as Shakespeare wisely pointed out, we all play many roles in our lives. The roles in dysfunctional family systems are different. They are not chosen or flexible. They are necessitated by the covert or overt needs of the family as a system…If the family system has no warmth, one child will be warm and loving to everyone. If the family system is ravaged with unexpressed anger and pain, one child will become the Scapegoat and act out all the anger and pain. In every case the person playing the role gives up his own unique selfhood… The whole family is dis-eased and each person gives up his true self to play a role in keeping the family together. Every single person becomes a Co-dependent.

Right now let's hone in on how Co-dependency continues to play out in your *adult* relationships.

Examining the Co-dependency Cycle Inside a Person

We already said that The Lover/Romantic is often the culprit who gets us entwined in this mess, especially as it pertains to romantic relationships. Her main partner in crime is The Rescuer, who is harboring that hidden agenda deep inside of desperately wanting and needing to be loved. The way she was always taught to go about getting it was by being good and helpful. This subconscious motivation, which is rewarded in childhood, paves the way into this tender trap.

Our heroine in this tragedy is so busy going out and doing things for everybody else, she leaves no time and attention for herself. Subconsciously believing this will earn her love, she remains dedicated to her path, but she begins to notice that she is often left holding the short end of the stick. As she realizes that true happiness is eluding her, it leaves her depleted and sad. The tendency would be to say that *The Rescuer* is sad, but we must remember in dividing the psyche into its component parts, as we are doing here, that a Rescuer *cannot* be sad. That's when the wheel turns to the next character around the cycle.

Her constant caretaking of others without having anyone do anything to help her, turns that Rescuer into the poor innocent Victim. Realizing that she is all alone inside she cries out from the inequity, but with no one to hear her tears. This is because The Rescuer refuses to acknowledge her as she is so busy taking care of other people who have *real* problems. People experiencing this might acknowledge feeling blue or depressed, but if and when they do, remember they are no longer in Rescuer mode. They are now accessing and expressing their Inner Victim.

If they are Rescuer-dominant, however, their coping mechanism will be to deny all those feelings and keep busy, perhaps by diving right into another project to help someone else, anyone who they are capable of feeling sorry for. *I don't have time to get a massage. I'm too busy helping the homeless and running the PTA.* She probably won't even be able to admit defeat, while secretly thinking that everyone else seems to be having a happy life and simply wondering why she can't have the same thing.

Since an unexpressed Victim often experiences her problems through physical symptoms, this could cause that phenomenon we spoke of in the previous chapter. It may actually take an illness or an accident to intervene in order for a person's Victim to be heard. Meanwhile, they won't make any connection between what they are doing and these things that are happening to them, even if it's a series of one thing after another. Common results include being passed over for promotions or actually losing a job or a relationship, being robbed, having accidents involving bodily injury (including car accidents), getting colds, the flu or allergies, and having severe backaches or headaches.

The Victim will be active on the inside, though, possibly even slipping into a funk or even a clinical depression. If she has spent a lifetime comfortable in The Victim persona, this might feel very natural. There are some people astute enough to wonder whether they are wearing an invisible sign that says, "Kick Me." She will feel helpless and resentful and be resigned to blame others for her lot in life, feeling incapable of taking any responsibility for what is happening.

While The Rescuer is keeping outwardly busy, The Victim is inwardly lamenting: *I'm so tired. I wish I could just spend a whole day in bed doing nothing. I have so much to do. I'll never get it done and there's no one helping me.* She may also blame her misfortunes, as she sees them, on flaws she finds with herself. *None of this would be happening if I weren't so stupid to agree to do this. Why can't I ever say no?*

Eventually this all gets very frustrating and something's got to give. After being down in the dumps long enough from trying and trying to be good, charitable and kind, and it never being reciprocated, the next logical reaction is to get mad at the injustice. This is how this cycle proceeds and it leads to the next character, since The Victim is not capable of harboring those emotions. As the wheel turns to the position of The Persecutor, however, there are two scenarios that can play out from that part who has had enough.

Here we have a very interesting choice of whether The Persecutor's reaction will be directed outwardly or inwardly. One scenario, if these actions are in a person's repertoire, especially if she is Persecutor-dominant, such as a typical bully or "bitch" is that she can come out with guns blazing against whoever it is that did not fulfill The Rescuer's expectations. Now she will act out by hitting, screaming, throwing dishes or slamming doors. *Well you can screw this! I'm out of here! You can just do it yourself!*

However, if this is a person who cannot express discontent because of programming to the contrary (such as many women receive), The Persecutor archetype can emerge in a self-inflicted way, as in self-persecution or self-judgment. The inner conversation will sound like The Judge's self-condemnation with an inner thrashing such as: *What a pushover you are to take all this on. They obviously don't respect you, but why should they? You're an idiot and everyone knows it.*

But, alas, in the Co-dependency cycle, the wheel ultimately turns back around and The Rescuer will feel obligated to finish the task after all. It could take minutes or days, but eventually The Rescuer won't be able to live with herself if she doesn't apologize and make up. A person could even experience the whole range of emotions in the blink of an eye. Then, just as a cat always lands on its feet, The Rescuer always ends up on top of this triangle (see Illustration 1).

The Co-dependency Cycle Diagram

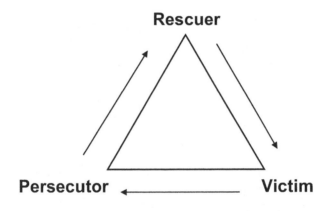

ILLUSTRATION 1

Let's listen to the way these characters would sound as they play out inside someone's head in real time. Imagine, for example, a woman in a working couple returning home from her job to prepare dinner and finding her boyfriend sleeping on the couch. We can dissect her thoughts and divide them up into each Sub-personality talking in turn to illustrate how insidious and ingrained this pattern is. The words in parentheses show which Co-dependency character is speaking and you'll see how quickly the thoughts fire and shift to the next character.

(starts as Rescuer): *Oh, my poor sweetheart, bless his heart, look at him, how tired he is. He must have had a hard day at work. I'm going to make a delicious meal. I bet he only ate fast food for lunch.*

(moves into Victim): *Well, I actually didn't even get a chance to eat my own lunch. I had an awfully draining day at work myself. My back is starting to hurt and my feet are killing me. I wish I could take a nap, but I have to cook or we'll never eat, and I'm starving.*

(then either to Persecutor): *Why is it he never helps me cook dinner? And then he leaves all the dirty dishes until I get sick of looking at them and I end up having to do them. I think I'll just eat a sandwich and leave him to fend for himself. If fast food is good enough for lunch he can eat it for dinner, too, unless he gets his lazy butt up and cooks something. This is the third day this week he's been asleep when I came home. He can starve for all I care.*

(or Self-Persecutor/Judge): *You are so stupid to let yourself fall for this act from this guy. He's just using you like every other man you've been with in your life.*

(back to Rescuer): *Oh, but I love him so much and he looks so cute sleeping. I wanted to try out this new recipe I know he'll love. I don't really mind doing it. I can get it whipped up in no time, and if he tried helping he'd just be in my way. Maybe tomorrow he'll take me out for dinner.*

(to Victim): *No, that's right, he says he's broke. Why can't I ever find a rich boyfriend?*

(to Persecutor): *You oughta leave his sorry ass. In fact, you could just leave him on the couch and go out to eat by yourself or with a girlfriend and let him figure out what to eat.*

(and back to Rescuer teaming up with The Lover/Romantic): *No, I've been away all day and I really miss him. I want to have dinner at home with him. He'll wake up with the smell of food cooking and we can have a nice romantic evening afterward.*

That is a good example of how these three voices slip so easily around in one's thoughts. This woman is stuck in a conundrum about a situation she can see is not totally satisfying, but is still serving her needs. As innocuous as it seems, it creeps into all of a person's interactions in a disempowering way that's beyond conscious control. If this woman does not get help in breaking the cycle, she will repeat it in all of her future relationships, just like with a battered woman's situation.

There are millions of people in similar relationships with clearly defined roles and that same conversation has probably gone through many women's minds. The merry-go-round continues to turn, both internally as illustrated above and three-dimensionally, drawing in another to do this dance with. Life feels right because the roles we are used to playing are easy since we are creatures of habit. But doing what's easy by simply staying in a relationship that doesn't serve our needs isn't always what is best for our highest good. Instead, we must sometimes do what seems hard in order for our lives to get easier.

I often illustrate Co-dependency at work in terms of how two people can make a seesaw go up and down with perfect precision, but when one gets off without another's knowledge, it can cause quite a disruption. The person who was "up," suddenly falls fast and hard and often feels hurt, confused, or may even seek revenge. Also, it's impossible to play on a seesaw alone. Even though life may feel like it's in perfect balance because it all fits together so naturally, when one person decides to stop playing his or her role, what felt so copasetic suddenly feels very uncomfortable. This fear of discomfort can keep people stuck going up and down and round and round. So, let's look at the way *out*.

Getting Clear

We've looked at the traits of these three individual characters: the way they entwine, the cycle that ensues, the causes from within the family and how it can play out not only as internal dialogue, but also in the way we interact with others. Now let's begin the process of untangling this massive ball of twine. Even though it may take some effort and cause some discomfort and disruption in one's life—if a person is interested in getting off this merry-go-round, or seesaw, of Co-dependency, there is a specific way to go about it.

We've seen how its origins come from within a dysfunctional family. It was no coincidence that as the characters were being described, it was pointed out that each one represents the traits of one member of a nuclear family: a mother, father and child. Therein lies the key to the solution. While wounded members of a dysfunctional family system inappropriately attempt to bring it into balance by blindly playing out reactive roles, in order to heal this pattern we need to *consciously* establish the archetypal roles of a *healthy* family into our psyche. Then purposely act out their healthy character traits. First let's dissect the dysfunction once more.

Notice how in the well-documented and pervasive Co-dependency cycle the traditional role of the Mother—The Rescuer/Caretaker—in the process of taking care of everybody else's needs, ends up neglecting her own and slips into The Victim. We said that position represents The Child (as well as the body). This needy, neglected child inside gets no attention while The Rescuer (Mommy) stays busy going out and taking care of everyone else in the world, *except* her own Inner Child.

When The Victim/Child/Body becomes whiney and depressed, or hurt and sick, The Persecutor (Daddy), instead of acting in his rightful role of Protector, gets mad and blames someone or something rather than looking within himself at the pain. Or perhaps he merely self-persecutes and shames himself. Or (as we see in emotionally abusive relationships), there could be a vacant space altogether, causing an external person to be sucked into the vacuum, to get mad at us and kick us while we're down.

Of course, once again, as the wheel turns, The Rescuer doesn't know any other way to react, so she goes back to her modus operandi and looks for someone else out in the world to take care of, perhaps as a way to ease her own pain and guilt. This vicious cycle continues, looking outside oneself in order to be of service, then experiencing pain or emptiness inside, which leads to blaming and shaming. An easy metaphor to draw is that first you bend over backward until (second) you get a backache, and (third) you lash back. So how do we stop this vicious circle?

The Road Map to Healing

We keep discussing who it is that leads us into Co-dependency, but which of these three characters is the one who can lead us out? Is it that sweet Rescuer who wants everyone to be happy? Is it the poor, innocent Victim who always ends up getting hurt? Or is it the mean old Persecutor? Congratulations if you guessed that it is our Victim who pulls us out of Co-dependency! Remember that one of its most important characteristics is to know how and when to ask for help. Now let's look at how it works.

Going back to our comparison to a healthy family, how would a responsible mother and father react if their child told them she was hurt or sick? It certainly wouldn't be to ignore her and look for some other distraction that needs their attention. And it wouldn't be to yell at her and blame her, or to seek blame somewhere else out there. A healthy response would simply be to hold her, listen to how she's feeling, acknowledge her, and protect her in every way possible from hurting.

It's a vital part of being human to have an inner barometer that can register pain and discomfort. People with neurological illnesses that prevent them from feeling the nerves signaling pain are in grave danger of doing irreparable harm to themselves unknowingly. The discourse on listening to the pain signals in our body was started in the chapter on The Inner Child. We will delve into it again in the chapters on Inner Guides. Suffice it to say that if a tea kettle is whistling on the stove, it would not serve us to ignore it, to get mad at it for making noise, nor to yell at whoever turned it on.

The Victim/Child/Body is performing its vital function by letting us know when we are out of our comfort zone, physically or emotionally. We then have a choice to respond appropriately or in a dysfunctional way. The place where most forms of therapy go wrong is because of a very subtle, yet vital, distinction. Therapists, self-help books, and leaders in the field all say the very same words that are so easy to hear and understand, but so hard to do: "You need to love yourself." The only problem is - they don't teach you how. When your very self has been masked by a false persona, damaged to the core, or is simply lost, it's much easier to love others.

People are quick to minimize their own suffering as bearable, when they compare it to the plight of so many others worse off in the world. Yet, feelings of altruism aren't necessarily the appropriate response. It is, however, the ingrained response from childhood, when being good meant being loved and rewarded by a kind word, a cookie, or perhaps a pat on the head. It's easier to understand the reason people keep reverting back to doing good deeds when we can see it as a conditioned response. Just like Pavlov's dogs would continue to salivate and expect food every time the bell was rung, adults continue to believe that they will be rewarded with some form of love for caretaking and pleasing others.

We can no longer fail to acknowledge the pain of a childhood where mistakes were made by generations of dysfunctional parenting. It's time for more people to admit to being one of the walking wounded, which will ultimately be the greatest way to help themselves and those they love. Children are instinctively bound to believe their parents are right because they are helpless to fend for themselves, and survival of the species dictates it. Now it is time to grow up and take off the blinders. Seeing and admitting the truth can eliminate the trap of passing down the sins of the fathers to future generations through blind obedience to some illusion of reality.

Yes, it is true, as many people like to point out, that it was a long time ago and you're a different person now. But the younger person you were when it happened got frozen in time when the pain occurred. That younger self (we're calling your Inner Child), has not gotten over it. The scenes of pain or neglect are still playing back deep inside you, over and over like a broken record. If you don't believe it, just notice that when a present event resonates with an old pain, the same reactions are triggered, as if you were right back there today.

Remember that list of traits we compiled in Chapter 5 to describe people walking around with an unhealed Inner Child? We said they grow into *spoiled, bratty, loud, dependent, ungrateful, demanding, selfish, messy, mean* and *needy* adults. No one was available to respond or even listen to the needs of that child back then, and in this dysfunctional pattern, there is still no one listening now. Since so many people have grown up physically without the benefit of being able to mature emotionally, they keep looking for outer "mommies and daddies" (Rescuers and Protectors) to keep taking care of the needs of their own Inner Child (Victim).

The Rescuer is the perfect part of us to take care of that Inner Victim/Child because it's in keeping with what she already is wired to do. So instead of The Rescuer/Caretaker going out there in the world and continuing the Co-dependent behavior of rescuing everyone else's wounded parts as she is prone to do, *she can rescue that part of herself* who needs someone's love. Then she can speak directly to the part that truly needs to hear it. This is the new healing paradigm. The old advice most people are following is still to look in the mirror and spout some typical New Age textbook-style affirmation the mind doesn't even believe, such as, "I'm good enough and smart enough and I love myself just the way I am."

We need to begin to see that even though we did mature and did get beyond our painful past, we did so by brushing certain things under the rug. As hokey as it might sound to so many adults who are grateful to be all grown up and past all that now, it's really not healthy to go on and never look back. People want to believe that all that Inner Child stuff is "woo-woo" or passé, but *this is the way to emulate a healthy family paradigm.* Can you discern the difference between deciding to love *yourself,* and declaring your love *for that child inside of you* who is still very much alive and listening to your words?

Just as a good mother would never have the heart to turn a deaf ear to her child's pain, we must access the compassion of our Inner Rescuer to acknowledge and listen to the pain of our Inner Child/Victim. In my case, I might say words like: *"I love you, Little Debbie. I'm sorry you're feeling scared but don't worry—I'm here with you. Let me give you a hug and you can tell me what's wrong."* This is a simple recipe for health as long as you can get past thinking of how it looks (that's The Judge!). It's very simple. It's so simple that children do it all the time.

When they need comfort, they immediately go to their doll or stuffed animal, hold it to themselves, talk to it, and it makes them feel better. We need to learn from children to have that same compassion for ourselves, and pick up our own wounded child inside and hold him or her. The actual act of hugging a stuffed animal, or even a pillow, that we are thinking of as our Inner Child, has an immediate calming neurological effect. It's built into the body on a kinesthetic level, so don't let your mind sabotage you.

Try both methods and *feel* the difference. Looking in the mirror and speaking nice words to yourself does not work the same way. We may go through the motions, but our mind and body can stay detached as this remains a cerebral and intellectual exercise. The way this new behavior works is to create a paradigm shift by modeling a healthy family experience inside of you. It allows your brain to reset itself to the original template of a healthy, loving family that we all innately know we deserve.

After we allow The Rescuer/Mother to embrace and comfort that Child, there is still something else that has to happen. Otherwise we are left in the unfortunate dynamic of a single mother family, which is just as unsatisfying on the inside as it is for all of them out there in the world. As healing as the unconditional love of a mother is, it is not complete without the absolute certainty of the safety and shelter of a Protector/Father. We don't need to wall ourselves off with protective armor against the world if we feel safe within the eyes of a watchful father who we know is waiting to defend us.

Im the Rescuer to My Inner Child (victim)

Putting it All Together   *Wrestler - Inner Protector*

Let's revisit the session my client Ellen had around her alcoholic fiancé. The way I got her Inner Rescuer to play the role of a new loving Mother for her child was simple. I encouraged her adult self to let her little child know that she didn't need to get sick in order to get a man's love and attention anymore. Then that became kinesthetically anchored into her body when she hugged her stuffed animal at that moment. Now every time she holds her teddy bear it will reinforce the bond between her adult self as The Rescuer and new Mommy to that little girl.

The next vital step was to eliminate the possibility of her going back into her Co-dependent pattern, which meant she needed to access an Inner Protector (who sometimes can develop into an Inner Father). Because she remembered her big brother playing the role of protector for her, we tried to bring him into her inner world. But we found him incapable of taking the action necessary to communicate his displeasure to her fiancé with the way he was treating his sister. In real life their relationship was not that close, so there could have been danger of cognitive dissonance anyway.

His discomfort with that confrontation simply meant we had to look deeper to find that archetypal energy inside of her, which is a more powerful solution that Alchemy provides anyway. It was available in the form of a Polynesian Warrior who appeared from her subconscious mind when we asked for someone who could handle that job. He immediately sprang into action by rushing to Ellen's defense and giving that fiancé a piece of his mind.

Just as was the case with this true story, similar sad scenarios play out in thousands of relationships all the time. Because nature abhors a vacuum, when a person is not in touch with that protective part of him or herself it is almost certain that he or she will pull some External Persecutor into that position, such as an alcoholic or abusive partner. By filling that space with someone from inside herself, Ellen is assuring herself of a way out of the Co-dependency cycle, as long as she continues to utilize that inner resource of her Polynesian Warrior/Protector.

In her case, rather than merely accessing an Inner Protector Sub-personality, she actually met an Inner Guide (more on this in Chapters 11 and 12) to fill that role inside of her. As is appropriate for a Guide, he was able to advise her on how to make better choices in the future. He told her:

For a man to be a candidate for an intimate relationship with you, he needs to be confident, maybe a little older than you, well put together, and independent. He should be with you out of choice and respect you, who you are, and what you have to offer. You should feel your connection with yourself when you're with him, like when you do T'ai Chi. And you should be able to be in the relationship without holding anything back.

That's just the kind of words of advice we want to hear from a Protector or from a loving and protective Father. Now we have broken that damaging cycle by directing the energy of the Rescuer (Mother) and Protector (Father) in the direction of The Victim (Child) and kept it from going round and round (see Illustration 2). The members of the Co-dependency cycle are now acting as a functional family unit and Ellen can stop looking for love in all the wrong places and for all the wrong reasons.

The Co-dependency Cycle Solution

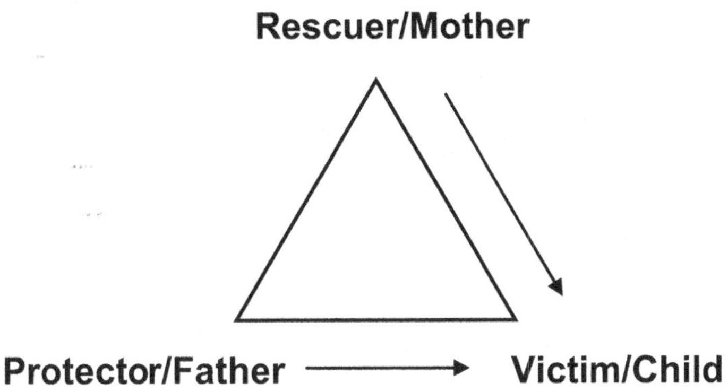

Rescuer/Mother

Protector/Father ⟶ Victim/Child

ILLUSTRATION 2

Breaking the Cycle

The way to create positive and beneficial behavioral change with all Sub-personality work is to take the contaminated aspects of all the characters and teach them how to maintain the positive traits of each character instead. We call that giving them new jobs, and we always make them consistent with the dynamics of the character. There's a magical transformation that happens when these three characters work together. When they align properly we end up with a wonderful alchemy of the three empowered personalities.

We saw how The Persecutor must take that *yang* male energy and use it to exhibit its most positive form as The Protector. His most important new job is to do anything necessary to diligently, or you could almost say ruthlessly, protect his own Inner Child just as a caring father would do for his children. The role of a father in a family is to provide, protect, lead and teach and those same traits can be used by The Protector with the Inner Child. He is also the part of us who is in charge of protecting one's personal time and space by having good boundaries and setting limits with oneself and others, including with one's own Rescuer.

Of course, The Rescuer must end the temptation to look outside for her next "rescue mission," and she is held accountable by her limit-setter, The Protector. Instead, for her new job, she tunes into her Victim/Child/Body with a mother's instinct and acknowledges any pain inside so she can attend to her own physical and emotional needs with her natural caretaking abilities. This is completely in keeping with what she likes to do anyway, so it's just a matter of redirecting her energy in a healthier way.

She must come to realize, after all, that there are many people who can answer the cries of the needy people in the world, but she is the only person who can hear the cries of her own Inner Child. Plus, it appeals to The Rescuer's altruism to understand that as long as any part of her remains hurt and neglected, there is less energy available for her to go out and help the suffering of the world. She won't even be valuable to her own family if she ends up sick. It also allays her sense of guilt to see how she can alleviate her Victim/Child's suffering.

The Rescuer in its highest form reaches out those loving arms that yearn to help, by holding that long forgotten Inner Child or the shunned Inner Victim just as a nurturing mother would. Then she can use her wonderful qualities of caring and compassion to be a healer or a teacher or even just a good friend. As long as she does it within limits, without over-stretching or burning herself out, it will prevent the danger of martyring herself, which could happen with a Rescuer who is left totally unchecked. We will visit the behavioral traits of The Martyr in Chapter 9.

Reframing even the good qualities of The Victim with a positive slant, however, presents a bigger challenge. No one likes a victim. Yes, we've pointed out the necessity of its positive traits of acknowledging pain, asking for help and knowing how to rest. And we know that the body and The Child are part of this character, and they can be lovable. Yet it's still not something that elicits a lot of pride or motivation to embrace and learn to love your Inner Victim. Maybe the problem is in that name itself. It's such an important part of this threesome that we really need to give it a new name that people can wish for and aspire to, that still maintains the integrity of the position.

One possibility is to call it The Victor, especially for people who literally were a victim and suffered some form of abuse from which they recovered and emerged even stronger. The word Survivor is often embraced by people who have experienced any extreme trauma or abuse and healed from the scars of it in therapy. It can be very empowering for them to realize they have gone from Victim to Victor or Survivor. Both can be used to re-name the positive aspects of The Victim persona.

However, although they don't make very catchy names, the best adjectives to describe an empowered and healed Victim, are actually *vulnerable* and *authentic*. It may sound strange to hear the word, vulnerable, framed as something to desire. That is because generally in life, and especially while growing up, there are many people who will prey on others' vulnerability. That is what can happen when you don't have an Inner Protector available. You remain at the mercy of all those External Persecutors who swim around like sharks smelling blood, waiting for their next innocent victim to prey upon.

But the ability to simultaneously feel vulnerable and protected is a powerful stance to take. It goes hand in hand with acting authentically, and is there anything greater to strive for than to be able to say that you have lived an *authentic* life? Imagine the freedom of truly knowing yourself, your needs and wants, your heart's true desire, and spending each day fulfilling them?

So many people look back at their youthful days and say, "If I only knew then what I know now!" How many people would choose instead to take the road that would lead them to what they truly wanted to do even if it would have made them vulnerable to ridicule or gone against popular opinion? The ability to walk our talk and be completely congruent with what we say, do, think, and believe is a gift not many people possess. Reigning in our Rescuer to take care of our needs first and having a Warrior/Protector to be our champion and fight for our rights allows us to be Victorious!

Coming Full Circle

These three Emotional Characters are responsible for letting us slip back into old and dysfunctional established patterns. Then because we feel incomplete, our answer to feeling whole is to find other people out there who have what we are missing. The reason we feel something is missing from our lives is because we remember it being present in our families of origin where everyone took on roles in order to establish family harmony. Even if it *was* dysfunctional—that's the view of the world that now seems right.

More specifically, people who were channeled into the caretaker role growing up (Rescuers) are statistically over-represented in the healing professions, yet they will still feel empty if they don't have someone to take care of at home. People who used to get attention in their families growing up by getting sick or yelled at (Victims), might protest about it, but will still draw people to them to treat them the same way. People used to creating crises and dramas all around them (Persecutors) will continue to create them, and keep pulling in people to help get them out of trouble.

The most important part to know now, though, is what keeps us out of trouble is having a balance of the *good* qualities of all three of the

Co-dependency characters within ourselves. Remember that all three roles need to be filled, and the fact is that if we don't possess the qualities of one or more of them within ourselves, they will be filled by someone outside of ourselves instead.

Because the pull is so strong, if the energy of one of the characters is absent in us, we are drawn to another person to supply the missing quality, just so the space does not remain void. It depends on which character is absent within us to see what scenario will most likely be played out with others. Of course, all this happens without any conscious knowledge of it. The more you understand this cycle, the more you will come to understand its complexities and how many possible situations exist for how it plays out in the world.

Breaking the cycle is the best way to feel fully empowered, autonomous, and in complete control of your life. Then you can begin to have relationships built on love and reverence that are "Co-Creative" and build upon each partner's strengths in an "Inter-Dependent" way. The relationship itself becomes a third entity and gets treated with the respect that it is due. When arguments arise and we find ourselves getting sucked into this old familiar cycle we can be aware of it and stop it through our conscious insight into it.

Stepping out of Co-dependency can be as easy as the simple steps outlined here. If you consciously use the principles delineated in this chapter, you will find yourself among the thousands of people who have discovered that loving, caring for, and protecting their Inner Child resulted in their own healing.

Now it's time to see how you fit into the picture of Co-dependency with a special exercise that lets you test yourself and see where the traps may lie in your life.

EXERCISE

This Co-dependency Quiz will help you learn whether Co-dependency is affecting your life now and if so, how, and where to go next.

Directions:

For Questions 1 – 5 on the following pages, count how many times you answer "yes" (out of eight possible answers) in the bulleted list for each section, then notate it in the space provided. When you've finished, take those answers and circle the appropriate numbers in the "Answer Grid" provided below. Read "Scoring" to hear what it all means.

1. (*Record number of "yes" answers for question 1 here.*) _|||| |||_ 8

- Do you go out of your way to help others even if it means neglecting your own needs when you already may be feeling drained?

- Are you in a profession or service industry that entails taking care of others?

- Do you over-commit your time for projects or errands you are not being paid for?

- Do you notice you are the person people call with their problems and you always listen, (you may even have trouble getting off the phone with them), but no one's there for you when you need to talk?

- Have you always felt a compulsion to help others?

- Do you stay on the phone longer than you'd like to?

- Do you sometimes buy things you don't really need from people, or give money to people on the street, because you feel sorry for them?

- Do you have trouble asking anyone for help?

2. *(Record number of "yes" answers for question 2 here.)* |||| | 4

- Do you find yourself thinking that you can't do anything right, or that bad things always happen to you?

- Are you prone to accidents, injuries, illnesses or suffer from frequent colds, flu's or allergies?

- Do you take prescription medication or miss work for injuries, headaches, stomachaches or backaches?

- Do you tend to call or lean on others to help you with your problems?

- Have you been a victim of robbery, rape, rip-offs, ugly break-ups, or physical or sexual abuse?

- Do you whine, complain, cry uncontrollably, feel depressed or suffer from fears, phobias, or obsessive/compulsive thoughts?

- Do you find yourself the brunt of people's jokes or ridicule; feel that the world is against you; or have a boss or manager who singles you out when you didn't do anything wrong?

- Do you cling to relationships, or have trouble being alone?

3. (*Record number of "yes" answers for question 3 here.*) ⎯⎯⎯⎯⎯⎯⎯⎯ ~~IIII~~ III 8

- Do you have difficulty setting limits and keeping personal boundaries?

- Do you get angry at yourself, judge yourself and find faults with yourself, while finding it difficult to get angry at others?

- Have you been in physically or emotionally abusive relationships or family situations?

- Do you like to have someone else around in order to feel safe?

- Do people that you consider your friends turn on you?

- Do you have difficulty asking for what you need?

- Do you find friends and family are often critical of you?

- Have you been bullied as a kid or an adult?

4. (*Record number of "yes" answers for question 4 here.*) II 2

- Do you act like a bully until you get your way and hate losing at games and sports?

- Do you often find yourself yelling at family, friends, or even strangers?

- Do people tell you that you're awfully critical of people and things?

- Do you have a short temper or sometimes notice people are scared of you?

- Do you get angry at inappropriate times despite the surroundings?

- Do you act destructively toward people or property?

- Do you display road rage?

- Do you often lose your temper and spank your children or take things out on them verbally?

5. (*Record number of "yes" answers for question 5 here.*) _____

- Do you have an easy time saying "No!"?

- Do you set limits with your time and money?

- Can you say no to sex or intimacy when you want to?

- Is it easy for you to stand up to people who try to push you and others around?

- Do you turn off your phone and let it go to voice mail when you're busy doing things?

- Are you willing to speak truthfully to people about something that's bothering you even if you know it will be unpleasant to confront them and might hurt their feelings or make them mad?

- Do you feel empowered and in charge of your life most of the time?

- Can you get appropriately angry in situations that warrant it?

ANSWER GRID

Put a circle around the number of "yes" answers you had recorded for each question.

Q 1:   0   1   2   3   4   5   6   7   (8)

Q 2:   0   1   2   3   (4)   5   6   7   8

Q 3:   0   1   2   3   4   5   6   7   (8)

Q 4:   0   1   (2)   3   4   5   6   7   8

Q 5:   (0)   1   2   3   4   5   6   7   8

SCORING

0 – 3 "yes" answers to Questions 1-3 means:
- You *might be free of Co-dependency.* Congratulations.
- The less "yeses" the better.
- **If it is accompanied by 4 or more "yes" answers to Question 5 and only 1 or 2 "yeses" in Question 4:**
- You have *probably conquered Co-dependency* in most of your relationships. Great!

4 or more "yes" answers to Questions 1-3 indicates:
- *Classic Co-dependency.*

THE KEY

Question **1** concerns **The Rescuer/Caretaker/Pleaser**

6 or more "yes" answers to Question 1 shows:

You have the possibility of a *Rescuer-dominant personality.*

Question **2** concerns **The Victim**

6 or more "yes" answers to Question 2 shows:

You have the possibility of a *Victim-dominant personality.*

Question **3** indicates the possibility of inviting in the presence

of an **External Persecutor**

6 or more "yes" answers to Question 3 (especially combined with only 1 or 2 "yeses" in Question 5) shows:

You might want to *stay clear of relationships* until you have learned to

develop your Inner Warrior/Protector.

Question **4** concerns **The Persecutor**

4 or more "yes" answers to Question 4 shows:

You have the possibility of a *Persecutor-dominant personality.*

Question **5** concerns **The Protector**

6 or more "yes" answers to Question 5 shows:

There is a good chance that you have a *well-developed Warrior/Protector* and know how to display good personal boundaries. Excellent!

(*However*, **combined with 4 or more "yes" answers to Question 4**, you may be *overly self-protective* and still be displaying *some traits of The Persecutor.*)

Where do you go from here?

➤ If the answers you gave to the above questions suggest you may be engaging in Co-dependency from the perspective of one or more of the three Characters, it could be helpful to re-read these last two chapters paying special attention to advice regarding those characters. As a shortcut, you could try just reviewing the sections on: **Examining the Co-dependency Cycle Inside a Person, Putting it All Together** and **Breaking the Cycle**.

➤ If you decide to seek out a therapist for help, I would advise you look for a Certified Alchemical Hypnotherapist who would be specifically equipped to deal with this issue in the way I've outlined it here. As a resource in finding one, you could refer to the Website, www.AlchemyInstitute.com

➤ (Optional) For fun, you can do this exercise imagining you were different ages in your life and see how you've changed through the years. For instance, thinking back ten years ago or twenty years ago, how would you have answered these questions?

In my case, the answers right now in my life are 2-2-2-2-8. If I thought back thirty years they would be 6-6-8-2-0. They say you teach what you most need to learn. Now you know why I'm in this occupation!

➤ (Advanced) If you were not happy with your results at this time, keep studying these chapters until you can put the principles into practice in your life. Then take this quiz again six months from now and see how the results differ.

THE MARTYR

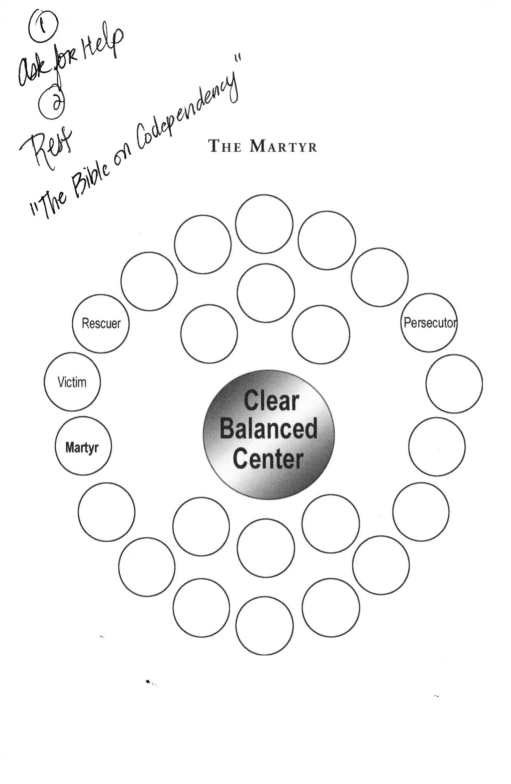

We do not have to visit a madhouse to find disordered minds; our planet is the mental institution of the universe.

— Johann Wolfgang von Goethe

Chapter 9

Religion

Misery Loves Company - The Martyr

The last Emotional Character we'll examine is one of the most difficult to understand and to explain. How in the world does it serve anyone to martyr himself? Why would anyone choose to live as a martyr (much less die as one)? One reason may be because many religions hold the values of the martyr in high regard. "Christ died for our sins," Christian children are taught in the family, church and parochial schools. Who wouldn't want to be Christ-like and turn the other cheek the way we are told He did?

The list of positive attributes that accompanies The Martyr is a short one that describes a few historical and religious icons such as Abraham Lincoln and Jesus. The uncontaminated Martyr is someone who believes in a higher cause and will die for his beliefs. He or she often becomes a rallying figure, either while still alive or often posthumously. Martyrs know how to be of service and are there to help when needed, even to the point of being self-sacrificing. Their good qualities also include being honorable with noble intentions. The big problem is that it is hard to find many martyrs who are not contaminated and toxic.

Of course, Christianity hasn't got the market cornered on martyrdom. The classic martyr that comes to many people's minds and is the brunt of many comics' jokes is the stereotypical Jewish mother who is always doing, doing, doing for her family and never receives enough thanks for it. We'll look more into this dynamic later on in this chapter.

Within the past few decades the world has seen different religious cults commit mass suicides or go down together in fiery flames. Were their motivations to martyr themselves? In Islam, the Koran states, "God rewards those who martyr themselves for God." There are now scores of Muslims signing up to be martyrs, and mothers who couldn't be prouder of them even if it means they are prepared to take on a suicide mission. Isn't that counter-intuitive when supposedly the greatest loss a person can suffer is the death of a child?

The Hindus preach non-violence which could be a way to end up at the wrong end of a gun. One of the greatest martyrs of the modern era was the Hindu sage Mahatma Gandhi, who was murdered for his efforts to build a united India. Martyrs of many faiths, both religious and sectarian, serve to inspire others through their lives and their deaths. In the last century alone, as well as Gandhi, we've also seen the suffering of Mother Theresa, Nelson Mandela and even the Reverend Martin Luther King, Jr., who predicted his own assassination yet kept preaching in public.

I had the opportunity in the 1980's to see a man named Brian Wilson (not the same one as is in the Beach Boys), get up on stage and speak poignantly about a cause he sacrificed his legs for. He and his fellow protestors were willing to lie down across the railroad tracks to stop U.S. trains from carrying bombs that were on their way to South America to support a tyrannical regime. One day during the well-organized protests, one of the trains approached Brian and the line of his colleagues' bodies lying along the tracks, and the conductor did not stop.

Many of the other protestors jumped up and ran out of the way, but Brian stood up on his prosthetic legs at the podium and told us he still believed his legs were a small price to pay to bring this issue to light. He also knew he was only one person and there were hundreds of others who were losing their legs to minefields every day all over the third world.

Some of our greatest literature deals with themes of martyrdom. We weep for the hero in *A Tale of Two Cities* as he marches willingly to the guillotine in the place of the man whom his beloved is in love with, and utters those immortal words, "'Tis a far, far better thing I do than I have ever done before." We feel for Heathcliff in *Wuthering Heights* when he fulfills his promise to become worthy of Catherine only to find that she has martyred herself by marrying a man she never loved until it kills her; then again as Heathcliff chooses the role of martyr for himself as well, spending the rest of his years alone with Catherine's ghost in the moors as his only companion.

You could almost say there is a sense of glamour, and certainly valor, in dying a martyr's death. In literature, true to the Greek tradition, tragedies must contain an element of doom and the death of the hero, such as Romeo and Juliet's star-crossed lovers. But can't we keep that in books and movies? Why *choose* to embrace that stance in one's life? Does God really want us to suffer? Are martyrs holier than the rest of us? We see priests, monks and nuns take vows of celibacy, poverty and silence. Does that give them a step up on the stairway to heaven?

Is there a chance that people have misinterpreted the intentions that were handed down as the word of God? In Barbara Walter's Holiday Special, aired first in 2005, "Heaven, Where is it? How do we Get There?" she examined faith from the perspective of all the world's major religions. Her expert on the Koran gave an interpretation of the idea of "martyring oneself for God" as doing "service for God"; that is quite different than how some people are interpreting that command today.

Spiritual Madness

Maybe times are also changing, or at least that's what Caroline Myss purports in her CD called *Spiritual Madness*. Myss started off as a medical intuitive and in the 1990's she began to see a pattern in the illnesses that were plaguing her clients. She diagnosed the phenomena as a "metaphysical disease of epidemic proportion." The diseases we call depression, anxiety, chronic fatigue, and a host of other physical ailments, she saw as all having their roots in people's fears of waking up to who they truly are. That is why she came to label the maladies she saw in so many people as *spiritual* madness.

Myss noticed that the more people tried to preserve order in their lives, the more often they found their lives falling apart. People were spending so much energy working to maintain the status quo, and the world around them was changing so fast, it was literally beginning to feel like they were going mad! Myss contends we have to let go of the idea of how we want God to be and what we want Him to do for us in our lives. One problem is that we as human beings like things to work in an orderly fashion by our human standards. But, as we've heard a thousand times, *the only constant in life is change*.

In my life, I can tell you that my Inner Control Freak could certainly do without so much change if I were in charge. I hate when my favorite restaurant closes, or friends and neighbors I've grown to love move away or die. I hate being slowed down or detoured due to road construction and sometimes I even wish I could keep kids from growing up. But of course, I'm not running the universe, so I've had to learn to make peace with the concept that "change is good" and have even used that as a mantra at times in my life to keep myself from going mad. I have also come to appreciate the fact that God works in mysterious ways.

Magicians understand that people get dazzled by their tricks because most of us define magic as having events and other external things cooperate with us. So what magicians know to be sleight of hand, we see as pulling rabbits out of a hat. Once we come to accept that change is the only constant in life, we can begin to understand that *chaos* is an essential element in *Divine Order*.

Caroline Myss says, "The moment you recognize chaos as the voice of God is the day you see clearly." She says the path of mysticism is the path of *release from order* and that the Divine Mind works in paradox, for instance, in order to be big you need to get small. In fact this is a time when there is a calling for *all* people on earth to become small and let God work through us, only it goes counter to the programming so many have been brought up with to leave that to the clerics among us.

In the past, seekers who wanted to be on a spiritual path used to take vows, leave the material world behind, and surround themselves with other like-minded souls. She says the goal now is to "find the extraordinary within ordinary life." That's not so easy to do at home with all the distractions of work, relationships, children, and financial obligations. Plus there are no role models, "book" or rules to follow.

Perhaps we think we can remain safe within our ingrained beliefs and the comforts of our everyday world, but when we feel that sense of malaise coming on, or begin to get the urgings to do or have or know something more, it may mean we are being called to enter the mysteries of our own inner world. Vicki Noble, the creator of the *Motherpeace* tarot, claims, "If one is afraid to enter one's own astral territory, one can never know oneself—and the mystery of initiation is about little more than this."

The fact is that the path of contemporary mysticism has now been brought to the personal level and is available to the masses instead of the few who have historically cloistered themselves in a life of service to God. Noble explains the concept well in her interpretation of the major arcana card of the Moon. "...Jungian psychology today reflects the idea that modern people experience initiation rites and symbolic ventures into the ancient mystery realms through the unconscious—mainly our dreams and our artistic expression…If you can enter the darkness with eagerness and courage; if you can trust in the higher powers to guide you intuitively through the journey of darkness and the unknown, then you will learn from the voyage and gain consciousness as your initiatory gift."

Myss advises people who are living in fear or suffering from spiritual madness to counteract it by developing "Spiritual Self-Esteem," defined as *the ability to hear God speaking to you directly in personally meaningful ways* and then taking the responsibility to *act on the advice* you receive. We will speak in depth about this concept and how to do just that in Chapters 11 and 12 when we delve into a lengthy discussion on Inner Guides.

Myss alleges that when the ailments of spiritual madness manifest in people, they are often being suppressed with drugs; but she claims it is really God speaking to us saying: *It's time to wake up now. Open your eyes and see the miracles all around you!* Becoming aware of those small everyday miracles allows everyone to experience *mystical* moments in *normal* life. This is how we're meant to find our true calling. We can build our spiritual self-esteem and find our own divinity through following God's advice directly, without the need for a third party to interpret it for us or dictate it to us.

It may even be possible to open our ears and hear the voice of God speaking to us in our heads. We no longer need to view that as "going mad." Unfortunately, too many people who hear this calling are afraid to take flight into the unknown. It feels scary to do something new, which is why so many people who may be right on the brink of waking up to who they truly are, ignore their inner promptings and instead end up feeling lost, lonely and sad. They choose to stay in the safety of the nest forever and get trapped in their depression, pain and illnesses, instead of jumping out and discovering they were meant to fly.

Martyr-dominated people are particularly unwilling to take that leap because they can't let go of their strong desire to control all aspects of their lives. For some of them, the results of watching everyone else enjoying life and feeling like they're doomed to be no more than an onlooker, can result in manifesting some of the more toxic aspects of The Martyr. Martyrs often have a passive-aggressive energy. They can learn to use pain to their advantage to control others into feeling sorry for them and getting them to do their bidding.

Other negative traits of The Martyr include blaming everyone else in the world for his or her own misery by making others feel guilty. They can be master manipulators, often full of hidden agendas. As might be expected, some martyrs may be misguided and fanatical because they are dealing with serious religious programming. It's important to also mention the possibility of a genetic heritage or past life trauma that could be at the root of The Martyr in some people.

The Martyr in Action

One of the students who went through my Alchemical Hypnotherapy training program was brought up by the "proverbial" Jewish mother and a father who had been the sole survivor in his family of the Nazi concentration camps where he spent his childhood from age eight until his liberation when he was fourteen. Her own childhood was evidently colored by those factors. When class began and she was asked to use three words to describe herself, she answered, "Skeptic, skeptic and skeptic."

At the beginning of the course, her belief system was telling her that she was alive to be miserable. As the weeks went by she began to question whether any of us were really created and put on this earth to live a miserable life? She revealed this secret to the class on the last day when she was asked to make a speech and she began to speak of her own metamorphosis, actually likening it to the chrysalis, or cocoon, stage of a butterfly where she saw herself and so many other people stuck living their lives.

She described to people how she could help them take the same journey she had just been through. She called it, "the way for each of us to come out of our cocoon, to spread our wings, transform, and become whatever our dreams are...Looking within, experiencing life as life is, without the masks that we wear, without the parts that we play to simply survive." She continued, "You get to rip the skins off that protect you, tear the masks off and look at each part of you: the beauty, the fire, the stillness, the excitement behind the characters that play the roles in your life."

Then she concluded that, "I know now through Alchemical Hypnotherapy that I was not put on this planet to be a miserable human being. I was put here to experience life to its fullest, to experience the air as the breath which feeds my body; to experience other people as integral parts of how I love and am the person who I am. I invite you all to take the journey, to feel the life beyond the life you have been living."

Dissecting the Martyr Complex

The Martyr is a slippery character because although it can exist in and of itself, it is generally comes out as a "Martyr's Complex" which is made up of all the positions in the Co-dependency triangle. In its complex form it is part Rescuer, part Victim and part Persecutor, all wrapped up into one. Since it is vital to get into rapport and pace (agree with) each Sub-personality we work with in order to allow them to transform, we have our work cut out for us with The Martyr.

Just when we think we have developed rapport with one part of it and we begin to ask it what it really wants, another part of it pops up with a completely different set of desires and it's back to the drawing board. Therefore, we must have a way to counteract that dynamic. One of the best ways to deal with The Martyr is through the tactic of "divide and conquer." By dividing that one character up into his or her component parts and speaking to them each individually we can contain it. Otherwise it will be like trying to hold onto a fish and it will squirm right out of our grasp.

Here's a good example of how a Martyr-dominant Jewish mother might sound both in a normal conversation and inside her head: *I've tried so hard to be a good mother to my boys. I worked my fingers to the bone, cooking and cleaning and working nights until my back was breaking. But now you think they would care enough to call or write? Not even a postcard! They say they love me, but they're busy. What kind of love is that? I was busy, too, but not too busy to make them chicken soup anytime they got sick! I should just forget about them and go on with my life, let them feel what it would be like to not have me around! But it breaks my heart. If I was smart, I'd just write them out of the will. They probably only stay in contact to make sure I'll leave them something. But they do work hard and they are good boys, God bless them.*

Can you hear the way the conversation is being run by The Rescuer, Victim and Persecutor all at the same time, switching to another character with almost every sentence? If I came back with a statement like, "Oh, I'm sure they love you," she would be able to spin around and tell me all the reasons why they don't. Conversely, if I paced the Persecutor in her and agreed that she would be smart to write her sons out of the will, (God help me!) she would come to their rescue and attack me.

Our best solution sounds like this, "I know there's a part of you that really loves your sons," and if I was speaking to a client I might ask what we can call her. "Can we call that part of you 'The Mama'?" Then after we came up with a name she agreed with, I would go on and add, "But it sounds like they have hurt you a lot and you're feeling a little left out right now. Maybe we can call that part 'The Sad One'."

Finally I'd have to deal with the Persecutor by acknowledging, "And it sounds like there's a part of you who's sick and tired of being treated that way and isn't going to take it anymore! Could we call her 'Mrs. Over It'?" We'd take as long as necessary for her to come up with and get comfortable with the names for all the parts, and then we'd be able to start getting somewhere."

Working with The Martyr in Therapy

Of course Martyrs can come in all shapes and forms. Dr. Alan D. came to see me for a session because of back pain that was almost crippling him. When he looked at the X-rays of his own spine, he said it was in the worst shape of anyone he'd ever seen. I learned there was a deep, permeating sadness in his life because of the fact that his son had been diagnosed a few years before with a congenital illness that put him in a lot of pain and could possibly prove terminal. As a doctor Alan was feeling completely powerless to help him, and resorted to prayer as the only solution he knew of. Only there was a problem in the way he was praying.

In his despair as Dr. Daddy, who was being sidelined when he wanted to be in the game, he tried playing The Hero; but in his desperation it came out as The Martyr, and the words he prayed came back to bite him. Alan was being eaten up by guilt, perhaps inherent from his Catholic upbringing, and prayed with all his might every morning and night to God for him to be able to take his son's pain. Obviously God was listening, and gave the doc what he asked for.

He had the whole Martyr Complex going. His Inner Hero was playing the part of The Rescuer trying to perform miracles. However, knowing he was powerless to do anything for his son made Alan feel like a helpless Victim. He was so riddled with guilt, it made him feel better to actually hurt and Persecute himself with this horrific pain in his back which was rendering him useless to his family. He was in so much pain he could hardly work, and was almost ready to sell his practice. But meanwhile his true-to-form Martyr part, who we named Mr. Guilty, felt good about being in rapport with his son, because at least now the boy didn't have to suffer alone.

I began to frame the situation in a new way for Alan to see what the results of his thinking and his actions were really doing to him and the people he loved. His Inner Child was perceptive enough to say a lot of the words for me. As the session opened his Child immediately started to tell him, "Stop trying to control everything, learn to say no, nurture yourself more, and stop feeling so guilty...Sing more and spend more time with your friends and family...Enjoy your life and stop doing everything for everyone." He has a smart kid. Too bad Alan wasn't listening. Mr. Guilty was too busy believing that misery really does love company.

When he heard those words spoken by his Inner Child in the session Alan finally was able to listen to that inner wisdom, but his guilt was still dominating him. The next thing it made him want to do was to communicate to his son that sometimes he doesn't feel he does enough for him, and then to ask God if any of this was his fault. He admitted that his idea of being a dad meant that he *should* take on the pain. I knew it was time to intervene and let him see the future consequences of his beliefs.

I had him look twenty years into the future from the vantage point of two different scenarios. First he looked ahead to see his life as it would be if he continued this way, and when he saw a decrepit old man it really scared him. Then I suggested what a difference it would make, not only to him, but even as a role model for his family, if he could model a man living his life without guilt. Otherwise, he would be bringing up another generation of martyrs by example.

Even as exciting as it was for him to see himself taking a different fork in the road and to instead see a future free of pain, happy, healthy, and much more financially independent, Alan still had a question he needed to ask his son before he was willing to accept that future for himself. He needed to know if he would still love his dad as much if Alan was healthy. When his son answered, "of course," he was ready to tell his back it was time to get strong again, to which his back answered him, "It's about time!" He then declared, "I'm *back*!"

We did a little more work to give him a chance to make a list of all the burdens he saw that he was carrying on his back and he made a decision to let some of them go. Then he "prescribed" for himself a list of things he needed to do in order to heal, including light exercise, more R&R, and better nutrition. After all of that he was then able to connect with his dead father as a Spiritual Guide and hear him urging him to add to that list: following his heart's desire to sing more.

The first person he got to be a good role model for was his Inner Child who was very glad to hear him getting with the program and told him it was better late than never. Alan then admitted it wasn't working to think he knew what was best. He was now ready to use a different prayer than he had been for so many years. He changed it from his old Martyr's stance of, "Give me their pain. Let them fly, not me," to the same words he prayed for everyone else to now apply to himself, too, "Let us all be happy and filled with blessings."

Alan was amazed that he had practically made himself a cripple with the words he was affirming everyday with his prayers. The change in his entire life was enormous, and it always is when we put a stop to any kind of unconscious self-sabotage, such as that which comes from The Martyr. He even got a new trick to put into his Doctor's bag. He has started to ask people what words they use when they pray and to pass on words of advice when he hears the tones of guilt in anyone else's prayers.

We will revisit the doctor again in Chapter 11 for more about his profound life-changing encounter during this session with his long-deceased father, who guided him onward in his quest to become a singer. But, as we saw here, he had a lot of work to do before he could connect with and hear the inspiring words of his dad. Yet, as almost always is the case, when we cleared the contamination of his self-inflicted martyrdom, he was able to soar out of his pain and into his life's purpose, just as you heard the daughter of the concentration camp survivor acknowledging above in her own words.

EXERCISE

This chapter began by posing many questions including the big one: are martyrs holier than the rest of us? Perhaps a few pages later, you are ready to answer the same way I would with an unequivocal "no!" This is not in any way meant as disrespect to those people who have been dealt a hand that includes suffering from some illness or disability that they were born with or sustained. I am a firm believer in Karma as a private pact made with our soul to work out lessons from previous lives by choice before we were born.

But the way of The Martyr is toxic; somebody always gets hurt. We can write a new chapter in the 21st century that reads, "Suffering is no longer necessary." It will take each one of us doing our own personal work to make this a reality, but we *can* make a turn from Suffering to Surrender. Surrendering may seem more difficult to some people because it involves letting go of control and trusting in something we can't see. But just because we can't see it doesn't mean that there isn't something better than we can imagine awaiting us—and that something might just be our life's purpose.

Here are some questions to help you explore The Martyr and ponder the existence of it in your life:

➤ Have you ever had the thought that you were put on this earth to suffer?

➤ Do you feel like you may be suffering from any of the emotional symptoms or physical manifestations of what we've called "spiritual madness"? These can include depression, anxiety, cancer, chronic fatigue, feeling lost, alone or afraid, being on medication for an emotional or physical condition, or even simple malaise.

➢ Where are you in your metamorphosis from caterpillar to butterfly? Are you still slinking along the ground as the caterpillar? Are you stuck in the chrysalis stage and afraid to come out? Have you had the experience of spreading your wings and flying?

➢ How is your "Spiritual Self-Esteem"? Do you feel connected to a spiritual source that you can go to for answers in your life? Do you see and acknowledge everyday miracles?

➢ (Optional) Is there a Martyr inside you or do you know anyone who displays the characteristics of The Martyr? What are some of the lines that he or she uses that make you think so?

➢ (Advanced) Can you divide those lines up into the three Co-dependency characters within The Martyr and differentiate the voices of the Rescuer, Victim and Persecutor?

Rescuer   Victim   Persecutor

overdoing   #   #
people
pleasing

*Everything that irritates us about others
can lead us to an understanding of ourselves.*

— Carl Jung

Chapter 10

THE DARK SIDE OF THE MOON

As the moon revolves around the earth, it appears to grow from a crescent shape to a full circle and back again because of the shadow the Earth casts as the sun's light is reflected back to us. Of course we know that it is always circular whether we can see its full round form or not. The phases of the moon showing us its changing face during a month can be likened to the various faces we show the world, as different Sub-personalities reflect our behavior patterns during the days and nights of our lives.

All the characters in the previous chapters that you have recognized and acknowledged as a part of yourself are connected to the "sunny" side of you that you are willing to admit to or "own." They are basically within our normal conscious awareness even if they may have been hidden from view until this book shed some light on them.

However, the book would not be complete without exploring the "dark side" of us as well. As the ancient Mystery Schools have known for centuries, the answer to the greatest mystery is to be found in the deep dark recesses of our unconscious mind. Therefore, we will move now from the exploration of our ego side to the more hidden, shadowy side of ourselves.

In this chapter we will, in fact, be introduced to the most hidden character, The Saboteur, who lives in the depth of The Shadow. We will see how being in the dark can create the circumstances for self-sabotage or even lead people down a path to total self-destruction. Also, we will see that if we stop and take the time to listen to this desperate character, we find that it miraculously holds the key to giving us everything we've always wanted in life.

The Shadow

The Shadow is that area in which we are asked to leave the safety of the known and are tested to explore the deepest, darkest regions within. The journey to "know thyself" will never be complete without the willingness to dive deeper beneath the surface to ferret out all aspects of the Self. Our soul will continue to call us to this task, and until we are willing to answer it we may experience bouts of pain and martyrdom, or, as Caroline Myss tells us, spiritual madness—our own dark night of the soul.

Myss believes it may be necessary for millions of people to experience just that at this time. She construes what John of the Cross really meant when he said, "You cannot find God unless you are born again," was that we all need to enter the darkness in order to find the light—quite a different idea from the usual interpretation. Just like the birth canal through which we all enter the world, the only way out is to go through it; and we must do it alone.

We have been born at this time, not to just be content with what the world presents to us externally, but to get to know our own shadow side and truly become fully awake and conscious. We can have the guidance of others who have been there before, but no one's journey will be the same as another's. We all have our own darkness to enter and Shadow to face. It is the mythical "Hero's Journey" of which Joseph Campbell speaks. In Alchemy we call it finding your own "personal mythology."

It may seem preferable to stay on the surface and not look beyond the nice, polished front we've worked so hard to present to the world. Most of us are unaccustomed to taking any ownership or personal responsibility for those traits that live in our Shadow (out of sight, out of mind). We don't realize that our normal state of consciousness is like that of an ostrich with its head in the sand.

So, just as the moon has a dark side we never see because it never faces the sun, there is similarly a side of everyone's personality that we keep tucked away behind us, and that is what psychologists call "The Shadow." Of course we can decide to simply go on living on the sunny side even choosing, albeit unconsciously, to "disown" our Shadow. However, unlike the view we have of the moon from Earth, we don't walk around where we are always facing others. The irony is that since other people can see behind us, they can often see our Shadow much easier than we can.

On the other hand, as you know if you've ever tried to see the back of your own head, the only way you can do it is by looking in a mirror. Since we have done such a good job of putting our disowned parts behind us (even though our friends may be able to see them clearly), having those traits "mirrored" back to us through other people who have matching ones is now often the only way we have of seeing our own Shadow. Dr. Phil McGraw says there's an old saying in psychology that illustrates how we do this. It goes, "There's something about that old boy that I just can't stand [in me!]"

You see, we have inner radar that tunes right into those things we reject in ourselves, and they continually show up all around us in the form of other people who become "mirrors" for us. There are two easy ways to get an inkling of your own Shadow. One of them is to think of the people who really "push your buttons" or you despise passionately. Another is to think of the people you truly love and admire and are, in fact, quite envious of.

You may feel that you could never be like those people, do what they do, or have what they have, because they seem either so terrible or, conversely, so wonderful. This will begin to give you an idea of both your "negative projections" and "positive projections." The concept of projection is simply: *those things we reject in ourselves are spotlighted for us when we see them in others*. The Universe purposely places those people in our lives to help us accept the truth about ourselves. That is how they become a "mirror" to help us see our own Shadow.

Many people are afraid of the dark and would immediately think of it as negative and sinister. That's an accurate assessment of one aspect of The Shadow and it's easy to see that "shadowy" side of people who possess those traits, but it's not the only way it presents itself. There are also many people who actually disown the strongest, most beautiful and *positive* parts of themselves and that issue is not addressed often enough in discussions of The Shadow.

When I used to go to Jones Beach in the summer with my high school girl friends on Long Island, it never made sense to me why at least one of them would inevitably point out the most beautiful woman on the beach with her perfect bikini-clad bronzed body and declared emphatically, "Look at her. I hate her!" Now I've come to understand that like most high school kids, my girlfriends had been far too willing to own their self-proclaimed flaws, while they had placed their beauty in their Shadow.

Sometimes it's easier to be in awe, or even go so far as to fall in love with people because of particular traits we see in them, when those people are really in our lives to help us nurture and develop those same traits within us. I used to find myself very attracted to people who had what I saw as amazing healing abilities: they seemed to know intuitively just how to touch people to take away their pain. I felt so powerless to help people stop hurting, and was attributing to these massage therapists and healers supernatural abilities of almost god-like proportion. I finally realized that I needed to take that envy and admiration I had for them and develop those traits and claim them for myself.

Over a number of years I made it a point to take classes in acupressure, Reiki and other mind/body and somatic healing techniques. Now what I used to see as a mystical healing power that I assumed was a skill that

I needed to seek out in others with that gift, I learned to take out of my Shadow and develop in myself. If I hadn't already had the propensity for it, it would not have held such a special place of longing in my heart and soul. Presently I've relegated other healers into a peer group of which I consider myself a member, and the awe I was in of them has disappeared.

In contrast, I can be in awe of musicians gifted with beautiful voices and abilities, but never gravitated toward them with jealousy or passion because a musical propensity is not a trait that's buried in my Shadow. However, there may be many "air guitar" players out there dying to pick up a real electric guitar and be just like Carlos Santana or singers who would never admit they yearn to be crowned the next American Idol.

Those people who really do try out for talent shows aren't keeping those feelings in their Shadow because, although they may be deluding themselves, they are up front about their desire. The way you know what may be lurking in your Shadow is through the *secret* obsession or passion you possess about something or someone. Remember that the passion can feel like love and desire *or* like hatred and jealousy. As long as it's *not* a *neutral* feeling, it can be a case of positive or negative projection of your Shadow side onto others. *dancers*

Positive projections such as love, beauty, social skills, self-worth, independence, sensitivity, strength, success, fame and fortune abound. The shortcut most of us rely on is the common feeling of attraction to another person or people who happen to have the traits we want. That's how the mirror goes up. Then we can simply idolize or blindly "fall in love" with them because they have those things we yearn for, rather than putting forth the effort to develop those traits in ourselves. This could be one explanation for why so many marriages fail.

We usually learn the hard way, through the repeated heartaches from broken relationships that another person can't be a substitute for what our soul is lacking. The best chance for achieving true love is by doing our own

Shadow work. We can then look forward to enjoying a healthy relationship in the full light of the sun. At least then when we awaken from the bliss of the honeymoon to the realization that our beloved is mortal after all, we can accept him for who he really is.

We can also live our own lives without any worry of someone not loving us if they really knew everything about us, because as long as you live with any secrets hiding in your Shadow you are constantly in fear of being "exposed." Think back to my Mr. Together client who was married to a Ms. Together who would never let him see her naked except in total darkness, or even without her make-up on. What do you think she may have living in her shadow?

Without the willingness to explore and face our Shadow, it's like looking for love in a "house of mirrors" full of false reflections and projections. Sooner or later the magic mirror that we believed was reflecting our beloved becomes a more accurate reflection of reality. We begin to see that The Shadow has been lurking all along, and the face looking back at us in the mirror is ultimately our own.

Perhaps the other person stops playing the role we had cast them in and we feel confused or betrayed. We may even end up distraught, like the witch in Snow White, as we are caught staring right at the truth we were afraid to admit. There's no replacement for the dedication it takes to own our power and grow into the person we were truly meant to be. It's not always easy, but if we're lucky some light is shed on the situation. Remember, all you need to do to eliminate the darkness is to turn on the light.

As you learn to know and accept yourself (and your *selves*) and to love all of you, you'll notice a new feeling of peace and alignment inside. There will also be less self-judgment, persecution, and sabotaging behavior from parts of you who were feeling isolated, rejected and deserted by you. But first you must realize that the longer these parts have been left alone, the more opportunity they've had to become toxic. For instance, there may be a part of you that can rage at your loved ones, even though you like to be known as peace-loving, because you keep this part of yourself hidden until those times when you lose control and it just comes out.

Since our Shadow is full of those parts that we try to deny, suppress and keep secret, they are love-starved. You could liken it to a feral child who has been left to fend for himself and when he's brought back to civilization he appears to be primitive and savage. Even the child's own mother upon being reunited might be repulsed and have no desire to care for him in that state. She may even feel a mistake has been made and try to disavow any connection to him. All the child needs is to be loved and cared for to restore him to acting human again, yet even a mother's instinct can be fooled.

The Judge and/or Preacher are often the jailers of these orphaned parts, attempting to keep the Sub-personalities they deem unacceptable to be presented to the outside world, hidden, out of sight, in the Shadow. They may call them *weak, ugly, pathetic, selfish, mad, mean, lazy, wrong, sinful, perverted, or disgusting*, yet their undesirable behavior persists. Of course it's to no avail, as has been discussed, since people can see behind (and through) us. It just seems to be easier for most people to continue to act reprehensibly and lie to themselves and others about these traits than to deal with them.

The Shadow Unmasked

One way to rationalize our actions is by dehumanizing our victims through euphemisms ("collateral damage"), labels ("geeks," "cockroaches"), or placing blame ("I was just following orders"). Soldiers in Vietnam were forced to take part in acts of warfare that made them face the darkest parts of themselves. The 1960's and 70's saw veterans coming home unable to rectify their civilian life with the dark secrets they attempted to bury through military debriefings and medications. For many years Americans were forced to face their collective Shadow for what our government did to innocent people in campaigns such as the Mei Lei massacre.

Brave men such as Hugh Thomson, a helicopter pilot, and his crew who tried to stop the murders by rescuing women and children at Mei Lei, were actually court-martialed and treated like traitors. It wasn't until decades later, when as a nation, our leaders admitted to the atrocity of those acts, that these men were finally honored and touted as the heroes that they truly were.

There is a long history of people projecting their own dark sides onto others. Many are all too willing to project the things about themselves they feel guilty about and cannot reconcile with their socially acceptable "sunny" personalities. They instead hone in on these Shadow traits they think they see in others as evils to be destroyed. Centuries ago missionaries covering themselves in clothes from head to toe out of sexual repression and religious modesty, tried to change "savage natives" in Hawaii and around the world into what they defined as civilized, often resulting in near genocide.

During the Middle Ages in Europe millions of women who were adept in the healing arts and herbology were burned as witches because of a heretical connotation to their powers, and the unwillingness of the male patriarchy to accept the more powerful, yet subtle, feminine gifts of intuition and healing. Just decades ago Jews, homosexuals, and gypsies were thrown into concentration camps to be exterminated by the insane dictates of a man who *had Jewish blood* running in his veins.

Perhaps we could understand a natural fear of others very different from ourselves out of pure ignorance. Yet how often is the object of hatred and vengeance actually someone extremely similar? Look at the long struggle between the Irish and the English or the Arabs and the Jews. Likewise, the parallels between fundamentalist Muslims and fundamentalist Christians are undeniable. Our attachment to our ego identity and the resistance to *owning* those traits that we wish to attribute to others, keep us blindly striking out in our feeble attempts to eradicate what we don't like in ourselves.

You may recall that J. Edgar Hoover, during his years as the FBI Director, was a closet homosexual who viciously exposed and prosecuted other gay men of his time. Too often in the news we hear the secrets of those we trusted in political office or looked up to as role models in business, sports or entertainment, being exposed for fraud, indecency or dishonesty. Politics in this decade has been strewn with similar examples including New York's Governor Spitzer who won his office through his tough stance on prostitution only to get caught in his own trap.

Until people can embrace and make friends with their own Shadows we will continue to see cases of politicians telling bold-faced lies and preachers being caught doing the very things they are preaching against. The more vocal we hear people getting on their podiums, the more we should remember the perceptive words Shakespeare wrote to describe the guilt of Lady Macbeth, "The lady doth protest too much."

Since food and sex are two areas we may have been shamed about in our past, they are typical areas for shadowy behavior to take place. Maybe it shows up in the way you stash food in places and eat it secretly so people won't see you "pigging out." It could even be the fact that you've been engaging in sexual practices you espouse to be against. Or perhaps you have been carrying on an affair with someone who's married. Inevitably these acts will come back to sabotage us.

The Saboteur

As I said before it is not uncommon for a Shadow Character to also be the part of ourselves that sabotages us. Unlike all the Sub-personalities presented thus far in the book, which conform to certain identifiable traits, the Saboteur shows up differently in everyone. The pattern of behavior may exhibit certain similarities, but the form anyone's Saboteur takes is unique. There are markers they all have in common including the fact that the Saboteur is shrouded in secrecy, shame, and denial, but it is the effect he has, or the havoc he wreaks that is his distinguishing mark.

The main way he makes himself known is that we never can get what we really want in life. We may get close, but somewhere along the way to reaching our goal, the Saboteur pops up, foils us again, and just like with that card in Monopoly, we're sent directly to jail without collecting $200. It could be a relationship, a job, a promotion, a new car or good health—the Saboteur will choose whatever would be our most prized possession to deny us. Some signs of having an Inner Saboteur could be suffering from chronic pain, a life-threatening illness, addictions, or being prone to accidents or procrastination in your life.

Our Saboteur is relegated to the deep, dark dungeon within, in the company of all the traits we don't like about ourselves that we keep in our Shadow. Just as slipping into the shade is a natural thing we do to get out of the sun on a hot day, our Saboteur tries to slip back into our Shadow when things get heated up in our lives. But the more we desire to live in Truth, the harder it is to stop those rumblings down in the dungeon from interfering with our lives. Eventually the time comes in the life of every person desiring to live consciously when we choose to turn on the light to dispel the darkness.

The origin of the Saboteur has its roots in one of three scenarios. There may have been some moment in time when it stopped believing it would or could ever have its needs met, so it started taking pleasure in foiling all our best laid plans. Or perhaps the Saboteur could be there because it is mad at us for having been too weak to be able to fight and protect ourselves against past abuse in our life; or thirdly, because of guilt over something we actually did that our Saboteur is now punishing us for.

In the case of actual guilt over a real overt act, the incident could be something we have a clear recollection of, which has been plaguing us with guilt, similar to Lady Macbeth; or it could be from a past life action which is buried deep within the subconscious memory, and needs to be ferreted out through past life regression therapy. For instance, I had two single mothers who came to see me because they were having trouble supporting their children, and, coincidentally, they both found out they had former lives as corrupt tax collectors during the Roman Empire. After they committed to doing some present-day atonement, their financial situations turned around.

However, in my practice I have found fewer clients plagued by real guilt, and more of them who are punishing themselves over something they merely *think* they did wrong. Most of the Saboteurs I've dealt with pop up because of either a feeling of utter hopelessness, or to punish us over *falsely perceived* guilt which riddles us with anger at ourselves over our *perceived* impotence. (Our Saboteur doesn't realize or care that we may only have been four years old when we were abused.)

It sounds in our heads like either beating up on ourselves or deep regret with a lot of *would'ves and should'ves* that can play like a broken record, possibly even keeping us awake at night. It's necessary to find the real reason for our despair or the true target of our anger and correct our perception of past events. The amazing thing we know about dealing with the Saboteur is that when we find and satisfy him, therein lies the key to resolving our core issues in life, just as with the single mothers!

Saboteurs I've Known and Loved

Interestingly, one way I've heard clients describe their Saboteurs when they see them in their minds is that they look like a "Blob." Here's an examples of one of those Saboteurs I found very early on in my practice with a man I'll call Charles, who was trying to write a book. When we went in to do a Conference Room around that subject, all the characters who showed up around the table seemed to be in favor of writing it. The only problem was that he wasn't getting any work done. I had worked with Charles many times before, often at his house, but when I arrived there this time I was aghast at the condition it was in.

Every room was a mess—the place looked like it hadn't been cleaned in weeks and the kitchen had dishes piled up almost to the ceiling. I asked all the Sub-personalities that had shown up at his Conference Room if the one responsible for the client's obvious self-sabotaging behavior was present around the table yet. They were all too willing to say, "No," at that point and play tattletale, because they were all sick of his behavior. A whole chorus of them chimed in to tell me that not only was he not here yet, but in fact, he was where he always was: in bed reading comic books and masturbating.

Since the Saboteur had been caught in the act he finally made his way unwillingly to the table. He proceeded to take his seat at the head of the table, in the position of power. We named him The Blob, and he immediately declared that he was in charge and wouldn't let anything get done because he knew writing a book would never work out just like nothing ever had in the past. However, the fact that we had been able to pull this character out from the Shadow into the light for Charles and all his parts who wanted to write this book to see, was the beginning of a new life for him.

The Blob watched as we went back and rescued Little Charles from being a child who never got the attention and love he deserved. The characters at the table were able to have an open dialogue with The Blob and finally bring him into an alliance for change. He even admitted he was getting sick of the mess in the house and tired of doing nothing. With all the attention his fellow Conference Room characters were willing to show him, The Blob transformed into The Writer he always dreamed of being, but was afraid he never could be.

There was an immediate shift in Charles's life after that session. He reported that he never let dishes pile up in the sink again and began to take pride in his house and do work outside in his garden as well. Most importantly, he went on to write and publish a trilogy of books over the next five years. Secondly his new, clean environment also helped him attract a girlfriend, which was an issue he had been working on unsuccessfully for months. He now has a beautiful child and has become a model dad. You can see that when a person finally comes face to face with his Saboteur and deals with it once and for all, it can completely change his life.

Another client, Bob J., was in dire straits after a serious fight he had with his girlfriend the previous evening turned physical, which resulted in the police being called and a restraining order being placed against him. His Saboteur/Persecutor had reared his ugly head publicly and Bob's Romantic was completely heartsick about it. I began to dialogue with those two parts.

The Saboteur was still close to the surface, so he was easy to access. We discovered he was perceiving Bob as weak because he saw him staying home cooking, cleaning and taking care of his girlfriend's daughter while she went to work. Most of Bob was enjoying that arrangement. He had been on the road to sobriety and connecting with his softer side for two years already. But his Saboteur saw it as emasculating and would pop up to counter it, especially whenever Bob drank. We named him Macho Bob.

The other side of Bob we called The Poet was happy to have alone time to pursue his passion as a writer and poet. This angered his Saboteur who retorted by getting drunk and playing with guns to prove his maleness. It was clear to Bob after his girlfriend left him for his dangerous acting out, that he was being sabotaged by Macho Bob who was punishing him for his perceived sins. The session proved to be a mini-intervention with himself and a major turning point in his life.

I knew we needed to change Macho Bob's perspective about what it really meant to be a man. I contended that being a real man meant having the guts to do what's hard and that playing with guns and drinking alcohol was easy. I suggested that what would *really* show that he had the fortitude to prove how macho he was, would be for him to have the strength to finally stop drinking for good. That way, Macho Bob had an alternative way to maintain his feeling of machismo while channeling it into a behavior that would actually help rather than sabotage him.

He said he was up for the challenge. (Notice how I reframed the definition of being macho without trying to make his desire to be macho wrong.) That day was literally the start of more than twenty years of sobriety and throughout that time he's been helping other men to do the same. Now I'd say Macho Bob has become a *real man*. This is an excellent example of how the Saboteur actually holds the key to solving someone's core issue.

Here's another example of how self-sabotage works in the case of a woman whose real name is Zoilita Grant, MS, CCHt. When I did this session with her in the early 1990's she was struggling with a bothersome addiction to hamburgers and coffee. The strange part was that she didn't even like to drink coffee and had been a vegetarian from the time she was fifteen years old (she was then the mother of two teenage kids). The craving she was experiencing to go through the Wendy's drive-up window was quickly becoming more uncontrollable.

I found the dynamics going on inside her like a war between two Sub-personalities, each full of shame about the other. On one side was Ms. Together, the successful business woman and therapist, who was very ashamed of her recent pattern of bingeing. It was especially embarrassing to Zoilita since she specialized in healing people with eating disorders. You can see how this self-sabotage was undermining Zoilita's career. She felt like a fake; she didn't feel good about going to work and helping clients do something she couldn't even do for herself.

Meanwhile, it turned out that Zoilita's Rebel was feeling powerless now because she was afraid she had "sold out" to the enemy after her younger days as a rebellious hippie. Unbeknownst to Zoilita, her Rebel was secretly ashamed to be a therapist taking insurance reimbursements, because she felt that insurance companies were corrupt. The Rebel was acting out by making her eat junk food as a way of punishing her. I needed to open up a dialogue between these two parts of her and find some way to satisfy them both.

I began to dialogue with The Rebel first, because in this case she was the Saboteur, and asked her a key question in dealing with self-sabotage due to a feeling of powerlessness, "How would you run Zoilita's life if you were in charge?" Her first response was that she wanted to have the feeling of freedom she used to get in her youth driving around the country in her VW van, but after further probing, that really didn't resolve the anger she was feeling at Zoilita for what she perceived as "selling out" and taking money from insurance companies.

pay others to like me *please others* *$ not deserving*

Anger at oneself is one of the primary dynamics going on with self-sabotage, just as we saw with Macho Bob. When it's coupled with a feeling of impotence to do anything about it, the uprising begins. The direction I took *no one spat on me* was to attempt to reframe the way this Rebel/Saboteur looked at taking money from insurance companies. Instead of seeing it as selling out, I presented the idea that what Zoilita was really doing was "taking from the rich" (insurance agents), and "giving to the poor" (deserving clients), just like Robin Hood!

You can see that because I was able to give a new framework of rebellion to the same activity of being a therapist, I was enrolling The Rebel to join her rather than sabotage her. The Rebel was actually delighted with this new role of wearing business suits as a "disguise" so nobody would know she was really there to rob from the rich and give to the poor. Right after this session the sabotaging behavior of eating hamburgers and drinking coffee stopped and she and her Rebel began enjoying their time together working "undercover."

Now, fifteen years later, she is running a hugely successful school, the Colorado School of Counseling Hypnotherapy, where she teaches others to duplicate her formula. So you could say this "Robin Hood" now has gathered a following of her "band of merry men" (and women) who continue to proverbially take from the rich and give to the poor in a win/win/win situation. In the case of both Bob and Zoilita, the key was to come up with an alternative behavior that would satisfy the Saboteur. Without asking them to give up who they were, it allowed them each to refocus their damaging energy into a more appropriate behavior.

Often coming face to face with some of our disowned Sub-personalities makes us feel like we don't want to have any part of them, and we are even tempted to "de-possess" that part of ourselves. There are many schools of thought that adhere to that concept and encourage people to dispose of those parts that we don't like in ourselves. Even though it's a very tempting thing to do and seems logical enough, don't be fooled. Our attempts to rid ourselves of a part of us, no matter how nasty it seems, will make it come back to haunt us again and again until we are willing to make peace and embrace it.

We cannot disown anything that is truly an Internal Character, no matter how much we want to. Let me illustrate this point with a story of some of my students who learned this the hard way. I was assisting in a small practice group at an Alchemical Hypnotherapy Training where the students were learning the technique of Conference Room. (That is what I was doing with Charles about writing his book, where his Sub-personalities came to the Conference Table to align around an issue in his life in order to accomplish a goal.)

The student being worked on, Molly, by one of the other students had uncovered a female Judge who looked like an old biddy school teacher with glasses. Molly projected her pain onto her and blamed her for her lack of success in life. At the end of the session the student therapist allowed Molly to show her displeasure with that old biddy for being so judgmental by imagining herself taking those glasses off that teacher's nose and stomping on them while telling her to get out of her life.

I knew that there was no way you could do that to an Internal Character, which this Inner School Teacher/Judge definitely appeared to be. (If this had been an External Character—for instance, a real school teacher from her past—her reaction would have been fine.) However, I wanted my students to learn this lesson on their own and allowed the session to end that way, knowing I would be there to remedy any deleterious effects.

Well, no sooner did Molly sit up from her session still feeling triumphant for the way she broke those glasses, than she was suddenly rubbing her eyes and complaining of a headache. I immediately stepped in and reminded the group that you cannot fire, dismiss, disown or otherwise do away with *any* Internal Character no matter how much you don't like one. I was able to remedy this situation by putting this student back into trance for about five more minutes of work.

I had Molly dialogue with this Inner School Teacher, allowing her to explain her positive motivations. As a new job she was going to watch over the details Molly often tended to overlook in her life. That is consistent with the positive qualities of a Judge archetype and lets her feel useful. And, of course, we gave The Teacher back her glasses. Molly came back amazed, happy, and headache-free.

Ryan - strong, calm, patient, adventurer, rebel, play hard, work
fearless hard
Irfan - successful, admired/respected, smart, hard working
Robert - street smart, business manererer, special VIP treatment
Katie - Beautiful, soft, sweet, calm, spiritual, fearless
star of
Debbie - strong, smart, intellectual, spiritual
the show

Here are some questions to help you discover your positive Shadow↓

and fall in love with yourself.
fearless

Maryam - fun, free, playful, adventuree, fearless
gurus (Mooji Baba) — wisdom, imparting peace + love / protected

> Make a list of names of all the people you've ever been in love

with in your life.

> Add to that list the friends you have (of either gender) who
you truly look up to, love, and admire. These would be the
friends or relatives you have felt close enough over the years
to call your best friend or include in your list of best friends.
Include them even if you've fallen out with them over the
years.

> This next step may take some time and you may need a lot
of paper. Index cards would work well. Now, one by one put
each person's name on top of a page or card and really get in
touch with the energy of each individual. As you feel their
presence, list the traits that make you love or admire them.
Know that you can always go back later to add things you've
forgotten.

> When you're all finished, go back and notice those traits
that show up over and over again consistently among many
of your friends and lovers. Circle them, underline them or
highlight them (with a highlighter) so those traits stand out.

> Now make a new list with your name at the top and fill in that
list with all the words that have been highlighted. This is a
list of the things about yourself that you love, whether you've

NEGATIVE PARTS OF ME

Mom
demanding
self centered
bossy
pushy
mean
judgmental
takes adv. of others

Dad
stubborn
inflexible
judgmental
narrow minded
cheap
opportunistic
takes advantage of others

ever recognized them as you or not. Learn to own these traits as your best qualities. You may have been spending too much time disowning them and projecting them onto people who may or may not have been worthy.

➤ Look back at your original list of all the people you've been in love with. Are there any people on that list who you now feel were there to help you fall in love with *you*? all of them

➤ (Advanced) Repeat the first five steps with people you can't stand or who really "push your buttons" whenever you're around them or when you think of the things they've done that make you mad. Remember a neutral feeling toward a person you merely dislike does not qualify them for this list. The key is to really write down the people who make your blood boil. This may prove to be much more difficult, but if you stick to it, it will help you discover your negative projections you have relegated into your Shadow.

➤ (Optional) Have you ever experienced a "dark night of the soul" in your life? How did you get through it? What did you learn as a result?

Rabia
Fearless protected
Adventurer
hard working
admired "special" VIP
strong (mind + body)
spiritual
fun
free
wisdom, imparting peace → love

dance → fair

taking care of a
man →
(all of mom's side)

not standing
up for myself
financially

The most beautiful thing we can experience
is the mysterious.
It is the source of all true art and all science.
He to whom this emotion is a stranger,
who can no longer pause to wonder
and stand rapt in awe,
is as good as dead:
his eyes are closed.

— Albert Einstein

Chapter 11

THAT STILL SMALL VOICE

So far this book has explored the psychological, physical, and emotional aspects of the way we talk to ourselves in the privacy of our own thoughts. These next two chapters will explore the Spiritual dimension to the silent messages we receive. One of the most important reasons for doing the exercises (in the previous chapters) is to teach you the lesson of discernment as you learn how to discriminate between the voices of the various characters inside you. As I first noted, many of the voices we hear talking to us in our heads come from outside us—the External Characters. They belong to other people we've known in our lives and we can now choose to clear our heads and dismiss those outmoded thoughts.

Then we looked at the characteristics of over twenty different Sub-personalities, including the persona of the Child we once were. We discovered that many of the different Intellectual and Emotional Characters who blend to form the personality we display to the world today are direct results of adaptations we made to the outside circumstances we were exposed to when growing up. Now that you are identifying and piecing together the different puzzle parts that make up *how* you are, it's time to hear from the voice that can help you become *who* you were truly meant to be.

One thing you've probably noticed about all the Sub-personalities is that they come with their own myopic and self-centered view of the world. For instance, The Judge is always demanding social propriety, while Mr. Together is busy trying to get ahead, The Victim is feeling sorry for himself, and The Rebel just wants to have fun. But it is our Spiritual Guides who love and understand the needs of all the different parts of us and want them all to be happy. A whole new feeling of connectedness within ourselves and with the world opens up when we can discern the intuitive voice of our Inner Guides from the ordinary chatter in our head.

However, because we tend to have so many internal voices dominating our thoughts, the "still, small voice," as it is often called, of our own inner guidance is not always able to get our attention. The fears, judgments and second guessing that we spend much of our time listening to can keep us from hearing the healthy advice that is trying to come through. It's so important to learn how to tune into this wise part of you, who knows how to steer your life in the right direction for your highest good.

Listening to Your Inner Guides

Who or what are we to define as Guides? They may be known and described by many names such as Guardian Angels, Spiritual Guides, Internal Self Helpers, Ascended Masters, the Universe, God, Buddha, Jesus, Yahweh, Higher Self, Creator, Ancestors, Great Spirit, conscience, instinct and probably more depending on what school of thought or religious background you come from. I would argue one could use these names interchangeably for the purpose of explaining the information in this chapter, to describe the energy of the inner spiritual help they provide.

Mostly, you can think of the Inner Guides we'll be discussing here as having the knowledge you would expect from an Inner Teacher on your path on Earth. Interestingly, unlike all the other voices we have been delineating so far in this book, which can be heard conversing with you within the jumble of your thoughts, as well as heard and observed by others through your words and actions, the "voice" of your inner guidance must be discerned and recognized by the recipient of it.

Although it is by no means the only way Guides make contact, you may be one of the 7 to 10 percent of the population—roughly twenty million people (according to polls taken in England and the United States)—who, when surveyed, actually hear inner voices. Out of that group, virtually none of the respondents questioned had ever spoken to anyone about their experiences before. This is so even though 85 percent of those who reported having these experiences found them "extremely positive with beneficial results." That is how deep the fear is of being ridiculed or worse. However, if anyone did decide to speak openly they would find they were in good company.

Socrates was very open about the voice that he heard which he called, "The Sign." He claimed to have been accompanied throughout much of his life by what he described as a "semi-divine being" whose voice would often dissuade him from some undertakings through warnings with accurate and verifiable results. Joan of Arc was a seventeen-year-old peasant girl who heard a voice telling her she was supposed to help reinstate the King of France to the throne. Of course, we know there was good news and bad news: she accomplished the feat, and then was burned at the stake for it.

More recently, one woman who has come out publicly and is still made the brunt of jokes for it, because of the relationship she has with her Guide, is Shirley MacLaine. She writes about the first conversation she had with him in her book, *Dancing in the Light*. When he first appeared to her, she asked, "'Who are you?'… 'I am your higher unlimited self,' it said…'Oh, my goodness,' I heard myself saying stupidly to it. 'Are you really there?' 'Yes,' it said. 'I have always been here. I have been here with you since the beginning of time. I am never away from you. I am you. I am your unlimited soul. I am the unlimited you that guides you and teaches you through each incarnation.'"

Many authors have credited voices as helping them with their writing including Robert Louis Stevenson; science fiction writer, Ray Bradbury; and Judith Rossner, the author of *Looking for Mr. Goodbar*. Richard Bach, author of nine books, was walking on the beach one evening when he distinctly heard the words, "Jonathon Livingston Seagull." He reportedly went home and sat down with a pen and paper when, within an hour, the first part of his famous book wrote itself as if he were watching a movie.

Hollywood has explored the phenomenon of inner voices and visions throughout its history, many of which became classics. There is a great depiction of a man hearing an inner voice in the 1980's film, *Field of Dreams*. Kevin Costner's character clearly hears a phrase instructing him to, "Build it and he will come," which prompts the building of a baseball field among his crops into which his deceased father eventually comes to play. In the classic Capra film *It's a Wonderful Life*, Jimmy Stewart plays George Bailey who meets his Guardian Angel, Clarence, when he tries to kill himself by jumping off a bridge. When his Angel shows him a glimpse of the difference his life makes in the lives of so many people, he is transformed and chooses to live.

For the majority who will not experience such dramatic demonstrations of your Guides' presence, you can come to understand and identify many different ways that you are being led by the calling of your Higher Self. The "voice" of your inner guidance is a personal, subtle and subjective experience which can sometimes speak to you in your head like a voice, but there are many other ways it can present itself. Since we are a part of the universal wholeness, your Guides can even "speak" to you through external events, often coming as a series of meaningful symbolic occurrences.

Patricia Haggard, the office manager of the Alchemy Institute, describes her experiences this way: *My Guides bring messages, protection, healing and knowing in varying, fun and creative ways. When I was in my 20's dragonflies and butterflies began making dramatic fly-pasts, prolific visits to my dreams, and frequent landings on my clothes and hair. During the winter months in Canada they would be everywhere in print, photos or on fabric. Whenever they came to me it became a signal that there was something I needed to pay attention to. I learned to get quiet inside to feel or hear the intention of the contact.* Birds/Hawks

Maybe you've walked into a room for the first time and felt like you'd been there before. It's such a ubiquitous occurrence that the French phrase "déjà vu" (translated as "already seen") has been used in English for decades to explain it. You've probably had some moment of intuition in your life when you had a certain urge to try something new and it worked out great, or conversely that caused you to change plans because of a "bad feeling" you had about it, which turned out to be correct.

A very intuitive friend of mine tells a story about a day when she gave her whole gardening crew the day off and despite their protests that they wanted to go to work, she was not to be swayed. She just knew that it was something she needed to do even though she did not know why. Later that day when she went to the job site to pick up a check from the homeowner, she arrived just after a fatal motorcycle accident had occurred which sent the bike flying right through the bushes where her crew would have been working.

Perhaps you've actually had a premonition about the future that came true. My mother's best friend, Joan, and her husband were visiting my parents in New York in the winter of 1975. The day before they left to drive back home to Massachusetts, Joan had a premonition—as if she'd been given a window though which to glimpse the near future—that she would never see her sixteen-year-old daughter, Andrea, again. It was her daughter's junior year of high school and she was on a ski trip that weekend with a group of friends.

The same night Joan and her husband were driving home from New York, the van their daughter was driving home in with her friends crashed. Andrea was the only one killed. That instinctual bond between a mother and her young is primal. They say forewarned is forearmed, and although no one can prepare oneself for the loss of a child, the fact that she had heard the warning inside her gave Joan extra courage to go on with her life and the strength to accept her devastating loss.

Why do so many brilliant ideas come to people in their dreams, or upon the first moment of waking? This was often the case with Albert Einstein who was quoted as saying that *imagination is more important than intellect.* You may have had the experience of taking a test and feeling as if an answer just popped into your head out of the blue. They say when taking exams, the first answer you come up with is usually the correct one. Sometimes the best thing you can do is to stop trying so hard; relax and get out of your own way. Become the hollow instrument through which your Inner Teacher or Guide can channel. Trust those hunches, even if you don't know why.

Maybe you've had the experience of not being able to get a song out of your head, until you stop to listen to the words and realize they are giving you just the message you need to hear. In my early 20's I took a job with a company I really admired, but in a position that didn't suit me. On the 4th of July I couldn't get the song, "I Can See Clearly Now" out of my head, until I could see my way clearly to make the decision that the next morning I was going to "declare my independence" from my job as a bookkeeper.

numbers

x3

RK

(222)

Synchronicities and Inner Knowing

Some people swear they receive messages from license plates, bumper stickers or billboards. Many people recount stories of opening a book or turning on a radio to hear something that answers a question that they have been wondering about. Most people have had the experience of thinking of someone and running into them or getting a call from them out of the blue soon afterward. These supposed random occurrences that can put you in the right place at the right time may not be as coincidental as they seem.

Naming something gives you power over it. So what may have previously seemed supernatural, if it was acknowledged at all, can suddenly be understood when there is a name for it. Swiss psychiatrist, Carl Jung, a peer of Sigmund Freud's, first coined the term, *synchronicity* in 1930 to explain meaningful coincidences as an "acausal connecting principle" that links together seemingly unrelated and unconnected events.

By naming them, Jung was acknowledging the power of those meaningful coincidences that are completely subjective, yet are often life-changing to the individual experiencing them. Synchronicities are actually one of the best ways our Guides have of speaking to us. Carl Jung not only wanted to give individuals the ability to experience the extraordinary within their ordinary lives as Caroline Myss says, but also to have a personal definition of this phenomenon which would completely divorce it from religion.

Until he did, these experiences were couched in the context of "the hand of God" stepping in, and they needed to call in a committee of experts to decide whether or not an actual "miracle" occurred. Now we can see the magic all around us as disparate elements of the Universe conspire to align on our behalf—while a more unenlightened audience might brush it off as coincidence or not notice it at all.

It is always a sign to pay attention when synchronicities occur three times or more on the same subject. The first thing we need to do is to

3x

believe in the power of our internal world and our imagination in the same way that Einstein did. The next step is to consciously pay attention to what is all around us. This attunement will be evident by the ability to get into a flow of life that feels like you are being carried downstream as doors open and life gets richer.

We cannot learn very much about Spirit from the five senses alone since Spirit is not of the physical or material plane. Spirit can be thought of as the breath of life and many spiritual practices involve deep breathing. You may recall how my chronic stomach aches began to go away when I was able to stop trying to fit into the mold others wanted of me, and learned to breathe in my "Debbie-ness." But most importantly, we can all learn to tune into Spirit through our sixth sense of *knowingness* by reconnecting our five senses with our hearts. Carlos Santana, who considers Spirit to be the source of his music says, "You touch the Light when you listen to the voice within your own heart."

When learning to discern the "voice" of your Guide it is easiest heard through the feelings in your heart, because they do not lie, the way the head can. Just as music can evoke emotions without the need for lyrics, we can easily "hear" what is right for us when we listen with our hearts. It is difficult to even use words to explain when we just *know* something is right for us. It is a common human experience many have shared, to hear a call from deep in our soul at critical times in our lives or when we are very quiet. met Ryan... marned Irfan... Robert's death...

These powerfully moving experiences are certainly heart-opening moments, which often are accompanied by laughter or tears, and can quite literally bring us to our knees. They often change people's lives completely. Where do these flashes of intuition or epiphanies that strike us like lightning bolts come from? Psychologists and scientists can pinpoint their origins as located in the temporal lobe in the right hemisphere of our brains, while religious people will credit God as the source for these inspirations.

Yet, even though they're often called "religious experiences," they are not the private domain of any particular religion. With over 10,000 separate and distinct religions in the world today (according to ABC News), the events reported during these phenomena, *including sudden total knowing and an eternal moment of unity*, are more universally similar than any theological teachings. They not only cross all religious boundaries, a belief in God is not even a pre-requisite for having one.

These ecstatic, mystical experiences have been reported by one-third to one-half of all adults according to four separate surveys. Less dramatic moments of clarity and insight such as the ones cited in this chapter are available to all of us freely throughout our lives, and on a daily basis. The purpose of this chapter is to help you learn how to listen to the voice of your intuition, your Guides, Spirit, the Universe, God or whatever you want to call it, which is always calling to you.

Whether you think of it as a premonition, gut feeling, hunch, instinct, ESP, or "women's intuition," it's always a good idea to pay attention to that very soft voice inside that whispers advice. It might sound like the way you'd imagine the voice of your conscience would speak to you. In addition to the many other intuitive ways we've covered that exist for our Guides to lead us, sometimes it's helpful to go straight to the source in order to develop a more personal connection with them and receive more specific advice.

Finding My Inner Guidance

We find the source of this inner wisdom in the peace and quiet of our subconscious mind. Although we get a chance to make contact every night when we go to sleep, our dreams are generally out of our control, and often slip from our memories before we awake. By deciding to go into hypnosis with a Certified Hypnotherapist (CHT) trained in these techniques, we can be introduced "in person" to the various Guides who are here to help us. It gives a chance for the other 90 percent of us, who have not had an experience of hearing our inner guidance speaking to us during our waking hours, to take a journey with professional help to formally introduce them to us.

In 1983 when I first started learning Alchemical Hypnotherapy, I couldn't wait to meet my Spirit Guides. Before that can happen in a session or in your life, however, it is generally necessary to let go of some of the pain we have been holding onto through erroneous thinking, which cloud our inner clarity and become blockages in our life. Change is always perceived by the ego as scary, thus we get into a rut and end up repeating the same destructive patterns, even though our Guides continually provide life lessons arranged to give us another chance to do things differently.

In my case I was living alone and wanted to work on my history of jumping from one Co-dependent and dysfunctional relationship to another. I had been going to psychics and friends for answers and companionship. When they were around I felt good, but I fought to keep my spirits up when I was alone. I was stuck in my head, constantly analyzing everything and had buried my feelings so deeply that I was out of touch with my own emotions.

In my first session with David Quigley I saw that in my most recent relationship, I had allowed another person's opinions to replace the wisdom of my own guidance. It felt oppressive, like a hand pushing down on the top of my head. I communicated in no uncertain terms I would not put up with that any longer, and by stating my intention to honor myself I was suddenly in touch with my Higher Self. I did not "see" anyone, but I heard a message in my mind telling me: *you are going to be entering the world as a well-known creative person in the arena of writing or film and turning people onto the idea of love through your work.* It told me the cosmos was behind me if I would hold fast to my vision and I got a picture of myself as a flower unfolding.

I soon got another session from a classmate I was studying Alchemy with because my Rebel was being very defensive and causing problems in my life. In it I saw an Angel flying over me who told me her name was Wind and she was here to help give me strength, direction and heal my emotions. She told me that every time I felt something or someone, such as my Rebel, trying to distract me I should reach out and she would hold my hand and lead me back onto my path. My "homework" was to spend time bringing Little Debbie to her so we could feel her support in our lives and not give my Rebel so much power.

Starting almost immediately and especially as the years went by, I began to get very evident messages that were connected to the wind. They ranged from small subtle breezes that occurred at significant times, to major gusts of wind that blew almost on cue as I spoke important words, to wind chimes that would ring in response to a thought I had. Sometimes they were humorous events, such as blowing my hat off into a boat while waiting for a photo to be snapped on a dock. Sometimes they were auspicious like the time I was on my way to do my first speaking engagement and the screen door literally blew out of my hand on the way out of the house.

There were many times when incidents would be corroborated by unsuspecting acquaintances on my travels to new cities who would invariably tell me apologetically, "It's unusually windy today." And on sacred occasions, such as those surrounding my mother's death, there were awesome displays of wind, tornados and high waves. I have come to understand that I indeed have a special relationship with the wind as evidenced by the many wondrous ways that my Guide has convinced me that the name I heard was indeed correct.

However, in real time back in 1983, I was still having trouble following through with my homework from Wind about coming to her with Little Debbie for support. During my next session I saw that my Inner Child was trying to get me to play with her but I just felt blocked and dejected. My Analyzer was thinking and worrying so much that my head felt as if there was a vice gripping it. I was instructed to ask my head what that pain was trying to tell me and I heard that while I very much wanted to be appreciated for my mind and my creativity, it was scary because I was shown a string of incidents from childhood where people had ridiculed me for my thoughts.

Wind had told me when I first met her that she was going to teach me how to fly with her. In this session she had me imagine I was speaking to an audience full of people who all had their own egos and might be judging me, but had me float way above them. I saw myself turn into a white bird and fly so high that the audience became small, looking like waves beneath me. It was suddenly easy for me to let go of caring about what they were thinking. *Beautiful*

When she had me imagine expressing myself again in front of an audience, my head felt better and I saw flames shooting out of it. Then a door opened in my forehead and the white bird flew into it. My Alchemical Hypnotherapist told me to follow it and I saw a big A-frame room with nothing in it but the bird in a cage, a desk, a chair and a typewriter. The bird told me that I didn't need to be lonely anymore because I could talk to him all day and he would bring back messages from the outside world like the dove in Noah's ark. *Wow!, Motivational speaking*

I heard my inner guidance tell me that I might want to learn to use a computer, although it was another six years until I bought one. That was the year I moved into the home I lived in for nearly eighteen years. When I first walked through the house, I had a deja-vu experience as soon as I saw one of the upstairs rooms. It reminded me of that big room from my session that the white bird had shown me. I immediately began to use that space for writing and it subsequently became my therapy room.

Can You Hear Your Body Talk?

Imagine having the opportunity to hear and heed the call of your Soul as it softly beckons you onto the private path that leads to the fulfillment of your life's purpose. This is the most profound gift that your Guides can give you. Then you can begin to be aware of the oneness of everything and feel your connection with the world around you. You can find messages everywhere as you learn to hear how the Universe talks to you the way the wind speaks to me. Plus, just like I did in the session when I entered into my head to talk to it, you can also feel the way the whole body can be used as an antenna to tune into for answers.

There are many phrases we already use that affirm this body wisdom. *I had an uneasy feeling around him. It made me shudder to think about it. Something just didn't feel right. I was jumping out of my skin. It made my head spin. I was sick over it. It turned my stomach. I got chills when you said that. I had a gut feeling that it was right. It made the hair raise on my neck.* You can hear that if you pay conscious attention, the body itself acts as a metaphorical channel through which your guidance can intuitively help maneuver you through life.

However, when we're out of touch with our Body/Mind/Spirit Emotional connection, we don't notice the little clues our Spiritual Guides or the Inner Healer, the specific Guide of this realm, are always trying to show us to keep us safe and lead us to our greatest joy. The ultimate betrayal is that we've been trained to remain completely out of touch with our own bodies. We've been taught to run right to the doctor or the medicine cabinet instead of listening to our inner wisdom through the metaphorical messages our physical vehicle reveals through various pains and illness, (i.e. *I'm sick of it, It's eating me up inside, I'm itching to do something else,* or *so-and-so is such a pain in the neck*).

Ads directed at sufferers of colds, allergies, irritable bowel syndrome, migraine pain, ulcers, diarrhea, constipation, acid indigestion, arthritis, insomnia, and a host of others persuade us through the pages of magazines and barrage us on the evening news during dinner that there's a pill to cure what ails us. "Just ask your doctor if it's right for you," they promote. The prescription medications that are being doled out in astronomical proportions are not just "mother's little helpers" anymore either. Now our children are being diagnosed at tender young ages and in 2005, three million children were on medication for ADD. There are kids who may never know life without pharmaceuticals after the age of six.

If it's not a physical ailment you're dealing with, there are now designer drugs for obsessive compulsive behavior, depression, post traumatic stress, anxiety, phobias, weight loss, or any other of a laundry list of diagnoses. The idea of greater life through chemistry has caught on in the psychiatric community so fully that the medical field can now find a way to put anyone with a physical, mental or emotional complaint on some new drug which can be whipped up to make the brain or body act right. But while everyone's busy looking for the cure to our problems in a lab, who's looking for the cause? *pain → cause?*

Taking medicine does give us immediate relief as it reduces the symptoms of our complaints. But it also keeps us out of touch with our Inner Healer that is signaling something is wrong and is there to clue us in to a possible cause. We have a perfect sort of radar built right into our biological system to tune us in to the answers to our life's issues. Physical pain is a great way to get our attention. Healing can begin with our *intention to know the truth*. And the truth may be that what is ailing us is on a spiritual level.

Since so much of the population is on medications, could it mean that there is a greater societal issue that needs to be addressed? Let's get a second opinion from Dr. Andrew Weil, M.D., author of many books including his latest, *Healthy Aging*. Dr Weil states on his website that "depression, anger, loneliness and other emotions that suppress immunity and unbalance the nervous system – including human misery and disease – derive from self-centeredness. These are all rooted in the sense of self as an isolated, separate entity. There is ample medical evidence that people who fail to establish meaningful connections have more illness."

Dr. Weil contends that human beings have got to consciously cultivate a sense of connection to a larger group, such as an extended family, community, or tribe because we are not intended to achieve full health as isolated, separate beings. He claims, "Health means wholeness, and wholeness implies connectedness—to family, friends, tribe, nation, humanity, the Earth, and whatever higher power you conceive of as the creator of the universe."

Western civilization has compartmentalized our spiritual life as something to do on Saturday or Sunday inside a building dubbed, "a house of God," by listening to someone designated as a "man of God." Because we are a society that likes to defer to specialists in different fields, we have grown accustomed to giving our health to the doctor, our money to the banker, our kids to the school system, and our souls to the rabbi, priest or preacher. However, in doing so, *we may be giving up the spiritual authority to guide our own lives.* It is a far cry from the feeling of connectedness to a higher power.

Albert Einstein wanted people to realize that they are actually a *part* of the universe. However, through an "optical delusion" of their consciousness people believe themselves to be separate. (The Sanskrit word, *maya*, describes the illusion created by our five senses which conceals the unity of absolute being.) Einstein went on to say that by experiencing one's thoughts and feelings as separate from the rest of humanity it becomes a kind of prison restricting our personal desires and affection to those few persons nearest to us. He proclaimed our task is to "free ourselves from this prison by widening our circle of compassion to embrace all living creatures and the whole of nature in its beauty."

The truth is that many people feel the pangs of separation because they have put up self-protective defense mechanisms because of whatever insults, abandonments or traumas they've suffered. In the misguided belief that they are keeping their feelings safe from being hurt, these walls instead keep them disconnected from others. Since most people are blinded by the illusion of separateness from the wholeness of the universe that Einstein spoke of, they feel all alone inside their walls. In fact, these days there are so many people suffering from a sense of isolation, separation and loneliness, that the media has claimed that America is afflicted with an "epidemic" of loneliness. Let's see how long it takes before a pill is designed to cure that.

Feeling Connected

Not only do we feel separate from others but we've all but lost our natural connection with the world around us and the cycles of life. Many tribal cultures, such as Native Americans have historically lived their lives close to the land as a demonstration of their connection with it. They consider the Earth to be their mother, respecting her and seeing her as a living, breathing being. They openly acknowledge the Spirit of the creatures, the rocks, trees, wind, water and all the elements, and embrace them as their sisters and brothers. They have remained receptive to being led by internal direction from their ancestors, their animal totems, and the "Great Spirit" as a way of life.

When the original inhabitants of North America met the explorers who landed on their shores five centuries ago, the Native people, as a matter of course, shared everything with their newly embraced brothers and sisters. The fact they had no concept of ownership over anything, including land, was quickly exploited by white men who had no such universal understanding, and these indigenous people became an early casualty of

Western belief and culture. How far will modern civilization go to protect its misconception of the world?

Maybe we can learn something from another society that has been around a lot longer than we have. On the complete opposite side of the globe, in the southern hemisphere, lives a people with an oral history that dates back 400,000 years and a way of life that is the complete opposite from ours. The Waitaha Maori of Aoteoroa (New Zealand) is a matriarchal culture that honors the more feminine attributes of inclusion, intuition, gestation, nurturance and the cycles of birth, death and aging. They consider the Holy Trinity to be Grandmother/Mother/Sister.

Macki Ruka, a Maori spiritual elder, related a prophecy their culture has known about for thousands of years that spoke of a time around the year 2000. He said, "I am living a 'journey prophecy' to reactivate … certain energy points around the world. When it is complete, it will change the thought programming of humanity, and lead us back to a place of one knowing, or universal oneness."

He continued, "Gentleness is needed now, and the power to go beyond the endurance of the mind and let everything be directed by the heart…The ultimate result will be to allow humankind to reconnect with the higher 'star being' that is in each of us…All work, all changes, begin with the individual who is listening to their own heart. When complete, all sisters and brothers can listen with their hearts and to their essence and begin to formulate the actions needed in their own families and communities that will usher in the return to universal peace."

In the early 1970's, Dr. Charles Kaiser, a sociology professor declared "the 200-year-old experiment of the nuclear family" a miserable failure. Since then we've seen the divorce rate in America go up from about one in three marriages, to 57.7% in 2005. That means that as the wedding industry skyrockets and people continue to march down the aisle believing that they have found their other half who will keep them from ever being lonely again, they have more than a one in two chance they will be visiting divorce court, and then trying it all again many more times in their lives.

Turning to Andrew Weil once again, he explains that to love is to experience connection in its highest, purest form, but that we tend to confuse loving with other feelings. Most people equate loving with the joy and pain of romantic love, rather than the idea of loving as a deep feeling of intimacy, connection and attachment to another.

He explains that in intimate relationships that do work, the temporary state of being "in love," induced by dopamine and other hormones, which can sustain itself up to roughly one year, is replaced by mutual loving by two people who are committed to a life together. In a study by Rutgers University it was found that the happiest people were those in long-term committed marriages, even compared to people who were living together, but not married; and especially compared to divorcees and single people.

Unfortunately a stable home life is no longer something an American child can count on. The majority of children are now being raised in one-parent households or "blended" families. We're seeing more latch-key kids of two working parents getting by with less and less of the precious element the children need most—their parents' time. Especially sad is the loss of the extended family situation at home, whereby elders would replace daycare and be available to share their time and wisdom with their grandchildren.

Worse still the modern elders of Western society, rather than being honored, are instead segregated into senior communities and nursing homes. We keep them alive longer through miracles of medicine just so that they can be spoon-fed and diapered like babies. Each stage of life is supposed to be passed through gracefully, with dignity and rewards. The cycle of life includes the innocence and discoveries of childhood, the passage into the responsibilities of adulthood, the payoff of our labors, and the integration and passing down of the life lessons learned as we move toward the end of our own life.

Unfortunately, the Mr. and Ms. Togethers and Mr. and Ms. Perfects of the world have become so dominant in modern American society that only people in the prime of their lives are honored. We have become a population so mesmerized by youth and beauty that it's become chic to inject, shrink, or cut off the lines on our faces that reveal the passage of time. There is an innate danger in this beauty myth which people have bought into, and in trying to fool Mother Nature. The truth is we will only pass through the "right" age once, and we will be continually striving to reach for it when we're young or relive it as we get older. All of which keeps us from living in the present, even in the moment, and loving ourselves for who we are now.

The discussion of Guides will continue in the next chapter. An exercise to help you find the voice of your Inner Guides will be found at the end of it.

How do the geese know when to fly to the sun?
Who tells them the seasons?
How do we, humans, know
when it is time to move on?
As with the migrant birds, so surely with us,
there is a voice within,
if only we would listen to it,
that tells us so certainly
when to go forth into the unknown.

— Elisabeth Kübler-Ross

Chapter 12

LISTENING TO YOUR HEART SONG

Can you imagine if we could take the power of love that exists among family members and harness it to spread out like ripples that encircle the whole globe? It's a huge concept to embrace the notion of being a part of the "Family of Man" as one's primary identity. Yet that is exactly what the greatest mind of the 20th century, Albert Einstein, asked us to undertake when he told us our task was to widen our circle of compassion. And isn't that what is meant by the Golden Rule, which seems to sum up the thread of Truth that runs through all religions?

David Quigley contends that by contacting our Inner Guides they can build a bridge for us to tap into the vast unused portion of the brain, including the instincts we've been developing as a race through millions of years of evolution. Consider what might be possible if we could cultivate the knowledge that is hidden beneath the surface of the small percentage of the brain we are known to use. This is how we can find the key to unlock those instructions to the universal consciousness of what Carl Jung called the Collective Unconscious, the place where dream symbols and archetypes live. Quigley says, "Through daily contact with our Inner Guides we find the answers to how to become better human beings, mothers, fathers, neighbors and mates."

What if instincts have been built into the human race through millions of years to insure survival of the species by instilling parenting skills we have lost touch with? It seems most parents say they make their mistakes on their first child until they feel more comfortable with the job with each subsequent birth. Some people even joke about wishing a set of instructions would come out with the placenta. Perhaps the set of instructions has been with us all along if we only knew where to look for it.

Inner Parents

People get tired of everything being blamed on the parents, and although there is some truth in that accusation, the root runs much deeper. It's passed down through generations of children not getting their needs met and having babies before they've healed themselves. So when you realize it's been wounded children bringing up children, you can't blame them, but you still need to stop the perpetuation of this dysfunction. Instead of blaming anybody, let's look at a simple solution to the incomplete parenting and spiritual poverty which is the experience of so many people in our modern society.

One of the most important categories of Guides you can run across in your inner world would be the introduction to what we believe in Alchemy is essential to the healthy completion of developmental tasks from childhood, by the re-parenting of our wounded child. Since we can't expect our parents to have been perfectly attuned to our every need, although it is what we deserved, we can now take the responsibility to tap into the Collective Unconscious and discover the archetypes of the Inner Family to provide the perfect connection our soul aches for.

Inner Parents can be completely available to the Inner Child to understand and give her everything she ever wanted and needed from external parents, but they were too busy or otherwise unable to provide. Most importantly it is in the reflection of our parents' eyes that we learn emotional intimacy as we see their love of us. To hear the voice of our Inner Parents declare their unconditional acceptance can rebuild a fragile sense of self-esteem which is lacking in most clients I see.

When we're not sure of being loved for what is inside us, we begin to believe that we can get loved by what is outside us and begin to focus on what we can do to get love. We can wear the latest styles of clothes, carry the coolest i-pod, drive the hottest car, do what we need to look young, yet our deepest needs are never met no matter how much we make or do or buy. However, when we are fulfilled from within, we don't need to have our life externally validated. I watch my clients' whole demeanor change when they feel themselves held in the arms of their Inner Mommy or Daddy and hear that they are loved just the way they are.

Often one of the Inner Parents can be a real mother or father who died when the client was young. Some of the most satisfying sessions I witness are when a client is reunited with a dead parent. One such heart-warming reunion was Barry, who came to see me with his wife. Barry was out of work and had no drive to do anything, but had applied for a job as a fireman because that was what his family wanted him to be. He told me he really wanted to be a writer, but didn't believe he could get a job as a writer that would pay well enough to support him and his wife.

A week later he was in a downward spiral because he found out he didn't qualify for the position at the fire department. I urged him to explore his true love of writing, which was evident in the passion with which he spoke about it. When we went into his feelings about never being able to get what he wants, Barry went back to the day his mother died when he was fifteen, and the guilt he felt because he would have been in the car with her if he hadn't stayed home from school that day pretending to be sick. His guilt stopped him from hearing his mother's spirit trying to communicate with him.

Barry felt his heart had completely closed down since the day she died and in his subconscious mind he pictured it as if it were a huge hole in his heart that he was hiding in. He could actually feel himself wasting away in there. He saw how much that was hurting his Inner Child and his mother. During the session he heard her voice assuring him, *I'm right here with you, don't give up. You're my strong boy. You can do anything. You're tough.* Barry made the decision to finally climb out of that hole. When he got out he saw his mother hand him back his heart. He then felt her put it back in his chest, seal it up and kiss it.

He was transformed by her embrace and forgiveness of his misplaced guilt. He sprang up out of that session like a changed man and kept repeating, "My mother gave me back my heart." The next week Barry had three job offers for writing positions. He accepted one right in his own small town where a journalist at the local newspaper had suddenly decided to retire and they needed someone to fill that vacancy immediately.

We don't need to have lost a parent in our youth in order to feel that loss as a gaping hole in our heart at any age. How many Oscars and awards are dedicated to the memory of a recipient's parents who are now the inspiration for their achievements? Remember Alan, that doctor we met in Chapter 9 with the bad back, who was martyring himself for the sake of his son? His father, who died when Alan was an adult, knew how much his son had always wanted to be a singer.

Alan's father was a singer until his mother made him give it up for something more financially secure. He always compared himself as a performer to his dad, whom he had idolized, but he never felt that he was as good. Like father, like son, Alan believed he needed to tough it up and give his family the best life he could through his medical practice. However, the truth was his practice was beginning to suffer because his back was in such bad shape, he was under doctor's orders to reduce his workload.

When he came for that session, I began to teach Alan the Co-dependency cycle, since it was obvious his body was playing The Victim role and telling him he needed to make a change. But it wasn't until he heard it from the words of his father in trance that he was prepared to really listen. After we dealt with Mr. Guilty and the way he was martyring himself, Alan's father came to him. He told him: *although you are a great doctor and your patients love you, you could heal more people through your singing. Listen to your heart to hear God's plan for you and get out of your ego. You have songs in you that need to be sung.* His father gave him his blessing to start living his dream.

Alan asked his father to let him feel his presence every time he got on stage and he decided to dedicate every gig to his dad. Within a year, Alan's body began to heal and although he didn't give up his practice completely he was invited to sing in Las Vegas at the Bellagio Hotel and had a very successful engagement. He now has a plan to pursue his singing career as more than just the hobby it had been when I first saw him and to slowly pass on his practice to a protégé in a timely manner. Alan's wife and family are backing him 100 percent and couldn't be prouder of him.

My Journey Home

While dead parents can be excellent Guides for some people, more often it is necessary to enlist the help of the archetypal Inner Parents to replace the missing elements of our own birth parents. I had one early session where Wind showed me a scene from my childhood of my family sitting around the picnic table in the backyard. My father was standing at the head of the table and grilling hamburgers while my mother was sitting across from me doing the crossword puzzle. I saw my brother and myself as little kids looking very bored. It typified the dynamic I grew up with: a classic "Father Knows Best" scene from the '50's, but it left me feeling spiritually hollow.

Wind had me communicate with my parents and I told my father I wished he hadn't been so authoritative, and had nourished me with more spiritual understanding rather than so much emphasis on material things. I repeated my need for a more nourishing environment to my mother and my desire for her to have given me more physical affection and held me more. I pleaded with her to look up from her puzzle and show more interest in solving life's puzzles. I saw that she was scared and defensive and that my father felt burdened with the need to provide for his family and neither of them knew how to do any better.

Wind tapped a magic wand on the table revealing a vision of how different our family could have been with plenty of affection, playing, hugs and love. Then she asked me if I wanted to find new Inner Parents and I said I didn't want to leave my brother behind. She brought both of us to an open field where there was a stern, tall, bald, regal-looking man who looked like a Tai Chi Master. He told me that he was taking over my spiritual education and would teach me about energy, martial arts and how to be meditatively quiet in order to balance the body and mind. When I looked at my brother, he didn't really understand what was going on, but he wasn't bored anymore.

Then when I expected to find an Inner Mother, instead I saw a red-headed bubbly woman my age who revealed herself as an Inner Friend, which felt great since I was still dealing with loneliness. I actually immediately recognized her from a dream where she appeared in a chair that was previously occupied by my mother and told me her name was Janis. I felt that the combination of a disciplined and serious father with a new friend who was light and free was the perfect balance I needed.

In retrospect I can see now that it was a major step in my climb out of Co-dependency. Janis said she would be there to talk to and help me not feel lonely. She was taking the appropriate position as my Rescuer who was there to take care of, listen to, and play with my Inner Child. Little Debbie liked the thought of having her in our inner world and she was really excited at the prospect of learning the lessons our new Inner Father had to share. He was obviously there in the role of a Spiritual Warrior/Protector.

When I first began my journey of inner exploration one of the biggest complaints people had about me was that I talked too much. I was amazed when my new Inner Father addressed that issue with such practical advice. He told me:

You must stay centered and don't talk so much—silence is powerful. You'll be a mighty warrior with your words—don't waste them—a warrior for Truth. Your weapon is your mouth in this war. You should listen inside and speak when there's something of value. If you babble, people will see you contorted. You can see many things but you have a hard time expressing them. It makes you feel lonely, but you're not alone. I and others will help you to speak. I will help you mostly with discipline. I'm glad you came.

The Guides I met in my sessions gave me insight into myself and direction for living my life's purpose. The comfort they gave me was immediately evident in a feeling of not being alone with the thoughts in my head. I had an epiphany that changed my life. I realized I didn't need to always be talking out loud to someone in order to be heard. My Guides were available for conversation and comfort any time I needed them. I made myself a little saying: "What a lovely surprise to realize how unlonely being alone can be."

Find Your Inspiration

Guides don't have to look like Angels, or Tai Chi Masters, or deceased friends or relatives, or come out of your dreams. They can be as unassuming as the guy next door. They are so in tune with us that they know just what qualities are going to be the most healing to compensate for what we are lacking. That is why they can change over time as our needs and spiritual understanding changes.

The form they can come in is endless. Some people only see light or color. Others may only hear their voices, feel their presence, or know them by a scent. They can present themselves as any guru, saint, avatar or historical figure someone feels close to. They often come as animals. As long as the guidance they give is practical and they don't try to control our choices, we can probably trust that they are there to help us.

One sweet example of this was with a client who had a very difficult childhood and was still suffering from an illness that made his bones and the linings of his organs very brittle and delicate. Obviously, it can be torturous for a kid to have to sit on the sidelines during recess, especially when the other children tease you for it. In his session a Guide came to him in the form of another little boy his age who was suffering from the same illness who brought kites and jacks and toy trucks for them to play with together. My client let loose all the childhood energy that had been pent up for twenty years right there during the session. It was perfect.

In this chapter you began to learn how to tune in to the wisest part of you that is totally clear beyond the babble of random thoughts, fears and projections that parade through your brain. So many people go for spiritual counseling or for psychic readings, asking someone else to tell them what they are here for. The truth is that the answer is right inside of you, and that is the ultimate goal of the information provided in this book. For you to go on your own "inner treasure hunt" and come up with that answer for yourself. It's time to take your power back and to tune into the advice that is constantly coming to you from within.

The more in touch with your passion and purpose, the greater chance you are already being led by you Inner Guides. Everyone has an individual path to walk and our job is to discover ours. Pantanjali spoke 2000 years ago about how we can connect with our Source by being "In Spirit" or what we would now call "inspired." By definition straight from Webster, inspiration once again involves "drawing breath into the lungs," as well as "being influenced by divine guidance." When we feel a drive inside ourselves toward something that feels as important to us as food, water and air, then we have already been guided to our purpose and are on our path.

The important thing about your purpose is that it resonates with you. Please don't negate it if it seems too mundane, or because it's something that comes easily to you. It's not everyone's destiny to be rich or famous. If your passion is fixing things, doing math, sports, gardening, cooking, or whatever it might be—follow it and see where it leads. Do it because it feeds your soul. Pay special attention to what it was that you always loved and were attracted to doing from the time you were a child. Therein usually lies the key to your purpose, just like the singer and writer who were both spurred on by a departed parent who came to them as a Guide, encouraging them to do what they loved. *party, dance, play*

Notice when something makes you feel happy, and if it does, continue in that direction. Conversely, when something gives you a negative or constrictive feeling when you think about doing it, listen to that and give yourself permission to say no. Being polite and following the crowd is not always the right road for you to walk. Be willing to listen to your instinctual gut reaction that comes from deep inside before making decisions for yourself. The better you get at listening to the signals your body is giving you, hearing that voice inside that whispers to you, and reading the "signs" all around you, the sooner you will be on your way to living the life you were meant to live.

There may be times when you feel that you must make those tough decisions that are not going to please everyone around you. It is up to you to know if it is right for you or not. No one can tell you how to run your life. In the end, you must take full responsibility for the choices you have made. Let them be ones you feel proud of instead of ones you did because you were acquiescing to the will of others, or because you did what seemed to be easy at the time.

Exercise

If you have completed the previous exercises in the book, you have been able to eliminate the interference of other people's voices in your head, and to successfully categorize the voices of your many "selves." Now here are some steps you can take to differentiate those from the messages that are actually coming from your Inner Guides. This final exercise will help you tune into the sound of your Soul which can whisper its guidance to you as a welcome companion for the rest of your life.

truth — saved my life

> **Start by developing a clear connection with your intuition. The best way to do that is to keep a journal to track your progress. Every time you have a feeling about something and it comes true, write it down.**

sexual embodiment & empowerment

Think of it as exercising and building your intuitive muscles; if you don't use them, they will atrophy. Conversely, through practice, you can improve your intuition. Most of all, it is a matter of learning to trust yourself. The truth is that you probably have little thoughts all the time about different events and people in your life and there are most likely many ways you are already in touch with guidance, but you let it go as being inconsequential.

Be sure to include everything without believing something was too insignificant to count. For instance, you may have gotten an urge to drive home a different route and later found out your usual commute was obstructed by road construction. Maybe you were upset because you were out of ketchup, and then remembered you had some in your coat pocket from a take-out restaurant you'd been to. Write those down.

Notice how your life changes when you come to realize how _knowing_ you already are. You might title the page: "A List of Coincidences," because that's what they will seem like. Write down if you'd been thinking of someone and then they call. It often happens the opposite way with me. I call so many people who tell me they were just thinking of me. That still involves intuition. If that is your case, write it down. What made you pick up the phone to connect with them? Maybe some part of you was tuned in to receiving their thoughts.

> ➤ **Remember to notate the times when you had a thought to do something (or not do it, as the case may be), but went _against_ your intuition.** _Robert_

Haven't there been times when you've said to yourself some phrase such as one of the following? _I had a thought to bring that with me; I actually had it in my hand, but put it down. Why did I let them talk me into going? I knew I wouldn't have a good time at that party. Something told me to do it like that, but I thought it was stupid. I thought about going that way, but it didn't make any sense. I should have started out sooner like I had planned._ It often ends with you thinking _now I wish I'd listened to my intuition._ A common phrase we use is that we went against our better judgment. Not listening to your intuition can occur every day on this kind of mundane level.

While we know that The Judge might constantly be bugging us in our brain over what we should or shouldn't be doing, our Guides give us more gentle instructions which may be debated by many voices until we learn to listen to the voice that leads us to the most positive outcomes. This is how we can begin to differentiate between our Sub-personalities and our Guides. Through the process of seeing the positive and negative consequences of our actions, we come to learn discernment rather than disappointment. A journal can be a great aid on the journey because it keeps us conscious of the results.

We always have the free will to not listen to that still small voice that guides us toward our smoothest path. Our Guides are very patient with us. Here's a story illustrating a time I ignored my intuition. I had telephoned for Chinese food one weekend recently and was told I could come pick it up in twenty minutes. I wasn't even hungry yet and was in the middle of a movie that had forty-five minutes left. I kept hearing in my head that the food would be delayed because it was Saturday night and when I listened to my body it was feeling very reticent to get up and leave just yet.

However, my Caretaker and Judge didn't want to disappoint the owners of the restaurant by disregarding the time they told me to come because it had always been ready before, so I decided to record the end of the movie on my VCR and leave right away. When I arrived there was a huge line and when I finally got waited on it turned out they had run out of one of the things I ordered which pushed my order back even more. I felt stuck there, knowing I had disregarded my Guides and was held up for over a half-hour waiting.

When I returned home ready to eat and watch the rest of the movie, to add insult to injury, for some reason the VCR had not worked, so I missed the end of it. After my initial disappointment, I chalked it up to a good lesson and vowed to pay more attention next time. That's the type of thing for you to journal. It could simply be listed it as "Chinese restaurant disaster" or whatever would bring back the incident. It's easier when the amount of time that passed from your thought until the realization is relatively short. However, even after many months or years it's still possible to trace an intuitive warning.

When working with clients who have had relationships go sour, I always like to ask them the initial impression they had of their "significant other"

Childish
impulsive immature

the very first time they saw him or her. It's remarkable how often the reason
for the breakup is a direct parallel connected with that immediate intuitive
feeling. (Of course, there are times when first meetings are awkward and
we can make allowances for those.) However, very often a strong warning
system did go off inside saying not to get involved with a person which
got rationalized away until such a time as the reality could no longer be
ignored. This was the case with Ellen from the Co-dependency chapters
(Chapters 7 & 8) who was engaged to an alcoholic.

I ask them to remember the exact words they had heard in their head
and I have them go into trance to find that part of them who was issuing
the warning. That is the part of them who is intuitive. Sometimes it is a
Sub-personality who has a history of being silenced by more dominating
characters, such as a Romantic and Rescuer ganging up and suppressing a
Wounded Child. I am then able to tell the client, "It's time to let this part
be heard before you continue to make the same mistake." Once they listen
to the child, or whoever it was, the Guide is often right there with advice
on how to make better choices in the future, as was illustrated well with
Ellen and her Polynesian Warrior/Inner Man as well as Dr. Alan and his
dad.

RK   22 @ 222

> **Discover some personal symbol that has meaning to you
> as a special way to realize that a Guide or someone close
> to you is communicating.** *Chills*

Perhaps you can identify a channel through which departed loved ones
or any of your Guides can come to you that has special meaning for you. It
could be a discovery you make such as I did with the wind or Patricia did
with dragonflies and butterflies. It might be something significant between
you and someone special who has died that you actually shared while they
were alive. It could be a song you sang together, a scent they wore, a favorite

phrase, number, flower, bird, etc. Anything that begins to repeat itself or gives you chills or tears when it appears is a good indication that there is a communication happening.

Synchronicities and coincidences that continue to happen well beyond the realm of chance happenings often get our attention, but we are almost afraid to believe they could mean anything. It's not hard to find signs if we just remain open to them. Even my father, who is a huge skeptic, took it as a sign of approval when he met his second wife on my mother's birthday two months after she died. Life is so much more fun and rewarding when we remain open to the possibilities that are all around us showing us how connected we really are.

> ## Begin to pay special attention to your dreams.

Look for people you know to make appearances and send you messages in your dreams, even if it's only to let you know they're alright. After my mother died from a long bout with Alzheimer's in 2001, I always find it comforting to dream about her and hear her speaking normally again. Once in awhile a dream with her feels prophetic, but mostly it's just nice to see her, and I wake up feeling like I've had a visitation.

You may dream of people you've never met, as well, who fill you with a really good feeling during the dream or upon waking. It's much easier for Guides to visit you when you are already deep asleep in your unconscious mind where they can bypass any conscious resistance you may be unwittingly putting up to their presence in your life. Write down any dreams that feel important and notate messages you receive. Then look back on your entries to see if anything you dreamed about actually occurred or later seems relevant. I see many clients who met a Guide in a dream and didn't realize it. Rule of thumb: if you think someone from your dream is a Guide, they probably are.

> ➤ **Be open for answers to problems to present themselves to you in your sleep or especially just upon waking.**

We looked at how so many brilliant ideas and solutions come to people, including Einstein, in their dreams. How does it happen that the patent office can be suddenly inundated with several inventors quite independently coming up with almost identical new inventions? It sometimes seems as if they are floating there ready to be plucked out of the Universe at different moments of history. Ideas are always flowing freely to us during our sleep. You don't need to be a scientist or an Einstein to make use of this natural phenomenon.

I had a photo album with pictures from five generations of my family that I had worked very hard to put together many years ago. I took it out to pack with me on a trip to Florida to show at my father's 80th birthday party. I was so disappointed when I opened it up and saw that it was falling apart. I discovered one of the two pins holding the hundred page album together had been damaged and I couldn't figure out how to fix it. When I got there I showed it to my father, knowing how good he is at solving problems, and asked him to begin to think of some way he might be able to repair it.

He got very frustrated looking at it and told me it would be impossible, but I told him not to worry; just to wait and see if anything came to him. A few hours later I came back from shopping and he was all excited to show me the album. He said he had taken a little nap and woke up suddenly with an inspiration. He jumped up and had it fixed in two minutes by tying a shoelace around the pages in place of the pin. It looks a little funny, but it feels as good as new and he assures me now it will last forever.

➤ **Utilize the ability to access your subconscious mind directly in order to meet a Guide through a guided visualization, meditation or hypnosis session.**

For the best chance of success, find a qualified Hypnotherapist to assist you. I highly recommend finding one trained in Alchemical techniques, because the definition of Alchemical Hypnotherapy straight out of the course workbook is: "interactive trance work using archetypes/guides to empower clients in discovering, aligning with, and living their life purposes."

Otherwise, look for a tape or CD designed to bring you into contact with your Inner Guides or Angels. That will prepare you by putting you into a more relaxed and receptive state since it's important to quiet the mind in order to hear their messages. If you don't get anything at first, there could be a number of reasons why not. For one thing you may have a pre-conceived notion of what it will be like, and you may actually miss what comes. Remain open to whatever form the communication may take. Your reward will be the wisdom that comes with the deep search within for the truth.

Be aware that inner "hearing" sometimes comes through the mind as words, but more often it comes in the form of *feeling* and *knowing*. Kimberly Marooney created a tarot deck called *Angel Blessings* while she was recovering from a life-threatening illness and a near-death experience. She writes, "Angels do not speak through vocal cords; instead they know our thoughts and communicate with feelings through the heart." Have an open heart and a beginner's mind, like that of a child. Your feelings will be the cord to connect you with Divine Guidance and you must believe you can trust them.

Our minds are so tricky that when they don't like the feelings they receive, our Skeptics, Judges and other Intellectual Characters take control and convince us not to feel the way we really are feeling. So recovering our true feelings may be a necessary step to reclaim our own power to connect with our spiritual nature. It often takes extensive emotional clearing work such as the type I went through personally and I do with my clients, before you can build that bridge to the world of your Guides. Most of us were taught to raise our eyes up to the Heavens, and the truth is that we need to look down into our bodies and our feelings which are actually the doors that lead us there.

Unfortunately, I sometimes see the opposite happening. In the New Age community where it can be popular to know how to channel your Guides, I see people who are getting impractical and impersonal intellectual information because they have not cleared out their own emotional channels. As you free your emotional body, your inner hearing and vision will begin to open and your Guides will be waiting for you.

Another thing that can prevent us from hearing the voice of our Guides is that our belief systems can limit the flow of knowledge coming in and act as screens to filter out or criticize things that don't conform to our beliefs. This can sometimes keep us denying the truth. The ensuing conflict of our warring Sub-personalities battling so loudly within can block our inner hearing. This is particularly so if you are dominated by a Judge, Skeptic or Preacher/Guru.

In that case, the loudest voice your Guides may be able to manage is the voice of your conscience pulling you back onto your Path. Follow that voice by listening to your heart and allowing your true feelings to bring you back into a place of clear thinking where you find your judgment improving and fears lessening. Then you can begin to trust your *active imagination* which is needed on this journey of learning to hear the still, small voice of your Guides. Your Higher Self will not cease in its efforts to make contact. The key is in your heart.

Be patient. Don't give up. You may need to listen to a CD often to achieve success. The least you will get out of it is to have received the benefits of a deep state of relaxation which improves general health and is wonderful for getting a good night's sleep. If you do happen to fall asleep while listening, that's alright. There may be a relationship forming at the unconscious level that will make itself known when you are ready to receive it consciously.

> **Develop a personal relationship with your Guides. Feel the way you are divinely connected with the Universe and all that is. Allow for miracles and you will begin to see them everywhere.**

The Universe loves to conspire to make your wishes come true. People are always quick to pray for guidance during trying times, but why not allow divine intervention to accompany you anytime? Take delight in the little things of everyday life. Parking spaces and green lights can be a blessing when you're in a hurry. Seeing the first blossoms of spring or a rosebud opening can feel like unwrapping gifts bestowed by nature. Catching glimpses of beautiful birds, dolphins or sunsets can uplift our spirits.

One example from my own life that delighted me occurred a few years ago when I was really wishing I had some fresh rosemary to cook with, only I couldn't grow any because my gardens are all shaded. The very next day, out of the blue, my neighbor across the street, who has plenty of sunlight, began planting a row of rosemary bushes along the road as a border. Since then I have had fresh rosemary anytime I've wanted it.

I used to live in the rainforests of Northern California and I considered the umbrella to be something of a man-made miracle, because it lets you create a dry space in the midst of a downpour. However, since moving back to the east coast where rain is more irregular, I began to notice how seldom I ever needed an umbrella anymore. For awhile I carried one anyway out of habit, until I became more aware of a strange phenomenon that seemed to be following me around.

Time after time, season after season, situations continued to present torrential rains all around me, except when I needed to be outside. My windshield wipers would be flapping like crazy during my drive, and upon reaching my destination the sky would suddenly clear. About fifteen years ago, I finally gave a name to this personal miracle I seemed to be privy to, which I call, "walking between the raindrops."

It is my wish to all of you on your personal journey, to discover a similar feeling of being "umbrella'd" by your Guides to the extent that you can feel the joys of walking between the raindrops in your own life.

I've come to believe that all my past failure and frustration were actually laying the foundation for the understandings that have created the new level of living I now enjoy.

— Tony Robbins

Chapter 13

COMING HOME TO MYSELF

To say I was born a great thinker might sound a bit presumptuous. But it seems like forever that I can remember being obsessed with talking to anyone who would listen and asking a million questions to assure I was understood and I understood others. When I was three years old, in fact, I had invisible mice friends I used to talk to who sat next to me on chairs that I wouldn't allow anyone to sit on so they wouldn't be crushed.

In fourth grade I wrote a poem about my parakeet called, *I Wish My Bird Could Talk to Me*. My parents would come home from PTA meetings throughout grade school, where the teachers' only complaint about me was that I needed to figure out who was the student and who was the teacher. I also became interested in the workings of the mind very early. In sixth grade when I needed to choose a subject to research for a student specialty to present in front of class with visual aids, I chose to do it on The Brain.

I was always fascinated with psychology, personality theories, and communication between people. I wanted to penetrate the space between us that kept us apart, feeling different and alone. I knew we all had a right to our private thoughts, but I felt sad about the distance it created and the unkindness that sometimes accompanied our illusory separateness.

My response to the cliques and peer pressure of high school was to write a poem in eleventh grade entitled, *Who Am I?* which attempted to bridge that gap. I declared victory when the girl next door, who was a cheerleader and on the student council, hung it in her locker. For Driver's Ed. class I wrote a paper on how to recognize the personalities of different drivers by looking at them behind the wheel. I, myself, have always related to my road Rebel, Rhonda Racer, although I've learned to cool her engines a bit, as I grew older.

I continued my pursuit of the answers to my burning questions in college where I declared the interdisciplinary major of Interpersonal Communications with a Theater minor. I had a chance to look at this issue through the perspective of Anthropology, Sociology, Psychology, Linguistics, English and Speech Communications. I found the science of General Semantics founded by Alfred Korzybski around the early 20th century, shed enormous light on the subject of misunderstandings and arguments.

I took that on as a special field of study. I devised an experiment to study the ability of people to read the emotions that others are going through. I was so intrigued by it I repeated it twice during my undergraduate studies. It was a take-off on a psychology study I read about where they measured the ability to correctly identify the emotions people were displaying through non-content language. In other words, the subjects displaying the emotions did so through saying letters of the alphabet instead of real words.

I learned that the ability to show and identify some emotions such as anger and sadness was relatively easy, yet there was still a difference if it was women or men conveying or receiving the messages. However, it became clear that it was mostly a guessing game when it came to knowing what someone else was feeling concerning the more complex emotions such as love, jealousy, fear and even satisfaction. It was a fascinating discovery, but being armed with this statistical analysis still didn't give me any tools to help make communicating any easier.

During my college days Richard Nixon got elected for a second term, the Vietnam war was still being waged but winding down, and another great political wave was taking over on the home front: the women's movement. Feminism was in its infancy and I became involved in a consciousness raising (C.R.) group on campus. The intimate weekly meetings held in women's dorm rooms allowed me to explore new identities within myself that weren't painted through the patriarchal picture I had always tried to fit into.

It seemed natural for me to move to San Francisco after graduation to be in the center of new thought and cultural freedom. The great divide I was seeing in America then was between men and women. I was acutely aware of the second class citizenship of women in the 1970's workplace in America. Living in Paris during a semester abroad had alerted me to the plight of French women where abortion was still illegal and women were wounding themselves with knitting needles and throwing themselves down stairs in an effort to control their own bodies. I believed political action was the way to make things change and I found myself volunteering for the Mayor's Commission on the Status of Women under Mayor George Moscone.

However, soon something happened that shifted my agenda. I was presented for the first time with new spiritual perspectives on life including the concepts of karma and reincarnation. Suddenly, the big picture I was seeing of a universal order dwarfed the petty political problems of the day. Everything took on new meaning when I realized people were all here to learn lessons designed to balance out their karmic slate set up by their soul before they were even born. Much of my anger at men dissipated as I realized I chose to come into the 20th century as a woman, and at one time I may have been a man with the same traits I was now mad at them for.

Eventually I was invited by friends to live with them in a small town in Northern California among the redwoods and ended up making that town my home for nine years. My spirit was soothed by the grandiosity of nature and I later realized I was guided there for the teachings I would soon receive. I had strayed from working in my field after graduation and was attempting instead to make it as a photographer, but basically was living as the proverbial starving artist.

One night in 1983, four years after I moved there, I awoke from a dream that became a defining moment in my life. In it a friend of mine told me she had taken the money she owed me and invested it for me and I was rich! It intrigued me enough to investigate and when I found my friend to share it with her she was on her way home from a workshop at a local massage school.

After hearing my dream, my friend, Dianne, generously offered to buy me a session from the workshop leader. She told me his name was David Quigley and he was utilizing healing techniques from Carl Jung, Psychosynthesis, the ancient Alchemists, present and past life regression therapy, and Shamanism, which he added to, synthesized and called Alchemical Hypnotherapy or Alchemy. After the session David told me he was giving a free lecture in town on his technique.

My curiosity was piqued by the session, and I figured I had nothing to lose by attending. When I heard him talk for two hours, I was amazed by the fact that he had presented a more complete answer to the workings of the mind than anything I had heard in four years of college. I decided to take his course, still thinking I would learn things to help me with my photography business. I heard a clear voice in my head that got excited when I was sitting listening to him that first day and said, *I could teach this.*

Little did I know I was actually in the midst of changing the entire course of my life.

My Alchemical Journey

Alchemy has been understood for centuries as a mystical art for the transmutation of consciousness through the joining of opposites, such as the union of the physical and spiritual, or the male and female sides of a person. Carl Jung resurrected the term in the early twentieth century and brought it into the field of psychology. He used the word Alchemy to help define the process of individuation, or wholeness. Emphasizing the importance of spirituality in the psychic health of the modern man, he argued Alchemy was a sort of western yoga designed to facilitate an inner journey of transformation.

The fundamental concept of Alchemy stemmed from the Aristotelian doctrine that all things tend to reach perfection. Symbolically, many people understand Alchemy as the transmutation of common elements, such as base metals, into pure gold. Metaphorically that describes the process of modern day Master Alchemists in their ability to transform the disparate elements of human consciousness, such as confusion, envy, loneliness, and despair, into the gold of self-realization.

Even with such obvious external divisions between people of different classes, races, religions, and political parties, we remain oblivious to the internal divisions that exist within ourselves. Life keeps people feeling alone and separate, isolated within our own thoughts and memories which Jung refers to as the "personal unconscious." Many clues abound through dreams and synchronicities to prove the existence of what he termed the "collective unconscious" which is the realm of archetypes and Sub-personalities shared by all of humanity.

The synchronicities in my own life that led me to the exploration of my personal and collective unconscious through Alchemy is what allowed me to emerge from being the prisoner of my mind and step through the doorway to wholeness. Because I had always relied on my mind as the place to look for answers to everything I had to discover how to "get out of my head." My biggest challenges were: learning to listen to my body, accept my emotions and follow my intuition. That's where the ability to meet the voices in my head truly enabled me to become whole. I owe that success to the Alchemical Hypnotherapy sessions I underwent as a result of having that fateful dream.

As I began to clear away emotional debris from the past and get clarity on the voices in my head, my life changed dramatically. Whereas I thought I would be learning to organize my negatives, instead I was learning a system of organizing my psyche! Sub-personalities were falling into place in my head where I could recognize the ways they benefited or sabotaged me and could give them new jobs that would capitalize on their strengths. Within six months I had learned to keep my Inner Victim and Rescuer at bay to keep me out of the grips of Co-dependency with the help of my Inner Warrior who learned to say "no."

My biggest gift came from meeting my Spirit Guides whose words comforted me and led me through life and continue to guide me to this day. As I spoke about previously, the immediate and lasting effect they had was twofold. I lost a pervasive sense of loneliness accompanied by the thought that if I had no one to talk to, no one was listening. That made the biggest outward change in my personality because I no longer needed to talk all the time. I suddenly realized that I could talk to my Guides out loud or in my head anytime I wanted to.

Plus, I was especially delighted to realize that not only were they listening, they were also *answering* me. Their answers weren't always in words or imminent, but they eventually became apparent. And equally important, I had a new occupation because by learning Alchemy and getting in touch with the voices in my head, I had finally found a well-organized system to help people achieve the same ability to communicate their thoughts and feelings with others and themselves.

Alchemical techniques allow a person to delve into the world of dreams to make direct contact rather than rely on the skill of symbolic interpretation which was the best-scene scenario envisioned by Jung. We hold the power to direct our lives rather than being a victim of life's circumstances by exploring our emotional complexes head on, and making the acquaintance of the personas we have developed to deal with them. In the middle of the 20th century, late in his life, Carl Jung became afraid of what was in store for mankind if we continued heading in the same direction. He believed the only salvation for the future of humanity lay in people becoming more conscious.

I completely agree. I worry about the ease by which we can be seduced into distractions as the world becomes more electronically efficient. It has become a push-button world of instant gratification, sound bites, and tiny attention spans. Many people can go days without ever stepping on the natural world as more and more of it is being paved over. Workdays are becoming longer. There are already numerous ways that communicating can be accomplished without ever making eye contact with another human being, and I'm sure at this moment someone is coming up with yet another.

It's easy to put off getting to know ourselves when striving to get ahead is so much more highly valued. Yet the rewards of truly knowing yourself are beyond value. The collection of characters I am aware of who are part of my Inner Team are my most valuable resources. The joy I get from the connection I have with Little Debbie is something that accompanies me every day. When I wondered why I tended to hold in my emotions I was led to a past life journey to meet Laughing Eagle, a Native American warrior who watched his tribe get massacred and lost his smile, and I understood.

The ability to transform that situation through Alchemy and bring him back as an Inner Father for Little Debbie was magical. He was available to me in a more emotional capacity than my Tai Chi Master, who was more of a teacher. Continuing to appreciate my connection with my Angel, Wind, as a Guide until she revealed herself as Little Debbie's Inner Mother has been a divine unfolding of events over the last two and a half decades.

The session where I watched my Judge go from a stodgy patriarchal man with a white wig to a woman in an indigo wet suit emerging from the water and revealing her long blond hair was better than watching any movie ever produced. She came out of the ocean with the message that it was time to "ride the wave into a new future." It was electrifying. Equally exciting was the time a new friend emerged during a session on loneliness and said he could teach Little Debbie some new tricks.

I saw in my mind's eye a little ten-year-old boy levitate from the ground until he was sitting up on a tree limb. He looked like Peter Pan so I asked him if his name was Peter. He told me, "No. It's Pan." That helped move Little Debbie from Wounded Child to Magical Child. Of course a skeptical mind like mine does have trouble believing all these things and tries to put them off as wild imaginings. But every once in awhile something happens that makes me have to become a believer. One of those times was when I was doing a session about my mother during her early stages of Alzheimer's.

I went back during one of my sessions to her childhood to rescue her from painful incidents from when she was little and I kept her in my inner world as a play friend for Little Debbie. I saw her as a four or five-year-old and called her "Little Mommy Eileen." I never discussed my sessions with my parents, but the next time I went to visit them in Florida my mother had decided to put up a framed picture of herself as a five-year-old that I had never seen before and there it remained on her dresser until the day she died.

This is only a small sampling of the many past-life characters, Guides and Sub-personalities I have accompanying me now in my conscious mind. They have allowed me to emerge as the "Self" I knew myself to be as a child, but who got buried under the weight of shyness, self-consciousness and the excruciating pain of those undiagnosed stomachaches I spoke about in Chapter 5, that accompanied me as I retreated into a self-imposed shell through adolescence. My sensitive nature made it difficult to escape from painful memories of feeling different as the new kid in junior high school.

There was no severe abuse I needed to overcome, just the run-of-the-mill neuroses I didn't have the tools to tackle. So I brushed them under the rug like everyone else. Luckily, I was introduced to a technique that allowed me to solve the greatest mystery we are all here to solve—*me*! What more can we ask for than the freedom to truly express our authentic self? That is, of course, after we've come to know *who* that is. And after we've learned to get out of our heads and into our hearts.

I encourage you to embark on the greatest adventure any of us will be asked to participate in. Remember the part of you who is talking to you right now in your mind or body, feeling either excited or scared, is the first one for you to get ready to meet. Bring that part along to be a witness to the greatest task your Soul will ever ask of you, and begin right now talking to *your* selves.

Source Material and Suggested Reading

Assagioli, R. (1971) *Psychosynthesis.* New York, NY: Penguin.

Bass, E. and Davis, L. (1988) *The Courage to Heal.* New York, NY: Harper & Rowe.

Boyne, Gil. (1992) *Transforming Hypnotherapy.* Glendale, CA: Westwood Publishing.

Bradshaw, J. (1988) *On the Family.* Deerfield Beach, FL: Health Communications, Inc.

Bradshaw, J. (1988) *Healing the Shame that Binds You.* Deerfield Bch., FL: Heath Communications, Inc.

Bradshaw, J. (1996) *Family Secrets.* New York, NY: Bantam Books, Inc.

Branden, N. (1988) *The Disowned Self.* Los Angeles, CA: Nash Publishing Corp.

Bridges, C. (1991) *The Medicine Woman Inner Guidebook.* Stamford, CT: U.S. Games Systems, Inc.

Campbell, J. (2008) *The Hero with a Thousand Faces, 3rd edition.* San Rafael, CA: New World Library.

Cameron, J. (1992) *The Artist's Way: A Spiritual Path to Higher Creativity.* New York, NY: G.P. Putnam's Sons.

Carson, R. (2003) *Taming Your Gremlin.* New York, NY: HarperCollins Press.

Deann, A. (2006) *Release Your Magical Child.* Sacramento, CA: Mind Emotion Harmony.

Dragon, J. and Popp, T., Ed. ((1999) *Multiple Journeys to One.* Santa Rosa, CA: Dancing Serpents Press.

Duckett, M. (2007) *The Mental Codes—Secret Powers of The Mind.* Marietta, GA: Whitmire Publishing.

Edwards, B. (1989) *Drawing on the Right Side of the Brain.* Los Angeles, CA: Tarcher.

Erduman, R. (2001) *Veils of Separation: Finding the Face of Oneness.* Canada: Hignell Printing, Inc.

Geringer Woititz, J. (1983) *Adult Children of Alcoholics.* Pompano Beach, FL: Health Communications, Inc.

Gordon, M. (1991) *Healing is Remembering Who You Are.* Oakland, CA: WiseWord Publishing.

Griscom, C. (1988) *The Healing of Emotion.* New York, NY: Fireside.

Harris, T. (1969) *I'm OK—You're OK.* New York, NY: Harper & Row.

Hay, L. (1988) *Heal Your Body.* Santa Monica, CA: Hay House, Inc.

Hunter, Roy (1995) *The Art of Hypnotherapy.* Dubuque, IO: Kendall/Hunt Publishing Co.

Janov, A. (1970) *Primal Scream.* New York, NY: Dell Publishing Co., Inc.

Johnson, R. (1985) *We.* New York, NY: Harper and Row.

Jung, C.G. (1965) *Memories. Dreams & Reflections.* New York, NY: Random House.

Jung, C.G. (1968) *Psychology and Alchemy.* Princeton, N.J.: Bollingen Foundation.

Marooney, K (1995) *Angel Blessings: Cards of Sacred Guidance & Inspiration.* Carmel, CA: Merrill-West Publishing.

MacLaine, S. (1986) *Dancing in the Light.* New York, NY: Bantam Books, Inc.

Miller, Alice (2005) *The Body Never Lies: The Lingering Effects of Cruel Parenting.* New York, NY: W.W. Norton.

Miller, A. (2001) *The Truth Will Set You Free: Overcoming Emotional Blindness and Finding Your True Adult Self.* New York: Basic Books.

Miller, A. (1985) *Thor Shalt Not Be Aware: Society's Betrayal of the Child.* New York, NY: Penguin USA.

Moody, R. (1984) *Life After Life.* New York, NY: Bantam Books, Inc.

Myss, C. (2001) *Sacred Contracts.* New York, NY: Harmony Books.

Myss, C. (1999) *Spiritual Madness.* on Tape or CD: Sounds True Media.

Noble, V. (1983) *Motherpeace.* San Francisco, CA: Harper Collins.

Perls, F. (1974) *Gestalt Therapy Verbatim.* Moah, UT: Real People Press.

Quigley, D. (1989) *Alchemical Hypnotherapy.* Redway, CA: Lost Coast Press.

Rossi, E. (1993) *The Psychology of Mind/Body Healing.* W.W. Norton & Co.

Schaef, A. W. (1990) *Escape From Intimacy.* New York, NY: Harper and Row.

Small, J. (1991) *Awakening in Time.* New York, NY: Bantam Books, Inc.

Siegel, B. (1986) *Love. Medicine & Miracles: Lessons Learned About Self-Healing from a Surgeon's Experience with Exceptional Patients.* New York, NY: Harper & Row.

Siegel, B. (1990) *Peace, Love and Healing: Bodymind Communication and the Path of Self-Healing.* New York: Harper & Row.

Simonton, C., Matthew-Simonton, S. and Creighton, J. (1981) *Getting Well Again.* New York, NY: Bantam Books, Inc.

Stone, H and Winkelman, S. (1989) *Embracing Ourselves.* San Rafael, CA: New World Library.

Thayer, S. and Nathanson, L.S. (1997) *Interrview with an Angel.* Gillette, NJ: Edin Books, Inc.

Tolle, E. (2005) *A New Earth.* New York, NY: Plume.

Walkenstein, E. (1983) *Your Inner Therapist.* Philadelphia, PA: The Westminster Press.

Weiss, B. (1988) *Many Lives. Many Masters.* New York, NY: Fireside.

Whitfield, C. (1989) *Healing the Child Within.* Deerfield Beach, FL: Health Communications, Inc.

Zukav, G. (1990) *The Seat of the Soul.* New York, NY: Fireside.

Diagnostic and Statistical Manual of Mental Disorders, 4th Edition, (DSM-IV). (1994) American Psychiatric Association.

Intellectual Characters

Character	Strengths	Weaknesses	Possible Jobs	Could be Heard Saying
For Example				
The Judge King Solomon Sandra Day O'Connor Dr. Phil McGraw Simon Cowell Rush Limbaugh *Sam* ~~*Jasim*~~	Disciplined, Discerning, Decisive, Fair, Objective, Critical thinking, Good judgment, Social values, Propriety, Task-oriented, Penetrating, Balanced, Organized, Moral compass, Commanding, Evaluating	Judgmental, Mean, Critical, Hypocritical, Prejudiced, Condemnatory, Rigid, Self-righteous, Fault-finding, Conformist, Punitive, Controlling, Never satisfied, Opinionated, Task-master, Obnoxious, Guilt-imposing, Unsolicited advice,	Judge, Mediator, Critic, FDA, School Principal, Air traffic controller, EPA, Dean, Board member, Ship Captain, Film producer, Manager, Warden, Moderator, Stage Manager, Commander, Policy enforcer, IRS auditor, News editor	**Toxic:** *Guilty! Can't you do anything right? What were you thinking?!* **Healthy:** *Innocent until proven guilty. There are two sides to every story*
Skeptic/Cynic/ Scientist/Guard Jane Goodall Stephen Hawking Bill Maher Don Rickles Eddie Haskell *Jasim*	Scout, Reality tester, Not gullible, Objective, Scientific, Uncovers evidence, Gathers data, Shows common sense & healthy doubt, Deductive reasoning, Self-protective, Pragmatist, Fact-finding, Researcher, BS detector, Calculating, Good in emergencies	Distrusting, Unwilling to Risk, Pessimist, Atheist, Materialist, Greedy, Shifty, Paranoid, Demands proof, Cynical, Sarcastic, Sneaky, Misanthropic, Dishonest, Sly, Underhanded, Unenlightened, Negative, Aloof, Con-man, Cutting, Know-it-all	Statistician, Scout, Scientist, Protector, Engineer, CPA, EMT, Professor, Comptroller, Data analyst, Detective, Security Chemist, guard, Researcher, Systems analyst, Investigator, Surveyor, Computer programmer, Undercover agent, Investigative Reporter, Anthropologist	**Toxic:** *Sure, that's what they all say. Prove it! Show me the money. Life's a bitch & then you die. What's in it for me?* **Healthy:** *The proof of the pudding is in the eating. Let's wait and see.*
The Preacher/Guru/ Seeker/Believer Deepak Chopra Jesse Jackson Mother Theresa Jim Baker Jim Jones *Rabia the NUN celibate*	Transcendental, Sees the big picture, Not materialistic, Spiritual compass, Detached, Seeks meaning and truth, Has faith, Enlightened, Religious, Charitable, Kind, Modest, Moral values, Altruistic, Compassionate, Humble, Generosity of spirit, Self-actualizing	Spiritual arrogance, Bigoted, Sees evil, Moralistic, Self-righteous, Intolerant, Closed-minded, Inflexible, Pious, Preachy, sex & money, Cloistered, Proselytize, Guilt-inducing, Dogmatic, Condemnatory, Conservative, Negates needs of body, Repressed, Evangelical, Sanctimonious *Believer*	Charity worker, Volunteer, Fund-raiser, Missionary, Spiritual counselor, Clergy, Rabbi, Nun, Zen monk, Ascetic, Community garden director, Inspirational speaker or writer, Christian rock band, Gospel singer, Televangelist, Motivational speaker, New Age Filmmaker	**Toxic:** *You're going to Hell for that. My way is the right way. Money is the root of all evil.* **Healthy:** *This too shall pass. Have faith. Let go and let God. Everything in moderation.*

Character	Strengths	Weaknesses	Possible Jobs	Could be Heard Saying
For Example				
Mr. & Ms. Together Barbara Walters Suze Ormond Denzel Washington Jerry McGuire Bernie Madoff	Organized, Confident, Go-getter, Reliable, Ability to succeed, Upwardly mobile, Financially successful, Smooth talker, Socialite, Good image, Hard worker, Take-charge attitude, Impeccable, Well-groomed, Charming, Attractive, Debonair, Fashion-conscious *Tom + Kfan*	Fake, Front or Mask, Obsessed with appearance, Shallow, Snobbish, Insomniac, Workaholic, Controlling, Denial of own physical needs & emotional issues, Steps on others to get ahead, Lives above means, Stressed, Caffeine addict	Promoter, Business owner, Leader, Millionaire, Organizer, Literary Agent, Socialite, Personal Consultant, Sports agent, Marketing, Talent scout, Upper management, Head hunter, Executive, Beauty contestant, PTA president, Cheerleader, Lawyer, Investment banker	**Toxic:** *If you want something done right, you've got to do it yourself. Not now, I'm busy, Fake it 'til you make it.* **Healthy:** *Dress for success. Let's do it. Focus.*
The Entertainer/Comic Lucille Ball Ellen DeGeneris Johnny Carson Robin Williams Judy Garland Janis Joplin	Engaging, Enrolls people, Maintains interest, Funny, Can command a room, Holds attention, Comic relief, Outgoing, Charismatic, Extroverted, Popular, Loves the spotlight, Dramatic, Talented, Idolized, Exuberant, Huge fund-raisers, Charitable, Gregarious, Fun to be around *Robert*	Needs approval & adulation, Hides feelings, Denies pain, Lives for public life, Empty off-stage, False persona, Self-destructive tendencies, Acting out, Needs to be center of attention, Doesn't listen, Co-dependent with or addicted to an audience, Self-absorbed, Social impropriety, Pretense, Annoying, Interrupts, Drama queen/king	Storyteller, Public speaker, Communicator, Master of ceremonies, Actor, Singer, Comedian, Clown, Talk show host, Spokesperson, Star, Toastmaster, Fundraiser, Wrestler, Cruise ship entertainment director, Band leader	**Toxic:** *Let me entertain you. The tears of a clown, when there's no one around. I'm the great pretender* **Healthy:** *The show must go on. Make 'em laugh.*
The King/Queen Oprah Bill Clinton Jackie Kennedy Onassis Donald Trump Saddam Hussein	Delegates authority & tasks, Leadership, Benevolence, Noblesse oblige, Powerful, Empowers others, Sense of responsibility, Influential, Socially responsible, Respected, High status, Nobility, Commanding, Mandated, Midas touch *Mom* *Robert*	Pompous, Patronizing, Out of touch, Dictatorial, Self-righteous, Controlling, Narcissistic, Condescending, Disempowers others, Selfish, Decadent, Egocentric, Tyrannical, Misuses power, Sense of entitlement, Superiority, Miserly, Authoritarian, Demanding	Overseer, Leader, Financier, Ruler, Philanthropist, Head of state, CEO, Legislator, Peacekeeper, Billionaire, Rancher, Oil magnate, Supreme Court Justice, Airline pilot, Orchestra conductor	**Toxic:** *Let them eat cake. Off with their heads. You're either with us or you're against us.* **Healthy:** *Let the voice of the people be heard. Let freedom ring, With liberty & justice for all.*

Character	Strengths	Weaknesses	Possible Jobs	Could be Heard Saying
For Example				
Mr. & Ms. Perfect Emily Post Heidi Klum Tim Gunn Martha Stewart Mr. Blackwell	Reliable, Thorough, Crafty, Gets the job done, Precise, Craftsmanship, Impeccable, Tireless, Social Graces, Manners, Neat & Clean, Exemplary, Consummate, Above reproach, Presentable, Discriminating, Respected, Well-dressed	Picky, Never good enough, Never satisfied, Impossible to please, Fault finding, Won't accept faults in self, Covers up, Patronizing, Unforgiving Obsessive/Compulsive, Fussy, Burnout, White glove treatment, Judgmental, Snob, Persnickety, Nose in the air	Quality control expert, Researcher, Director, Charm school instructor, Fashion consultant, Hospitality, Film editor, Make-over artist, Couture designer, Decorator, Personal shopper, Fashion model, Westminster Dog Show judge	**Toxic:** *Can't you do anything right? One more time (til you get it right).* **Healthy:** *Practice makes perfect. Only the best.*
Mr. & Ms. Independent James Bond Katherine Hepburn Richard Branson Quentin Tarantino Howard Hughes	Autonomous, Self-starter, Strong-willed, Accomplished, Free thinker, Ingenious, Entrepreneurial, Comfortable alone, Self-sufficient, Can-do attitude, Private, Stamina, Unique, Capable, Innovator, Forward thinking	Bad team player, Rebellious, Self-protective, Cold, Aloof, Can't ask for/ accept help, Insubordinate, Loner, Tough exterior, Fear of intimacy, Withdraws from society, Closed off	Leader, Inventor, Traveler, Role Model, Consultant, Independent contractor, Rock climber, Spy, Entrepreneur, Massage therapist, Stock broker, Independent filmmaker, Think tank, Forest ranger, Truck driver	**Toxic:** *I am a rock, I am an island. Leave me alone.* **Healthy:** ✶ *I can do it myself. I love my space. I want to be alone.*

(handwritten) Memere / Step

(handwritten) Me / Iyla

(handwritten) ♡ solving mysteries ♡
(handwritten) Private Investigator!

256

EMOTIONAL CHARACTERS

Character	Strengths	Weaknesses	Possible Jobs	Could be Heard Saying
For Example				
The Inner Child Dr. Seuss Bill Cosby Miley Cyrus Walt Disney PeeWee Herman	Joyous, Playful, Intuitive, Spontaneous, Sensitive, Fun, Innocent, Curious, Authentic, Honest, Creative, Energetic, Imaginative, Affectionate, Unconditional love, Childlike, In the moment *Little Rabia*	Demanding, Dependent, Loud, Whiney, Selfish, Needy, Messy, Bratty, Clingy, Sneaky, Helpless, Childish, Bully, Temper tantrums, Insensitive, Stubborn, Lazy, Short attention span, Self-absorbed	Professional Athlete, Teacher, Empath, Nanny, Artist, Actor, Dancer, Comedian, Circus clown, Parks and Recreation supervisor, Children's author, Dog walker, Toy store owner, Toy inventor, Professional gamer	**Toxic:** *I want it now! Mine, mine, mine. I'm not listening.* **Healthy:** *Let's play! All I want to do is have some fun*
The Prince & Princess Michelle Kwan Jonas Brothers John F. Kennedy, Jr. Princess Diana Paris Hilton	Deserving, Know they're special, Indulge without guilt, Romantic, Worthy, Socialite, Well-groomed, Can receive, Good manners, Charitable, Noble, Innocence, Graceful, Entitlement, Giving, Feel like royalty, Pampered, Debutante *Princess Rabia*	Expect to be waited on, Spoiled, Prima Dona, Obsessed with being special, Live in a fantasy world, Spend money like water, Silver spoon, Self-indulgent, No self-sufficiency unless bankrolled, Dependent, Expects to be rescued, Bossy, Immature, Condescending, Sheltered, Sense of entitlement	Model, Escort, Ambassador, Philanthropist, Art collector, Chair charity benefit, Romance writer, Fashion consultant, Hollywood star, Beauty contestant, Heiress, Pop star, Ice skater *Actress*	**Toxic:** *I'd rather be shopping. Some day my prince will come. Diamonds are a girl's best friend. I broke a nail.* **Healthy:** *What part of treating me like a Goddess do you not understand?*
The Rebel Madonna Susan B. Anthony James Dean Ozzie Osbourne Jim Morrison	Risk-taker, Defies limits, Can say "no," Innovative, Fights conformity, Thinks outside the box, Mover & shaker, Challenges authority, Gutsy, Spunky, Exciting, Outspoken, Spontaneous, Creative, Righteous anger, Playful, Spirited, *young Katie*	Adrenaline junkie, Addictive personality, Confrontive, Need for excitement, Shock value, Exhaustion from burnout, Subversive, Menace to society, Destructive, Self-destructive, Disregard for others, Anti-social, In your face, Disruptive, Rabble-rouser, Crowd mentality, Need to conform with peers	Rock & roll singer, Satirist, Private eye, Defense attorney, Consumer advocate, Reality game show contestant, Disc jockey, Drug rehabilitation counselor, Political cartoonist, Social commentator, Film maker, Political or social activist, CIA agent	**Toxic:** *Sex, drugs, rock & roll! Too bad if you can't take a joke. Screw it! If it feels good, do it.* **Healthy:** *Question authority. I'll try anything once. Go for it.*

Character	Strengths	Weaknesses	Possible Jobs	Could be Heard Saying
For Example				
The Adventurer John Glenn Jacques Cousteau Amelia Earhart Hans Solo Evel Knievel	Physically fit, Outdoorsy, Never dull, Freedom lover, Curious, Entertaining, Gypsy, Fearless, Outgoing, Sociable, Trail-blazer, Thrill-seeker, Not afraid of the unknown, Likes to try new things, Innovative, Rugged, Good story teller, Competitive, Early adapter to new inventions *Rabia*	Impatient, Foolhardy, No roots, Shallow, Irresponsible, Fear of intimacy, Bored easily, No deep interpersonal connections, Wanderer, Tells fish tales, Untrustworthy, Addicted to drama, Ungrounded, Flirts with danger	Wilderness guide, Camp counselor, Circus performer, Pilot, Sailor, Ship captain, Tour guide, Tradesman, Taxi driver, National Guard, Gambler, Coach, Storyteller, Inventor, Stunt person, Mystery writer, Travel agent, Cruise ship staff, Astronaut, FBI agent, Photographer, P.E. teacher	**Toxic:** *A rolling stone gathers no moss. I'll sing in the sunshine then I'll be on my way.* **Healthy:** *Just do it! Try it—you'll like it! Off to my next great adventure. One small step for man; one giant step for mankind!*
The Hero/Heroine Rosa Parks Captain "Sully" Luke Skywalker Marion Jones Sen. Joseph McCarthy	Belief in a cause, Courage, Self-sacrificing, Dramatic, High integrity, Humble, Daring, Altruistic, Purpose-driven, Dependable, Idealistic, Good in crisis, Fearless, Takes action, Committed, Johnny on-the-spot. *Counselor* *Rabia*	Foolhardy, Opportunistic, Overly dramatic, Need for adulation, Glory monger, Delusions of grandeur, Can get hurt or become a martyr, Need for recognition and the limelight, Fanatical, Empty or angry when not needed for a rescue, Disempowers others	Fire fighter, Policeman, Environmentalist, EMT, Doctor, E.R. Nurse, Military enlistee, Activist, Local politician, Consumer advocate, Social reformist, Parent, Veterinarian, Marine, Investigative reporter	**Toxic:** *I don't care how dangerous it is.* **Healthy:** *Women and children first. I just did what anyone would have done.*
The Warrior/Amazon General Colin Powell Lance Armstrong John Wayne Lara Croft Darth Vader	Protective, Disciplined, Gives orders/takes orders, Loyal, Detachment, Physically fit, Strategic, Spiritual discipline, Intestinal fortitude, Mission-driven, Camaraderie, Feels an obligation to defend those who need it, One-pointed focus, Sets boundaries, Activist *Ryan*	Heartless, cruel, violent, "Hawk," Invulnerable, Sees warfare as only solution, Intimidating, Insensitive, Unconscionable, Objectifies the enemy and speaks in euphemisms (collateral damage), War monger, Hardened, Callous	Military lifer, Military strategist, Martial Arts instructor, Sharp-shooter, Body guard, Secret service, Police Woman, Paparazzi, Lawyer, Olympic Athlete, Green Beret, Navy Seal, Surgeon, Boxer	**Toxic:** *Kill them all and let God sort it out. I was only following orders. Kill for peace.* **Healthy:** *All for one and one for all.*

Character	Strengths	Weaknesses	Possible Jobs	Could be Heard Saying
For Example				
The Sex Pot/ Sex Goddess/Stud Hugh Jackman Jennifer Lopez Gypsy Rose Lee Marilyn Monroe Anna Nicole Smith	Sexy, Uninhibited, Sensual, Seductive, Free spirit, Juicy, Erotic, Fulfilled, Orgasmic, Expressive, Provocative, Hot, Pleasure-seeking and giving, In touch with creative energy, Enjoys body and its sensations, No fear of intimacy, Open, Honest, Vulnerable *Sexual Goddess, Ruth*	Exploitive, Sex addict, Sees people as conquests, Gamey, Insatiable, Multiple partners, Open to contracting and spreading STD's, Unfaithful, Desperate, Low self esteem, Commitment-phobic, Into pornography, Manipulative	Sex therapist, Sales person, Dancer, Model, Hairdresser, Lounge singer, Rock star, Ballroom dance instructor, Stripper, Wine connoisseur, Yoga instructor, Dominatrix, Escort, Gigolo, Playboy bunny, Cocktail waitress, Soap opera star, Demo model	**Toxic:** *Promiscuous boy. They all feel the same in the dark.* **Healthy:** *Make love, not war. I need some sexual healing.*
The Artist Isadora Duncan Annie Leibovitz Maya Angelou Andy Warhol Vincent Van Gogh	Sensitive, Gentle, Original, Intuitive, Perceptive, Hands-on, Colorful, Eccentric, Independent, Visionary, Free spirit, Passionate, Creative genius, Love aesthetics and beauty, Open-minded, Bohemian, Disciplined, Flamboyant, Focused, Exacting, Detail oriented *Kathy (Cheat)*	Perfectionist, Eccentric, Out of touch with reality and their body, Broke (starving artist), Spacey, Scattered, Obsessed, Irresponsible, Misunderstood, Impractical, Loner, Lost in their art, Suffering, Ungrounded, Finicky, Self-deprecating	Social commentator, Art teacher, Cartoonist, Author, Musician, Poet, Architect, Landscape designer, Graphic artist, Psychic, Interior decorator, Gardener, Florist, Painter, Editor, Craftsman, Cabinetmaker, Chef, Fine artist, Cinematographer, Wedding videographer, Fashion designer, Dancer	**Toxic:** *Anything for the sake of art. It isn't quite finished yet—just give met a little more time.* **Healthy:** *Dress to express. Beauty is in the eye of the beholder.*
The Lover/Romantic Brad Pitt & Angelina Jolie John Lennon & Yoko Ono Romeo & Juliet Elizabeth Taylor Brittany Spears & Kevin Federline	Empathetic, Sensitive, Poetic, Dreamer, Unconditional love, Sentimental, Caring, Giving, Sensuous, Devoted, Capable of deep intimacy, Expressive, Passionate, Optimistic, Faithful *Goddess*	Hopeless romantic, Love-addict, Co-dependent, Needy, Fear of abandonment, Head in the clouds, Living in the past, Unrealistic, Enmeshed, Rose-colored glasses, Melodramatic, Obsessed, Stalker, Needy	Romance novelist, Couple's counselor, Animal trainer, Matchmaker, Healer, Mentor, Nanny, Singer/songwriter, Acting teacher, Life coach, Cook, Symphony Conductor	**Toxic:** *Love hurts. Hopelessly devoted to you.* **Healthy:** *Love is the answer. Love will see us through*

Character	Strengths	Weaknesses	Possible Jobs	Could be Heard Saying
For Example				
The Rescuer Florence Nightingale Patch Adams Jerry Lewis Paula Abdul Edith Bunker	Caring, Giving, Selfless, Reliable, Loyal, Helpful, Kind, Likeable, Gentle, Compassionate, Dependable, Agreeable, Sympathetic, Humanitarian, Chivalrous, Motherly, Empathetic *Robert*	Enabler, Goes overboard, Denies own needs, Can burn out, Unsolicited help, Busy-body, Forces others into dependency, Oversteps boundaries, Classic Co-dependent, Disempowering	AA sponsor, Caregiver, Nurse, Doctor, Special needs teacher, Butler, Defense attorney, Therapist, Patient advocate, Social worker, Physical therapist, Nutritionist, Babysitter, Hospice worker, Cancer researcher, Psychiatrist	**Toxic:** *He needed me. I'll bend over backwards. Stand by your man.* ✱ **Healthy:** *Can I help you? Please allow me. I'm so sorry that happened to you.*
The Victim Charlie Brown Victor Frankel Michael J. Fox Little Orphan Annie Woody Allen	Willing to be vulnerable, Can ask for help, Knows how and when to rest, Can surrender, Sensitive, Receptive, High tolerance for pain, Humble, Survivor, Can cry, Pacifist, Courage *The Protector:*	Masochistic, Helpless, Nags, Hopeless, Gives up, Blames others, Often sick, In pain, No responsibility, Self-pity, Miserable, Powerless, Wet blanket, Depressed, Trapped, Resentful, Painfully slow, Unlucky, Wimpy, Co-dependent, Clinging *The Persecutor:*	Test new medicines, March of Dimes poster child, Patient advocate, Rape crisis hotline, Candy striper, Spokesperson, Funeral home director, Humane society volunteer, Veterinary assistant	**Toxic:** *Poor, poor, pitiful me. Why does everything always happen to me? It's not my fault.* ♥ **Healthy:** *I'm so tired. I surrender.*
The Persecutor/ Protector Erin Brockovich The Terminator Clint Eastwood Mike Tyson Michael Vick	Strength of character, Protects self & others, Stands up for himself, Knows how to say no, Sets limits, Has good boundaries, Knows when enough's enough, Tells people when to back off *Police officer*	Sadistic, Abusive, Bully, Violent, Blaming & shaming, Bossy, Controlling, Seeks revenge, Picks fights, Name-calling, Mean, Tells people where to go, Passive-aggressive, Prejudiced	District Attorney, Body guard, Football player, Boxer, Personal trainer, Guard, Child advocate, Detective, Sargent, Policeman, Congressional aid, Politician	**Toxic:** *You made me do it. It's all your fault! Put up your dukes.* **Healthy:** *I'm not going to take this abuse anymore! Talk to the hand. Why don't you pick on someone your own size?*
The Martyr Martin Luther King, Jr. Mahatma Gandhi Anne Frank Heathcliff Tammy Faye Baker	Self-sacrificing, Believes in a higher cause, Rallying figure, Honorable, Well-intended, Christ-like, Purpose-driven *Robert*	Guilt imposing, Misguided, Manipulative, Fanatical, Controls others through pain, Hidden agendas, Religious programming, Backdoor jabs, Creates Co-dependency with everyone, Insulting	Professional volunteer, Head up a homeless shelter, Run a food bank, Peace Corps worker, Salvation Army collector, Social activist, Greenpeace worker	**Toxic:** *You'll be sorry when I'm dead & gone. Ungrateful.* *Robert* **Healthy:** *It is a far, far better thing I do than I have ever done.*

ABOUT THE AUTHOR

Debbie Unterman, a Master Alchemist and Clinical Hypnotherapist in practice for the last twenty-five years, is one of only a handful of authorized Alchemical Hypnotherapy Trainers in the world. She describes herself as *a private eye for the soul, helping people find themselves and restore lost dreams.*

Debbie is well known for her skillful style in dealing with Sub-personalities, for her work with survivors of childhood abuse or neglect, for her innovative "cure" for Co-dependency, and for helping couples relate better through cutting edge communication techniques, including improving the relationship between their Sub-personalities.

Debbie's education began with a degree in Interpersonal Communications from the State University of New York College at Brockport, which included a minor in Theatre and a semester abroad in Paris. She earned her certifications in Hypnotherapy and Jin Shin Do Acupressure from Heartwood College of the Healing Arts in Northern California. She was also trained and certified by the State of Georgia as a Mediator and Resolution Specialist through the Conflict Resolution Academy in Atlanta.

Calling Atlanta home since 1988, Debbie is the founder of AHAA!—the Alchemical Hypnotherapy Association of Atlanta and Aoteoroa (New Zealand). She developed the Body/Mind program for the New Life School of Massage in Atlanta, where she was the Body/Mind the Instructor for seven years.

A skilled communicator, Debbie has hosted her own weekly radio talk show on health in Northern California, appeared on various radio and cable television shows, and presented workshops at venues such as Hypnosis Conferences, Mind/Body/Spirit Expos, and AT&T.

To provide a way to learn and grow outside the realm of the traditional therapeutic paradigm, Debbie created two therapy-based board games, *Clarity: The Game of Your Life* and *Satori: The Game of Radical Forgiveness*. Utilizing creative play, they have helped hundreds of people gain advice, focus and direction, in a fun, intimate and caring environment.

Debbie Unterman is a dedicated healer whose compassion, listening skills and spiritual clarity motivate her students and clients. Her expertise, authenticity and insights are inspiring, while her enthusiasm is contagious.

For more information about Debbie Unterman and her services, visit **www.TalkingtoMySelves.com**. To learn more about the Game of Clarity, visit **www.PlayClarity.com**.

Debbie would love to hear from you! Please call 404-289-2343 or email her with your questions and comments, or to schedule private telephone Inner-Voice Coaching or in-person Alchemical Hypnotherapy sessions.

You can also call or write to request information about events, certification trainings, Clarity Cruises, or to schedule a "playshop" in your area.

To book a speaking engagement or inquire
about bulk book discounts, special orders, or anything else,
contact Debbie at 404-289-2343 or
debbieunterman@gmail.com.

David Quigley

Made in the USA
Columbia, SC
20 February 2022